The Expositor's Bible
The Second Epistle To The Corinthians

By

James Denney

The Expositor's Bible
The Second Epistle To The Corinthians
by James Denney

Copyright © 2023

All Rights reserved.

No part of this publication may be reproduced, stored in a retrieval system, or transmitted in any form or by any means, electronic, mechanical, photocopying or Otherwise, without the written permission of the publisher.
The author/editor asserts the moral right to be identified as the author/editor of this work.

ISBN: 978-93-61152-99-3

Published by

DOUBLE 9 BOOKS

2/13-B, Ansari Road
Daryaganj, New Delhi – 110002
info@double9books.com
www.double9books.com
Tel. 011-40042856

This book is under public domain

ABOUT THE AUTHOR

James Denney was a Scottish theologian and preacher who lived from 8 February 1856 to 12 June 1917. His theological explanation of the meaning of the atonement within Christian theology—that is, that it is "the most profound of all truths"—is arguably what has made him most famous today. Many claim that he was well-known for supporting the penal substitution theory, but this is an incorrect understanding of his views. That being said, Denney himself objected angrily to this portrayal. Born in Paisley, Scotland on February 5, 1856, The Death of Christ Denney was the son of Cameronian (Reformed Presbyterian) parents. His dad was a Cameronian deacon and joiner. The family joined the Free Church of Scotland in 1876, joining the majority of the Reformed Presbyterian Church of Scotland. From 1874 to 1879, he attended the Highlanders' Academy at Greenock, University of Glasgow, and from 1879 to 1883, he attended Free Church College in Glasgow. While attending Glasgow University, he was awarded the Blackstone Prize and the Moral Philosophy Gold Medal. Edward Caird and Richard Jebb had a big influence on him. He also worked briefly as John Veitch's student assistant.

CONTENTS

INTRODUCTION 7
I   SUFFERING AND CONSOLATION 12
II   FAITH BORN OF DESPAIR 20
III   THE CHURCH'S ONE FOUNDATION 27
IV   CHRISTIAN MYSTERIES 34
V   A PASTOR'S HEART 41
VI   CHURCH DISCIPLINE 49
VII   CHRIST'S CAPTIVE 56
VIII LIVING EPISTLES 65
IX   THE TWO COVENANTS 73
X   THE TRANSFIGURING SPIRIT 82
XI   THE GOSPEL DEFINED 92
XII   THE VICTORY OF FAITH 100
XIII THE CHRISTIAN HOPE 110
XIV THE MEASURE OF CHRIST'S LOVE 118
XV   THE NEW WORLD 125
XVI RECONCILIATION 132
XVII THE SIGNS OF AN APOSTLE 140
XVIII NEW TESTAMENT PURITANISM 148
XIX REPENTANCE UNTO LIFE 155
XX   THE GRACE OF LIBERALITY 163
XXI THE FRUITS OF LIBERALITY 170
XXII WAR 179

XXIII	COMPARISONS	186
XXIV	GODLY JEALOUSY	194
XXV	FOOLISH BOASTING	201
XXVI	STRENGTH AND WEAKNESS	212
XXVII	NOT YOURS, BUT YOU	222
XXVIII	CONCLUSION	230
FOOTNOTES:		239

INTRODUCTION

Introduction, in the scientific sense, is not part of the expositor's task; but it is convenient, especially when introduction and exposition have important bearings on each other, that the expositor should indicate his opinion on the questions common to both departments. This is the purpose of the statement which follows.

(1) The starting-point for every inquiry into the relations between St. Paul and the Corinthians, so far as they concern us here, is to be found in the close connexion between the two Epistles to the Corinthians which we possess. This close connexion is not a hypothesis, of greater or less probability, like so much that figures in Introductions to the Second Epistle; it is a large and solid fact, which is worth more for our guidance than the most ingenious conjectural combination. Stress has been justly laid on this by Holtzmann,[1] who illustrates the general fact by details. Thus 2 Cor. i. 8-10, ii. 12, 13, attach themselves immediately to the situation described in 1 Cor. xvi. 8, 9. Similarly in 2 Cor. i. 12 there seems to be a distinct echo of 1 Cor. ii. 4-14. More important is the unquestionable reference in 2 Cor. i. 13-17, 23, to 1 Cor. xvi. 5. From a comparison of these two passages it is plain that before Paul wrote either he had had an intention, of which the Corinthians were aware, to visit Corinth in a certain way. He was to leave Ephesus, sail straight across the sea to Corinth, go from Corinth to Macedonia, and then return, *viâ* Corinth, to Asia again. In other words, on this tour he was to visit Corinth twice. In the last chapter of the First Epistle, he announces a change of plan: he is *not* going to Corinth direct, but *viâ* Macedonia, and the Corinthians are only to see him once. He does not say, in the First Epistle, why he has changed his plan, but the announcement caused great dissatisfaction in Corinth. Some said he was a fickle creature; some said he was afraid to show face. This is the situation to which the Second Epistle directly addresses itself; the very first thing Paul does in it is to explain and justify the change of plan announced in the First. It was not fickleness, he says, nor cowardice, that made him change his mind, but the desire to spare the Corinthians and himself the pain which a visit paid at the moment would certainly inflict. The close connexion between our two Epistles, which on this point is unquestionable, may be further illustrated. Thus, not to point to general resemblances in feeling or temper,

the correspondence is at least suggestive between ἁγνὸς ἐν τῷ πράγματι, 2 Cor. vii. 11 (cf. the use of πρᾶγμα in 1 Thess. iv. 6), and τοιαύτη πορνεία in 1 Cor. v. 1; between ἐν προσώπῳ Χριστοῦ, 2 Cor. ii. 10, and ἐν τῷ ὀνόματι τοῦ Κ. ἡμῶν Ἰ. Χ., 1 Cor. v. 4; between the mention of Satan in 2 Cor. ii. 11 and 1 Cor. v. 5; between πενθεῖν in 2 Cor. xii. 21 and 1 Cor. v. 2; between τοιοῦτος and τις in 2 Cor. ii. 6 f., 2 Cor. ii. 5, and the same words in 1 Cor. v. 5 and 1 Cor. v. 1. If all these are carefully examined and compared, I think it becomes extremely difficult to believe that in 2 Cor. ii. 5 ff. and in 2 Cor. vii. 8 ff. the Apostle is dealing with anything else than the case of the sinner treated in 1 Cor. v. The coincidences in detail would be very striking under any circumstances; but in combination with the fact that the two Epistles, as has just been shown by the explanation of the change of purpose about the journey, are in the closest connexion with each other, they seem to me to come as nearly as possible to demonstration.

(2) If this view is accepted, it is natural and justifiable to explain the Second Epistle as far as possible out of the First. Thus the letter to which St. Paul refers in 2 Cor. ii. 4 and in 2 Cor. vii. 8, 12, will be our First Epistle to the Corinthians; the persons referred to in 2 Cor. vii. 12 as "he who did the wrong" and "he to whom the wrong was done" will be the son and the father in 1 Cor. v. 1. There are, indeed, many who think that it is absurd to speak of the First Epistle to the Corinthians as written "out of much affliction and anguish of heart and with many tears"; and who cannot imagine that Paul would speak of a great sin and crime, like that of the incestuous person, in such language as he employs in 2 Cor. ii. 5 ff. and 2 Cor. vii. 12. Such language, they argue, suits far better the case of a personal injury, an insult or outrage of which Paul—either in person or in one of his deputies—had been the victim at Corinth. Hence they argue for an intermediate visit of a very painful character, and for an intermediate letter, now lost, dealing with this painful incident. Paul, we are to suppose, visited Corinth on the business of 1 Cor. v. (among other things), and there suffered a great humiliation. He was defied by the guilty man and his friends, and had to leave the Church without effecting anything. Then he wrote the extremely severe letter to which ii. 4 refers—a letter which was carried by Titus, and which produced the change on which he congratulates himself in ii. 5 ff. and vii. 8 ff. It is obvious that this whole combination is hypothetical; and hence, though many have been attracted by it, it appears with an infinite variety of detail. It is obvious also that the grounds on which it rests are subjective; it is a question on which men will differ to the end of time, whether the language in 2 Cor. ii. 4 is an apt description of the mood in which Paul wrote (at least certain parts of) the First Epistle to the Corinthians, or whether the language in 2 Cor. ii. 5 ff., vii. 8 ff. is becoming language in which to close

proceedings like those opened in 1 Cor. v. If many have believed that it is not, many, on the other hand, have no difficulty in believing that it is; and those who take the negative not only fail to explain the series of verbal correspondences detailed above, but dissolve the connexion between our two Epistles altogether. Thus Godet allows more than a year, crowded with events, to come between them. In view of the palpable fact with which we started, I cannot but think this quite incredible: it is far easier to suppose that the proceedings about the incestuous person took a complexion which made Paul's language in the second and seventh chapters natural than to come to any confident conviction about this hypothetical visit and letter.

(3) But the visit, it may be said, at all events, is not hypothetical. It is distinctly alluded to in 2 Cor. ii. 1, xii. 14, xiii. 1. These passages are discussed in the exposition. The two last are certainly not decisive; there are good scholars who hold the same opinion of the first. Heinrici, for instance, maintains that Paul had only been once in Corinth when he wrote the Second Epistle; it was the *third* time he was *starting*, but once his intention had been frustrated or deferred, so that when he reached Corinth it would only be his second visit. A case can be stated for this, but in view of chap. ii. 1 and chap. xiii. 2, I do not see that it can be easily maintained. These passages practically compel us to assume that Paul had already visited Corinth a second time, and had had very painful experiences there. But the close connexion of our Epistles equally compels us to assume that this second visit belongs to an earlier date than our first canonical Epistle. We know nothing of it except that it was not pleasant, and that Paul was very willing to save both himself and the Corinthians the repetition of such an experience. It is nothing against this view that the visit in question is not referred to in Acts or in the fist letter. Hardly anything in chap. xi. 24 ff. is known to us from Acts, and probably we should never have known of this journey unless in explaining the change of purpose which the first letter announced it had occurred to Paul to say: "I did not wish to come when it could only vex you; I had enough of that before."

(4) As for the letter, which is supposed to be referred to in 2 Cor. ii. 4, it also has been relieved of its hypothetical character by being identified with chaps. x. 1-xiii. 10 of our present Second Epistle. In the absence of the faintest external indication that the Epistle ever existed in any other than its present form, it is perhaps superfluous to treat this seriously; but the comment of Godet seems to me sufficiently to dispose of it. The hypothetical letter in question—in which Godet himself believes—must have had two main objects: first, to accredit Titus, who is assumed to have carried it, as the representative of Paul; and, second, to insist on reparation for the assumed personal outrage of which Paul had been the victim on his recent visit. This

second object, at an events, is indisputable. But chaps. x. 1-xiii. 10 have no reference whatever to either of these things, and are wholly taken up with what the Apostle means to do, when he comes to Corinth the third time; they refer not to this (imaginary) insolent person, but to the misbelieving and the immoral in general.

(5) Except in the points specified, the interpretation of the Epistle is little affected by the questions raised in *Introduction*. Even in the points specified it is the historical reference, not the ethical import, which is affected. Whichever view we take of them, we get on the whole substantially the same impression of the spirit of Christ as it lives and works in the soul of the Apostle. It is part of the man's greatness, it is the seal of his inspiration, that in his hands the temporal becomes eternal, the incidental loses its purely incidental character, and has significance for all time. It is the expositor's task to deal with the spiritual rather than the historical side, and it will be sufficient here to indicate in outline what I conceive the series of Paul's relations with the Corinthians to have been.

(6) His first visit to Corinth was that which is recorded in Acts xviii.; according to the statement of ver. 11 it extended over a period of eighteen months. In all probability he had many communications with the Church, through deputies whom he commissioned, in the years during which he was absent; the form of the question in 2 Cor. xii. 17 (μή τινα ὧν ἀπέσταλκα πρὸς ὑμᾶς κ.τ.λ.) implies as much. But it is only after his coming to Ephesus, in the course of his third missionary journey, that personal intercourse with Corinth can have been resumed. To this period I should refer the visit which we are bound to assume on the ground of 2 Cor. ii. 1, xiii. 2. What the occasion was, or what the circumstances, we cannot tell; all we know is that it was painful, and perhaps disappointing. Paul had used grave and threatening language on this occasion (2 Cor. xiii. 2), but he had been obliged to tolerate some things which he would rather have seen otherwise. This visit was probably made toward the close of the three years' stay in Ephesus, and the letter referred to in 1 Cor. v. 9—the one in which he warned the Corinthians not to associate with fornicators—would most likely be written on his return from it. In this letter he may very naturally have announced that purpose of visiting Corinth twice—once on his way to Macedonia, and again on his way back—to which reference has already been made. This letter, plainly, did not serve its purpose, and not long afterwards Paul received at Ephesus deputies from the Corinthian Church (1 Cor. xvi. 17), who apparently brought written instructions with them, in which Paul's judgment was sought more minutely on a variety of ethical questions (1 Cor. vii. 1). Before these deputies arrived, or at all events before Paul wrote the letter (our First Epistle) in which he addressed himself to the

state of affairs in Corinth which their reports had disclosed, Timothy had left Ephesus on a journey of some interest. Paul meant Corinth to be his destination (1 Cor. iv. 17), but he had to go *viâ* Macedonia, and the Apostle was not certain that he would get so far (1 Cor. xvi. 10: "But *if* Timothy come," etc.). In point of fact, he does not seem to have gone farther than Macedonia; and Luke in Acts xix. 22 mentions Macedonia as the place to which he had been sent. That he got no farther is suggested also by the fact that Paul joins his name with his own in the salutation of the Second Epistle, which was written in Macedonia, but never hints that he owed to *him* any information whatever on the state of the Corinthian Church. All that he knew of this, and of the effect of his first letter, he learned from Titus (2 Cor. ii. 13, vii. 13 f.). But how did Titus happen to be in Corinth representing Paul? By far the happiest suggestion here is that which makes Titus and the brother of 2 Cor. xii. 18 the same as "the brethren" of 1 Cor. xvi. 12, whose return from Corinth Paul expected in company of Timothy. Timothy, as we have seen, did not get so far. Paul's departure from Ephesus was apparently hastened by a great peril; his anxiety, too, to hear the effect produced by that letter which had cost him so much—our First Epistle—was very great; he pressed on, past Troas, where a fair field of labour waited for workers, and finally encountered Titus in Macedonia, and heard his report.

(7) This is the point at which the Second Epistle to the Corinthians begins. It falls of itself into three clearly marked divisions. The first extends over chaps. i.-vii. In this the Apostle makes his peace, so to speak, with the Corinthians, and does everything in his power to remove any feeling of "soreness" which might linger in their minds over his rigorous treatment of one particular offender. But embedded in this there is a magnificent vindication of the spiritual apostolic ministry, especially in contrast with that of the legalists, and an appeal for love and confidence such as he had always bestowed on the Church. Chaps. viii. and ix. form the second part, and are devoted to the collection which was being made in the Gentile Churches for poor Christians in Jerusalem. The third part consists of chaps. x. to xiii. In this Paul confronts the disorders which still assert themselves in the Church; the pretensions of certain Judaists, "superlative apostles" as he calls them, who were assailing his apostolic vocation and subverting his gospel; and the immoral licence of others, presumably once pagans, who used liberty for a cloak to the flesh. He writes of both with unsparing severity, yet he does not wish to be severe. He parts from the Church with words of unaffected love, and includes them all in his benediction.

I
SUFFERING AND CONSOLATION

"Paul, an apostle of Christ Jesus through the will of God, and Timothy our brother, unto the Church of God which is at Corinth, with all the saints which are in the whole of Achaia: Grace to you and peace from God our Father and the Lord Jesus Christ.

"Blessed *be* the God and Father of our Lord Jesus Christ, the Father of mercies and God of all comfort; who comforteth us in all our affliction, that we may be able to comfort them that are in any affliction, through the comfort wherewith we ourselves are comforted of God. For as the sufferings of Christ abound unto us, even so our comfort also aboundeth through Christ. But whether we be afflicted, it is for your comfort and salvation; or whether we be comforted, it is for your comfort, which worketh in the patient enduring of the same sufferings which we also suffer: and our hope for you is stedfast; knowing that, as ye are partakers of the sufferings, so also are ye of the comfort."—2 Cor. i. 1-7 (R.V.).

The greeting with which St. Paul introduces his Epistles is much alike in them all, but it never becomes a mere formality, and ought not to pass unregarded as such. It describes, as a rule, the character in which he writes, and the character in which his correspondents are addressed. Here he is an apostle of Jesus Christ, divinely commissioned; and he addresses a Christian community at Corinth, including in it, for the purposes of his letter, the scattered Christians to be found in the other quarters of Achaia. His letters are occasional, in the sense that some special incident or situation called them forth; but this occasional character does not lessen their value. He addresses himself to the incident or situation in the consciousness of his apostolic vocation; he writes to a Church constituted for permanence, or at least for such duration as this transitory world can have; and what we have in his Epistles is not a series of *obiter dicta*, the casual utterances of an irresponsible person; it is the mind of Christ authoritatively given upon the questions raised. When he includes any other person in the salutation—as in this place "Timothy our brother"—it is rather as a mark of courtesy, than as adding to the Epistle another authority besides his own. Timothy had helped to found the Church at Corinth; Paul had shown great anxiety about his reception by the Corinthians, when he started to visit that turbulent Church alone (1 Cor. xvi. 10 f.); and in this new letter he honours him in their eyes by uniting his name with his own in the superscription. The Apostle and his affectionate fellow-worker wish the Corinthians, as they wished all the Churches, grace and peace from God our Father and the Lord Jesus Christ. It is not necessary to expound afresh the meaning and connexion of these two New Testament ideas: grace is the first and last word of the Gospel; and peace—perfect spiritual soundness—is the finished work of grace in the soul.

The Apostle's greeting is usually followed by a thanksgiving, in which he recalls the conversion of those to whom he is writing, or surveys their progress in the new life, and the improvement of their gifts, gratefully acknowledging God as the author of all. Thus in the First Epistle to the Corinthians he thanks God for the grace given to them in Christ Jesus, and especially for their Christian enrichment in all utterance and in all knowledge. So, too, but with deeper gratitude, he dwells on the virtues of the Thessalonians, remembering their work of faith, and labour of love, and patience of hope. Here also there is a thanksgiving, but at the first glance of a totally different character. The Apostle blesses God, not for what He has done for the Corinthians, but for what He has done for himself. "Blessed be the God and Father of our Lord Jesus Christ, the Father of mercies and God of all comfort, who comforteth us in all our tribulation." This departure from the Apostle's usual custom is probably not so selfish as it looks. When his mind travelled down from Philippi to Corinth, it rested on the spiritual aspects of the Church there with anything but unrelieved satisfaction. There was much for which he could not possibly be thankful; and just as the momentary apostasy of the Galatians led to his omitting the thanksgiving altogether, so the unsettled mood in which he wrote to the Corinthians gave it this peculiar turn. Nevertheless, when he thanked God for comforting him in all his afflictions, he thanked Him on their behalf. It was they who were eventually to have the profit both of his sorrows and his consolations. Probably, too, there is something here which is meant to appeal, even to those who disliked him in Corinth. There had been a good deal of friction between the Apostle and some who had once owned him as their father in Christ; they were blaming him, at this very moment, for not coming to visit them; and in this thanksgiving, which dilates on the afflictions he has endured, and on the divine consolation he has experienced in them, there is a tacit appeal to the sympathy even of hostile spirits. Do not, he seems to say, deal ungenerously with one who has passed through such terrible experiences, and lays the fruit of them at your feet. Chrysostom presses this view, as if St. Paul had written his thanksgiving in the character of a subtle diplomatist: to judge by one's feeling, it is true enough to deserve mention.

[2]

The subject of the thanksgiving is the Apostle's sufferings, and his experience of God's mercies under them. He expressly calls them the sufferings of Christ. These sufferings, he says, abound toward us. Christ was the greatest of sufferers: the flood of pain and sorrow went over His head; all its waves and billows broke upon Him. The Apostle was caught and overwhelmed by the same stream; the waters came into his soul. That is the meaning of τὰ παθήματα τοῦ Χριστοῦ περισσεύει εἰς ἡμᾶς. In abundant measure the disciple was initiated into his Master's stern experience; he learned, what he prayed to learn, the fellowship of His sufferings. The boldness of the language in which a mortal man calls his own afflictions the sufferings of Christ is far from unexampled in the New Testament. It is repeated by St. Paul in Col. i. 24: "I now rejoice in my sufferings on your behalf, and fill up that which is lacking of the afflictions of Christ in my flesh for His body's sake, which is the Church." It is varied in Heb. xiii. 13, where the sacred writer exhorts us to go out to Jesus, without the camp, bearing *His* reproach. It is anticipated and justified by the words of the Lord Himself: "Ye shall indeed drink of My cup; and with the baptism with which I am baptised shall ye be baptised withal." One lot, and that a cross, awaits all the children of God in this world, from the Only-begotten who came from the bosom of the Father, to the latest-born among His brethren. But let us beware of the hasty assertion that, because the Christian's sufferings can thus be described as of a piece with Christ's, the key to the mystery of Gethsemane and Calvary is to be found in the self-consciousness of martyrs and confessors. The very man who speaks of filling up that which is lacking of the afflictions of Christ for the Church's sake, and who says that the sufferings of Christ came on him in their fulness, would have been the first to protest against such an idea. "Was Paul crucified for you?" Christ suffered alone; there is, in spite of our fellowship with His sufferings, a solitary, incommunicable greatness in His Cross, which the Apostle will expound in another place (chap. v.). Even when Christ's sufferings come upon us there is a difference. At the very lowest, as Vinet has it, we do from gratitude what he did from pure love. We suffer in His company, sustained by His comfort; He suffered uncomforted and unsustained. We are afflicted, when it so happens, "under the auspices of the divine mercy"; He was afflicted that there might be mercy for us.

Few parts of Bible teaching are more recklessly applied than those about suffering and consolation. If all that men endured was of the character here described, if all their sufferings were sufferings of Christ, which came on them because they were walking in His steps and assailed by the forces which buffeted Him, consolation would be an easy task. The presence of God with the soul would make it almost unnecessary. The answer of a good conscience would take all the bitterness out of pain; and then, however it tortured, it could not poison the soul. The mere sense that our sufferings *are* the sufferings of Christ—that we are drinking of His cup—is itself a comfort and an inspiration beyond words. But much of our suffering, we know very well, is of a different character. It does not come on us because we are united to Christ, but because we are estranged from Him; it is the proof and the fruit, not of our righteousness, but of our guilt. It is our sin finding us out, and avenging itself upon us, and in no sense the suffering of Christ. Such suffering, no doubt, has its use and its purpose. It is meant to drive the soul in upon itself, to compel it to reflection, to give it no rest till it awakes to penitence, to urge it through despair to God. Those who suffer thus will have cause to thank God afterwards if His discipline leads to their amendment, but they have no title to take to themselves the consolation prepared for those who are partners in the sufferings of Christ. Nor is the minister of Christ at liberty to apply a passage like this to any case of affliction which he encounters in his work. There are sufferings and sufferings; there is a divine intention in them all, if we could only discover it; but the divine intention and the divinely wrought result are only explained here for one particular kind—those sufferings, namely, which come upon men in virtue of their following Jesus Christ. What, then does the Apostle's experience enable him to say on this hard question?

(1) His sufferings have brought him a new revelation of God, which is expressed in the new name, "The Father of mercies and God of all comfort." The name is wonderful in its tenderness; we feel as we pronounce it that a new conception of what love can be has been imparted to the Apostle's soul. It is in the sufferings and sorrows of life that we discover what we possess in our human friends. Perhaps one abandons us in our extremity, and another betrays us; but most of us find ourselves unexpectedly and astonishingly rich. People of whom we have hardly ever had a kind thought show us kindness; the unsuspected, unmerited goodness which comes to our relief makes us ashamed. This is the rule which is illustrated here by the example of God Himself. It is as if the Apostle said: "I never knew, till the sufferings of Christ abounded in me, how near God could come to man; I never knew how rich His mercies could be, how intimate His sympathy, how inspiring His comfort." This is an utterance well worth considering. The sufferings of men, and especially the sufferings of the innocent and the good, are often made the ground of hasty charges against God; nay, they

are often turned into arguments for Atheism. But who are they who make such charges? Not the righteous sufferers, at least in New Testament times. The Apostle here is their representative and spokesman, and he assures us that God never was so much to him as when he was in the sorest straits. The divine love was so far from being doubtful to him that it shone out then in unanticipated brightness; the very heart of the Father was revealed—all mercy, all encouragement and comfort. If the martyrs have no doubts of their own, is it not very gratuitous for the spectators to become sceptics on their account? "The sufferings of Christ" in His people may be an insoluble problem to the disinterested onlooker, but they are no problem to the sufferers. What is a mystery, when viewed from without, a mystery in which God seems to be conspicuous by His absence, is, when viewed from within, a new and priceless revelation of God Himself. "The Father of mercies and God of all comfort" is making Himself known now as for want of opportunity He could not be known before.

Notice especially that the consolation is said to abound "through Christ." He is the mediator through whom it comes. To partake in His sufferings is to be united to *Him*; and to be united to Him is to partake in His *life*. The Apostle anticipates here a thought on which he enlarges in the fourth chapter: "Always bearing about in the body the dying of Jesus, that the life also of Jesus may be manifested in our body." In our eagerness to emphasise the nearness and the sympathy of Jesus, it is to be feared that we do less than justice to the New Testament revelation of His glory. He does not suffer now. He is enthroned on high, far above all principality and power and might and dominion. The Spirit which brings His presence to our hearts is the Spirit of the Prince of Life; its function is not to be weak with our weakness, but to help our infirmity, and to strengthen us with all might in the inner man. The Christ who dwells in us through His Spirit is not the Man of Sorrows, wearing the crown of thorns; it is the King of kings and Lord of lords, making us partakers of His triumph. There is a weak tone in much of the religious literature which deals with suffering, utterly unlike that of the New Testament. It is a degradation of Christ to our level which it teaches, instead of an exaltation of man toward Christ's. But the last is the apostolic ideal: "More than conquerors through Him that loved us." The comfort of which St. Paul makes so much here is not necessarily deliverance from suffering for Christ's sake, still less exemption from it; it is the strength and courage and immortal hope which rise up, even in the midst of suffering, in the heart in which the Lord of glory dwells. Through Him such comfort abounds; it wells up to match and more than match the rising tide of suffering.

(2) But Paul's sufferings have done more than give him a new knowledge of God; they have given him at the same time a new power to comfort others. He is bold enough to make this ministry of consolation the key to his recent experiences. "He comforteth us in all our affliction, that we may be able to comfort them that are in any affliction, through the comfort wherewith we ourselves are comforted of God." His sufferings and his consolation together had a purpose that went beyond himself. How significant that is for some perplexing aspects of man's life! We are selfish, and instinctively regard ourselves as the centre of all providences; we naturally seek to explain everything by its bearing on ourselves alone. But God has not made us for selfishness and isolation, and some mysteries would be cleared up if we had love enough to see the ties by which our life is indissolubly linked to others. This, however, is less definite than the Apostle's thought; what he tells us is that he has gained a new power at a great price. It is a power which almost every Christian man will covet; but how many are willing to pass through the fire to obtain it? We must ourselves have needed and have found comfort, before we know what it is; we must ourselves have learned the art of consoling in the school of suffering, before we can practise it for the benefit of others. The most painfully tried, the most proved in suffering, the souls that are best acquainted with grief, provided their consolation has abounded through Christ, are specially called to this ministry. Their experience is their preparation for it. Nature is something, and age is something; but far more than nature and age is that discipline of God to which they have been submitted, that initiation into the sufferings of Christ which has made them acquainted with His consolations also, and has taught them to know the Father of mercies and the God of all comfort. Are they not among His best gifts to the Church, those whom He has qualified to console, by consoling them in the fire?

In the sixth verse the Apostle dwells on the interest of the Corinthians in his sufferings and his consolation. It is a practical illustration of the communion of the saints in Christ. "All that befalls *me*," says St. Paul, "has *your* interest in view. If I am afflicted, it is in the interest of your comfort: when you look at me, and see how I bear myself in the sufferings of Christ, you will be encouraged to become imitators of me, even as I am of Him. If, again, I am comforted, this also is in the interest of *your* comfort; God enables me to impart to you what He has imparted to me; and the comfort in question is no impotent thing; it proves its power in this—that when you have received it, you endure with brave patience the same sufferings which we also suffer." This last is a favourite thought with the Apostle, and connects itself readily with the idea, which may or may not have a right to be expressed in the text, that all this is in furtherance of the salvation of the Corinthians.[3] For if there is one note of the saved more certain than another, it is the brave patience with which they take upon them the sufferings of Christ. ὁ δὲ ὑπομείνας εἰς τέλος, οὗτος σωθήσεται (Matt. x. 22). All that helps men to endure to the end, helps them to salvation. All that tends to break the spirit and to sink men despondency, or hurry them into impatience or fear, leads in the opposite direction. The great service that a true comforter does is to put the strength and courage into us which enable us to take up our cross, however sharp and heavy, and to bear it to the last step and the last breath. No comfort is worth the name—none is taught of God—which has another efficacy than this. The saved are those whose souls rise to this description, and who recognise their spiritual kindred in such brave and patient sufferers as Paul.

The thanksgiving ends appropriately with a cheerful word about the Corinthians. "Our hope for you is stedfast; knowing that, as ye are partakers of the sufferings, so are ye also of the comfort." These two things go together; it is the appointed lot of the children of God to become acquainted with both. If the sufferings could come alone, if *they* could be assigned as the portion of the Church apart from the consolation, Paul could have no hope that the Corinthians would endure to the end; but as it is, he is not afraid. The force of his words is perhaps best felt by us, if instead of saying that the sufferings and the consolation are inseparable, we say that the consolation depends upon the sufferings. And what is the consolation? It is the presence of the exalted Saviour in the heart through His Spirit. It is a clear perception, and a firm hold, of the things which are unseen and eternal. It is a conviction of the divine love which cannot be shaken, and of its sovereignty and omnipotence in the Risen Christ. This infinite comfort is contingent upon our partaking of the sufferings of Christ. There is a point, the Apostle seems to say, at which the invisible world and its glories intersect this world in which we live, and become visible, real, and inspiring to men. It is the point at which we suffer with Christ's sufferings. At any other point the vision of this glory is unneeded, and therefore withheld. The worldly, the selfish, the cowardly; those who shrink from self-denial; those who evade pain; those who root themselves in the world that lies around us, and when they move at all move in the line of least resistance; those who have never carried Christ's Cross,—none of these can ever have the triumphant conviction of things unseen and eternal which throbs in every page of the New Testament. None of these can have what the Apostle elsewhere calls "eternal consolation." It is easy for unbelievers, and for Christians lapsing into unbelief, to mock this faith as faith in "the transcendent"; but would a single line of the New Testament have been written without it? When we weigh what is here asserted about its connexion with the sufferings of Christ, could a graver charge be brought against any Church than that its faith in this "transcendent" languished or was extinct? Do not let us hearken to the sceptical insinuations which would rob us of all that has been revealed in Christ's resurrection; and do not let us imagine, on the other hand, that we can retain a living faith in this revelation if we decline to take up our cross. It was only when the sufferings of Christ abounded in him that Paul's consolation was abundant through Christ; it was only when he laid down his life for His sake that Stephen saw the heavens opened and the Son of Man standing at the right hand of God.

II
FAITH BORN OF DESPAIR

"For we would not have you ignorant, brethren, concerning our affliction which befell us in Asia, that we were weighed down exceedingly, beyond our power, insomuch that we despaired even of life: yea, we ourselves have had the answer of death within ourselves, that we should not trust in ourselves, but in God which raiseth the dead: who delivered us out of so great a death, and will deliver: on whom we have set our hope that He will also still deliver us; ye also helping together on our behalf by your supplication; that, for the gift bestowed upon us by means of many, thanks may be given by many persons on our behalf.

"For our glorying is this, the testimony of our conscience, that in holiness and sincerity of God, not in fleshly wisdom but in the grace of God, we behaved ourselves in the world, and more abundantly to you-ward. For we write none other things unto you, than what ye read or even acknowledge, and I hope ye will acknowledge unto the end: as also ye did acknowledge us in part, that we are your glorying, even as ye also are ours, in the day of our Lord Jesus." —2 Cor. i. 8-14 (R.V.).

Paul seems to have felt that the thanksgiving with which he opens this letter to the Corinthians was so peculiar as to require explanation. It was not his way to burst upon his readers thus with his private experiences either of joy or sorrow; and though he had good reason for what he did—in that abundance of the heart out of which the mouth speaks, in his desire to conciliate the good-will of the Corinthians for a much-tried man, and in his faith in the real communion of the saints—he instinctively stops here a moment to vindicate what he has done. He does not wish them to be ignorant of an experience which has been so much to him, and ought to have the liveliest interest for them.

Evidently they knew that he had been in trouble, but they had no sufficient idea of the extremity to which he had been reduced. We were weighed down, he writes, in excess, beyond our power; the trial that came upon us was one not measured to man's strength. We despaired even of life. Nay, we have had[4] the answer of death in ourselves. When we looked about us, when we faced our circumstances, and asked ourselves whether death or life was to be the end of this, we could only answer, Death. We were like men under sentence; it was only a question of a little sooner or a little later, when the fatal stroke should fall.

The Apostle, who has a divine gift for interpreting experience and reading its lessons, tells us why he and his friends had to pass such a terrible time. It was that they might trust, not in themselves, but in God who raises the dead. It is natural, he implies, for us to trust in ourselves. It is so natural, and so confirmed by the habits of a lifetime, that no ordinary difficulties or perplexities avail to break us of it. It takes all God can do to root up our self-confidence. He must reduce us to despair; He must bring us to such an extremity that the one voice we have in our hearts, the one voice that cries to us wherever we look round for help, is Death, death, death. It is out of this despair that the superhuman hope is born. It is out of this abject helplessness that the soul learns to look up with new trust to God.

It is a melancholy reflection upon human nature that we have, as the Apostle expresses it elsewhere, to be "shut up" to all the mercies of God. If we could evade them, notwithstanding their freeness and their worth, we would. How do most of us attain to any faith in Providence? Is it not by proving, through numberless experiments, that it is not in man that walketh to direct his steps? Is it not by coming, again and again, to the limit of our resources, and being compelled to feel that unless there is a wisdom and a love at work on our behalf, immeasurably wiser and more benignant than our own, life is a moral chaos? How, above all, do we come to any faith in redemption? to any abiding trust in Jesus Christ as the Saviour of our souls? Is it not by this same way of despair? Is it not by the profound consciousness that in ourselves there is *no* answer to the question, How shall man be just with God? and that the answer must be sought in Him? Is it not by failure, by defeat, by deep disappointments, by ominous forebodings hardening into the awful certainty that we cannot with our own resources make ourselves good men—is it not by experiences like these that we are led to the Cross? This principle has many other illustrations in human life, and every one of them is something to our discredit. They all mean that only desperation opens our eyes to God's love. We do not heartily own Him as the author of life and health, unless He has raised us from sickness after the doctor had given us up. We do not acknowledge His paternal guidance of our life, unless in some sudden peril, or some impending disaster, He provides an unexpected deliverance. We do not confess that salvation is of the Lord, till our very soul has been convinced that in it there dwells no good thing. Happy are those who are taught, even by despair, to set their hope in God; and who, when they learn this lesson once, learn it, like St. Paul, once for all (see note on ἐσχήκαμεν above). Faith and hope like those which burn through this Epistle were well worth purchasing, even at such a price; they were blessings so valuable that the love of God did not shrink from reducing Paul to despair that he might be compelled to grasp them. Let us believe when such trials come into our lives—when we are weighed down exceedingly, beyond our strength, and are in darkness without light, in a valley of the shadow of death with no outlet—that God is not dealing with us cruelly or at random, but shutting us up to an experience of His love which we have hitherto declined. "After two days will He revive us; on the third day He will raise us up, and we shall live before Him."

The Apostle describes the God on whom he learned to hope as "God who raises the dead." He himself had been as good as dead, and his deliverance was as good as a resurrection. The phrase, however, seems to be the Apostle's equivalent for omnipotence: when he thinks of the utmost that God can do, he expresses it thus. Sometimes the application of it is merely physical (*e.g.*, Rom. iv. 17); sometimes it is spiritual as well. Thus in Eph. i. 19 ff. the possibilities of the Christian life are measured by this— that that power is at work in believers with which God wrought in Christ when *He raised Him from the dead*, and set Him at His own right hand in the heavenly places. Is not that power sufficient to do for the weakest and most desperate of men far more than all he needs? Yet it is his need, somehow, when brought home to him in despair, that opens his eyes to this omnipotent saving power.

The text of the words in which Paul tells of his deliverance can hardly be said to be quite certain, but the general meaning is plain. God delivered him from the awful death which was impending over him; he had his hope now firmly set on Him; he was sure that He would deliver him in the future also. [5] What the danger had been, which had made so powerful an impression on this hardy soul, we cannot now tell. It must have been something which happened after the First Epistle was written, and therefore was not the fighting with wild beasts at Ephesus, whatever that may have been (1 Cor. xv. 32). It may have been a serious bodily illness, which had brought him to death's door, and left him so weak, that still, at every step, he felt it was God's mercy that was holding him up. It may have been a plot to make away with him on the part of the many adversaries mentioned in the First Epistle (xvi. 9)—a plot which had failed, as it were, by a miracle, but the malignity of which still dogged his steps, and was only warded off by the constant presence of God. Both these suggestions require, and would satisfy, the reading, "who delivered us from so great a death, and *doth deliver*." If, however, we take the reading of the R.V.—"who delivered us from so great a death, and *will deliver*; on whom we have set our hope that He will also still deliver us"—the existence of the danger, at the moment at which Paul writes, is not necessarily involved; and the danger itself may have been more of what we might call an accidental character. The imminent peril of drowning referred to in chap. xi. 25 would meet the case; and the confidence expressed by Paul with such emphatic reference to the future will not seem without motive when we consider that he had several sea voyages in prospect—as those from Corinth to Syria, from Syria to Rome, and probably from Rome to Spain. So Hofmann interprets the whole passage: but whether the interpretation be good or bad, it is elsewhere than in its accidental circumstances that the interest of the transaction lies for the writer and for us. To Paul it was not merely a historical but a spiritual experience; not an incident without meaning, but a divinely ordered discipline; and it is thus that we must learn to read our own lives if the purpose of God is to be wrought out in them.

Notice in this connexion, in the eleventh verse, how simply Paul assumes the spiritual participation of the Corinthians in his fortunes. It is God indeed who delivers him, but the deliverance is wrought while they, as well as other Churches, co-operate in supplication on his behalf. In the strained relations existing between himself and the Corinthians, the assumption here made so graciously probably did them more than justice; if there were unsympathetic souls among them, they must have felt in it a delicate rebuke. What follows—"that, for the gift bestowed upon us by the means of many, thanks may be given by many persons on our behalf" (R.V.)—simple and intelligible as it looks in English, is one of the passages which justify M. Sabatier's remark that Paul is difficult to understand and impossible to translate. The Revisers seem to have construed τὸ εἰς ἡμᾶς χάρισμα διὰ πολλῶν together, as if it had been τὸ διὰ π. ε. ἡ. χάρισμα, the meaning being that the favour bestowed on Paul in his deliverance from this peril had been bestowed at the intercession of many. Others get virtually the same meaning by construing τὸ εἰς ἡμᾶς χάρισμα with ἐκ πολλῶν προσώπων: the inversion is supposed to emphasise these last words; and as it was, on this view, prayer on the part of many persons that procured his deliverance, Paul is anxious that the deliverance itself should be acknowledged by the thanksgiving of many. It cannot be denied that both these renderings are grammatically violent, and it seems to me preferable to keep τὸ εἰς ἡμᾶς χάρισμα by itself, even though ἐκ πολλῶν προσώπων and διὰ πολλῶν should then reduplicate the same idea with only a slight variation. We should then render: "in order that, on the part of many persons, the favour shown to us may be gratefully acknowledged by many on our behalf." The pleonasm thus resulting strikes one rather as characteristic of St. Paul's mood in such passages, than as a thing open to objection.[6] But grammar apart, what really has to be emphasised here is again the communion of the saints. All the Churches pray for St. Paul—at least he takes it for granted that they do; and when he is rescued from danger, his own thanksgiving is multiplied a thousandfold by the thanksgivings of others on his behalf. This is the ideal of an evangelist's life; in all its incidents and emergencies, in all its perils and salvations, it ought to float in an atmosphere of prayer. Every interposition of God on the missionary's behalf is then recognised by him as a gift of grace (χάρισμα)—not, be it understood, a private favour, but a blessing and a power capacitating him for further service to the Church. Those who have lived through his straits and his triumphs with him in their prayers know how true that is.

At this point (ver. 12) the key in which Paul writes begins to change. We are conscious of a slight discord the instant he speaks about the testimony of his conscience. Yet the transition is as unforced as any such transition can be. I may well take for granted, seems to be the thought in his mind, that you pray for me; I may well ask you to unite with me in thanks to God for my deliverance; for if there is one thing I am sure of, and proud of, it is that I have been a loyal minister of God in the world, and especially to you. Fleshly wisdom has not been my guide. I have used no worldly policy; I have sought no selfish ends. In a holiness and sincerity which God bestows, in an element of crystal transparency, I have led my apostolic life. The world has never convicted me of anything dark or underhand; and in all the world none know better than you, among whom I lived longer than elsewhere, working with my hands, and preaching the Gospel as freely as God offers it, that I have walked in the light as He is in the light.

This general defence, which is not without its note of defiance, becomes defined in ver. 13. Plainly charges of insincerity had been made against Paul, particularly affecting his correspondence, and it is to these he addresses himself. It is not easy to be outspoken and conciliatory in the same sentence, to show your indignation to the man who charges you with double-dealing, and at the same time take him to your heart; and the Apostle's effort to do all these things at once has proved embarrassing to himself, and more than embarrassing to his interpreters. He begins, indeed, lucidly enough. "We write nothing else to you than what you read." He does not mean that he had no correspondence with members of the Church except in his public epistles; but that in these public epistles his meaning was obvious and on the surface. His style was not, as some had hinted, obscure, tortuous, elaborately ambiguous, full of loop-holes; he wrote like a plain man to plain men; he said what he meant, and meant what he said. Then he qualifies this slightly. "We write nothing to you but what you read—or in point of fact acknowledge," even apart from our writing. This seems to me the simplest interpretation of the words ἢ καὶ ἐπιγινώσκετε; and the simplest construction is then that of Hofmann, who puts a colon at ἐπιγινώσκετε, and with ἐλπίζω δὲ begins what is virtually a separate sentence. "And I hope that to the end ye will acknowledge, as in fact you acknowledged us in part, that we are your boast, as you also are ours, in the day of the Lord Jesus." Other possibilities of punctuation and construction are so numerous that it would be endless to exhibit them; and in the long-run they do not much affect the sense. What the reader has to seize is that Paul has been accused of insincerity, especially in his correspondence, and that he indignantly denies the charge; that, in spite of such accusations, he can point to at least a partial recognition among the Corinthians of what he and his fellow-workers really are; and that he hopes their confidence in him will increase and continue to the end. Should this bright hope be gratified, then in the day of the Lord Jesus it will be the boast of the Corinthians that they had the great Apostle Paul as their spiritual father, and the boast of the Apostle that the Corinthians were his spiritual children.

A passage like this—and there are many like it in St. Paul—has something in it humiliating. Is it not a disgrace to human nature that a man so open, so truthful, so brave, should be put to his defence on a charge of underhand dealing? Ought not somebody to have been deeply ashamed, for bringing this shame on the Apostle? Let us be very careful how we lend motives, especially to men whom we know to be better than ourselves. There is that in all our hearts which is hostile to them, and would not be grieved to see them degraded a little; and it is that, and nothing else, which supplies bad motives for their good actions, and puts an ambiguous face on their simplest behaviour. "Deceit," says Solomon, "is in the heart of them that imagine evil"; it is our own selves that we condemn most surely when we pass our bad sentence upon others.

The immediate result of imputing motives, and putting a sinister interpretation on actions, is that mutual confidence is destroyed; and mutual confidence is the very element and atmosphere in which any spiritual good can be done. Unless a minister and his congregation recognise each other as in the main what they profess to be, their relation is destitute of spiritual reality; it may be an infinite weariness, or an infinite torment; it can never be a comfort or a delight on one side or the other. What would a family be, without the mutual confidence of husband and wife, of parents and children? What is a state worth, for any of the ideal ends for which a state exists, if those who represent it to the world have no instinctive sympathy with the general life, and if the collective conscience regards the leaders from a distance with dislike or distrust? And what is the pastoral relation worth, if, instead of mutual cordiality, openness, readiness to believe and to hope the best, instead of mutual intercession and thanksgiving, of mutual rejoicing in each other, there is suspicion, reserve, insinuation, coldness, a grudging recognition of what it is impossible to deny, a willingness to shake the head and to make mischief? What an experience of life we see, what a final appreciation of the best thing, in that utterance of St. John in extreme age: "Beloved, let us love one another." All that is good for us, all glory and joy, is summarily comprehended in that.

The last words of the text—"the day of the Lord Jesus"—recall a very similar passage in 1 Thess. ii. 19: "What is our hope, or joy, or crown of rejoicing—is it not even ye—before our Lord Jesus at His coming?" In both cases our minds are lifted to that great presence in which St. Paul habitually lived; and as we stand there our disagreements sink into their true proportions; our judgments of each other are seen in their true colours. No one will rejoice then that he has made evil out of good, that he has cunningly perverted simple actions, that he has discovered the infirmities of preachers, or set the saints at variance; the joy will be for those who have loved and trusted each other, who have borne each other's faults and laboured for their healing, who have believed all things, hoped all things, endured all things, rather than be parted from each other by any failure of love. The mutual confidence of Christian ministers and Christian people will then, after all its trials, have its exceeding great reward.

III
THE CHURCH'S ONE FOUNDATION

"And in this confidence I was minded to come before unto you, that ye might have a second benefit; and by you to pass into Macedonia, and again from Macedonia to come unto you, and of you to be set forward on my journey unto Judæa. When I therefore was thus minded, did I show fickleness? or the things that I purpose, do I purpose according to the flesh, that with me there should be the yea yea and the nay nay? But as God is faithful, our word toward you is not yea and nay. For the Son of God, Jesus Christ, who was preached among you by us, *even* by me and Silvanus and Timothy, was not yea and nay, but in Him is yea. For how many soever be the promises of God, in Him is the yea: wherefore also through Him is the Amen, unto the glory of God through us."—2 Cor. i. 15-20 (R.V.).

The emphatic words in the first sentence are "in this confidence." All the Apostle's plans for visiting Corinth, both in general and in their details, depended upon the maintenance of a good understanding between himself and the Church; and the very prominence here given to this condition is a tacit accusation of those whose conduct had destroyed his confidence. When he intimated his intention of visiting them, according to the programme of vv. 15 and 16, he had felt sure of a friendly welcome, and of the cordial recognition of his apostolic authority; it was only when that assurance was taken away from him by news of what was being said and done at Corinth, that he had changed his plan. He had originally intended to go from Ephesus to Corinth, then from Corinth north into Macedonia, then back to Corinth again, and thence, with the assistance of the Corinthians, or their convoy for part of the way, to Jerusalem. Had this purpose been carried out, he would of course have been twice in Corinth, and it is to this that most scholars refer the words "a second benefit,"[7] or rather "grace." This reference, indeed, is not quite certain; and it cannot be proved, though it is made more probable, by using πρότερον and δευτέραν to interpret each other. It remains possible that when Paul said, "I was minded to come before unto you, that ye might have a second benefit," he was thinking of his original visit as the first, and of this purposed one as the second, "grace." This reading of his words has commended itself to scholars like Calvin, Bengel, and Heinrici. Whichever of these interpretations be correct, the Apostle had abandoned his purpose of going from Ephesus to Macedonia *viâ* Corinth, and had intimated in the First Epistle (chap. xvi. 5) his intention of reaching Corinth *viâ* Macedonia. This change of purpose is not sufficient to explain what follows. Unless there had been at Corinth a great deal of bad feeling, it would have passed without remark, as a thing which had no doubt good reasons, though the Corinthians were ignorant of them; at the very most, it would have called forth expressions of disappointment and regret. They would have been sorry that the benefit (χάρις), the token of Divine favour which was always bestowed when the Apostle came "in the fulness of the blessing of Christ," and "longing to impart some spiritual gift," had been delayed; but they would have acquiesced as in any other natural disappointment. But this was not what took place. They used the Apostle's change of purpose to assail his character. They charged him with "lightness," with worthless levity. They called him a weathercock, a Yes and No man, who said now one thing and now the opposite, who said both at once and with equal emphasis, who had his own interests in view in his fickleness, and whose word, to speak plainly, could never be depended upon.

The responsibility for the change of plan has already, in the emphatic ταύτῃ τῇ πεποιθήσει, been indirectly transferred to his accusers; but the Apostle stoops to answer them quite straightforwardly. His answer is indeed a challenge: "When I cherished that first wish to visit you, *was* I—dare you say I was—guilty of the levity with which you charge me? Or—to enlarge the question, and, seeing that my whole character is attacked, to bring my character as a whole into the discussion—the things that I purpose, do I purpose according to the flesh, that with me there should be the yea yea and the nay nay?" Am I, he seems to say, in my character and conduct, like a shifty, unprincipled politician—a man who has no convictions, or no conscience about his convictions—a man who is guided, not by any higher spirit dwelling in him, but solely by considerations of selfish interest? Do I say things out of mere compliment, not meaning them? When I make promises, or announce intentions, is it always with the tacit reservation that they may be cancelled if they turn out inconvenient? Do you suppose that I *purposely* represent myself (ἵνα ᾖ παρ' ἐμοί) as a man who affirms and denies, makes promises and breaks them, has Yes yes and No no dwelling side by side in his soul?[8] You know me far better than to suppose any such thing. All my communications with you have been inconsistent with such a view of my character. As God is faithful, our word to you is not Yes and No.

It is not incoherent, or equivocal, or self-contradictory. It is entirely truthful and self-consistent.

In this eighteenth verse the Apostle's mind is reaching out already to what he is going to make his real defence, and ὁ λόγος ἡμῶν ("our word") therefore carries a double weight. It covers at once whatever he had said to them about the proposed journey, and whatever he had said in his evangelistic ministry at Corinth. It is this latter sense of it that is continued in ver. 19: "For the Son of God, Christ Jesus, who was preached among you by us, by me and Silvanus and Timotheus, was not Yes and No, but in him Yes has found place. For how many soever are the promises of God, in Him is the Yes." Let us notice first the argumentative force of this. Paul is engaged in vindicating his character, and especially in maintaining his truthfulness and sincerity. How does he do so here? His unspoken assumption is, that character is determined by the main interest of life; that the work to which a man gives his soul will react upon the soul, changing it into its own likeness. As the dyer's hand is subdued to the element it works in, so was the whole being of Paul—such is the argument—subdued to the element in which he wrought, conformed to it, impregnated by it. And what was that element? It was the Gospel concerning God's Son, Jesus Christ. Was there any dubiety about what that was? any equivocal mixture of Yes and No there? Far from it. Paul was so certain of what it was that he repeatedly and solemnly anathematised man or angel who should venture to qualify, let alone deny it. There is no mixture of Yes and No in Christ. As the Apostle says elsewhere (Rom. xv. 8), Jesus Christ was a minister of the circumcision *"in the interest of the truth of God, with a view to the confirmation of the promises."* However many the promises might be, in Him a mighty affirmation, a mighty fulfilment, was given of every one. The ministry of the Gospel has this, then, as its very subject, its constant preoccupation, its highest glory—the absolute faithfulness of God. Who would venture to assert that Paul, or that anybody,[9] could catch the trick of equivocation in such a service? Who does not see that such a service must needs create true men?

To this argument there is, for the natural man, a ready answer. It by no means follows, he will say, that because the Gospel is devoid of ambiguity or inconsistency, equivocation and insincerity must be unknown to its preachers. A man may proclaim the true Gospel and in his other dealings be far from a true man. Experience justifies this reply; and yet it does not invalidate Paul's argument. That argument is good for the case in which it is applied. It might be *repeated* by a hypocrite, but no hypocrite could ever have *invented* it. It bears, indeed, a striking because an unintentional testimony to the height at which Paul habitually lived, and to his unqualified identification of himself with his apostolic calling. If a man has ten interests in life, more or less divergent, he may have as many inconsistencies in his behaviour; but if he has said with St. Paul, "This one thing I do," and if the one thing which absorbs his very soul is an unceasing testimony to the truth and faithfulness of God, then it is utterly incredible that he should be a false and faithless man. The work which claims him for its own with this absolute authority will seal him with its own greatness, its own simplicity and truth. He will not use levity. The things which he purposes, he will not purpose according to the flesh. He will not be guided by considerations perpetually varying, except in the point of being all alike selfish. He will not be a Yes and No man, whom nobody can trust.

The argumentative force of the passage being admitted, its doctrinal import deserves attention. The Gospel—which is identified with God's Son, Jesus Christ—is here described as a mighty affirmation. It is not Yes and No, a message full of inconsistencies, or ambiguities, a proclamation the sense of which no one can ever be sure he has grasped. In it (ἐν αὐτῷ means "in Christ") the everlasting Yea has found place. The perfect tense (γέγονεν) means that this grand affirmation has come to us, and is with us, for good and all. What it was and continued to be in Paul's time, it is to this day. It is in this positive, definite, unmistakable character that the strength of the Gospel lies. What a man cannot know, cannot seize, cannot tell, he cannot preach. The refutation of popular errors, even in theology, is not gospel; the criticism of traditional theories, even about Scripture, is not gospel; the intellectual "economy," with which a clever man in a dubious position uses language about the Bible or its doctrines which to the simple means Yes, and to the subtle qualifies the Yes enormously, is not gospel. There is no strength in any of these things. Dealing in them does not make character simple, sincere, massive, Christian. When they stamp themselves on the soul, the result is not one to which we could make the appeal which Paul makes here. If we have any gospel at all, it is because there are things which stand for us above all doubts, truths so sure that we cannot question them, so absolute that we cannot qualify them, so much our life that to tamper with them is to touch our very heart. Nobody has any right to preach who has not mighty affirmations to make concerning God's Son, Jesus Christ—affirmations in which there is no ambiguity, and which no questioning can reach.

In the Apostle's mind a particular turn is given to this thought by its connexion with the Old Testament. In Christ, he says, the Yes has been realised; for how many soever are the promises of God, in Him is the Yes. The mode of expression is rather peculiar, but the meaning is quite plain. Is there a single word of good, Paul asks, that God has ever spoken concerning man? Then that word is reaffirmed, it is confirmed, it is fulfilled in Jesus

Christ. It is no longer a word, but an actual gift to men, which they may take hold of and possess. Of course when Paul says "how many soever are the promises," he is thinking of the Old Testament. It was there the promises stood in God's name; and hence he tells us in this passage that Christ is the fulfilment of the Old Testament; in Him God has kept His word given to the fathers. All that the holy men of old were bidden to hope for, as the Spirit spoke through them in many parts and in many ways, is given to the world at last: he who has God's Son, Jesus Christ, has all God has promised, and all He can give.

There are two opposite ways of looking at the Old Testament with which this apostolic teaching is inconsistent, and which, by anticipation, it condemns.

There is the opinion of those who say that God's promises to His people in the Old Testament have not been fulfilled, and never will be. That is the opinion held by many among the modern Jews, who have renounced all that was most characteristic in the religion of their fathers, and attenuated it into the merest deistical film of a creed. It is the opinion also of many who study the Bible as a piece of literary antiquity, but get to no perception of the life which is in it, or of the organic connexion between the Old Testament and the New. What the Apostle says of his countrymen in his own time is true of both these classes—when they read the Scriptures, there is a veil upon their hearts. The Old Testament promises have been fulfilled, every one of them. Let a man be taught what they mean, not as dead letters in an ancient scroll, but as present words of the living God; and then let him look to Jesus Christ, the Son of God, and see whether there is not in Him the mighty, the perpetual confirmation of them all. We smile sometimes at what seems the whimsical way in which the early Christians, who had not yet a New Testament, found Christ everywhere in the Old; but though it may be possible to err in detail in this pursuit, it is not possible to err on the whole. The Old Testament is gathered up, every living word of it, in Him; we are misunderstanding it if we take it otherwise.

The opinion just described is a species of rationalism. There is another opinion, which, while agreeing with the rationalistic one that many of God's promises in the Old Testament have not yet been fulfilled, believes that their fulfilment is still to be awaited. If one might do so without offence, I should call this a species of fanaticism. It is the error of those who take the Jewish nation as such to be the subject of prophecy, and hope for its restoration to Palestine, for a revived Jerusalem, a new Davidic monarchy, even a reign of Christ over such an earthly kingdom. All this, if we may take the Apostle's word for it, is beside the mark. Equally with rationalism it loses the spirit of God's word in the letter. The promises have been fulfilled already, and we are not to look for another fulfilment. Those who have seen Christ have seen all that God is going to do—and it is quite adequate—to make His word good. He who has welcomed Christ knows that not one good word of all that God has spoken has failed. God has never, by the promises of the Old Testament, or by the instincts of human nature, put a hope or a prayer into man's heart that is not answered and satisfied abundantly in His Son.

But leaving the reference to the Old Testament on one side, it is well worth while for us to consider the practical meaning of the truth, that *all* God's promises are Yea in Christ. God's promises are His declarations of what He is willing to do for men; and in the very nature of the case they are at once the inspiration and the limit of our prayers. We are encouraged to ask all that God promises, and we must stop there. Christ Himself then is the measure of prayer to man; we can ask all that is in Him; we dare not ask anything that lies outside of Him. How the consideration of this should expand our prayers in some directions, and contract them in others! We can ask God to give us Christ's purity, Christ's simplicity, Christ's meekness and gentleness, Christ's faithfulness and obedience, Christ's victory over the world. Have we ever measured these things? Have we ever put them into our prayers with any glimmering consciousness of their dimensions, any sense of the vastness of our request? Nay, we can ask Christ's glory, His Resurrection Life of splendour and incorruption—the image of the heavenly. God has promised us all these things, and far more: but has He always promised what we ask? Can we fix our eyes on His Son, as He lived our life in this world, and remembering that this, so far as this world is concerned, is the measure of promise, ask without any qualification that our course here may be free from every trouble? Had Christ no sorrow? Did He never meet with ingratitude? Was He never misunderstood? Was He never hungry, thirsty, weary? If all God's promises are summed up in Him—if He is everything that God has to give—can we go boldly to the throne of grace, and pray to be exempted from what He had to bear, or to be richly provided with indulgences which He never knew? What if all unanswered prayers might be defined as prayers for things not included in the promises—prayers that we might get what Christ did not get, or be spared what He was not spared? The spirit of this passage, however, does not urge so much the definiteness as the compass and the certainty of the promises of God. They are so many that Paul could never enumerate them, and all of them are sure in Christ. And when our eyes are once opened on Him, does not He Himself become as it were inevitably the substance of our prayers? Is not our whole heart's desire, Oh that I might win *Him*! Oh that *He* might live in me, and make me what He is! Oh that *that* Man might arise in me, that the man I am may cease to be! Do we not feel that if God would give us His Son, all would be ours that we could take or He could give?

It is in this mood—with the consciousness, I mean, that in Jesus Christ the sure promises of God are inconceivably rich and good—that the Apostle adds: "wherefore also through Him is the Amen." It is not easy to put a prayer into words, whether of petition or thanksgiving, for men are not much in the habit of speaking to God; but it is easy to say Amen. That is the part of the Church when God's Son, Jesus Christ, is proclaimed, clothed in His Gospel. Apart from the Gospel, we do not know God, or what He will do, or will not do, for sinful men; but as we listen to the proclamation of His mercy and His faithfulness, as our eyes are opened to see in His Son all He has promised to do for us, nay, in a sense, all He has already done, our grateful hearts break forth in one grand responsive Amen! So let it be! we cry. Unless God had first prompted us by sending His Son, we could never have found it in our hearts to present such requests to Him; but through Christ we are enabled to present them, though it should be at first with only a look at Him, and an appropriating Amen. It is the very nature of prayer, indeed, to be the answer to promise. Amen is all, at bottom, that God leaves for us to say.

The solemn acceptance of a mercy so great—an acceptance as joyful as it is solemn, since the Amen is one rising out of thankful hearts—redounds to the glory of God. This is the final cause of redemption, and however it may be lost sight of in theologies which make man their centre, it is always magnified in the New Testament. The Apostle rejoices that his ministry and that of his friends (δι' ἡμῶν) contributes to this glory; and the whole connexion of thought in the passage throws a light on a great Bible word. God's glory is identified here with the recognition and appropriation by men of His goodness and faithfulness in Jesus Christ. He is glorified when it dawns on human souls that He has spoken good concerning them beyond their utmost imaginings, and when that good is seen to be indubitably safe and sure in His Son. The Amen in which such souls welcome His mercy is the equivalent of the Old Testament word, "Salvation is of the Lord." It is expanded in an apostolic doxology: "Of Him, and through Him, and to Him are all things: to Him be glory for ever."

IV
CHRISTIAN MYSTERIES

"Now He that stablisheth us with you in Christ, and anointed us, is God; who also sealed us, and gave *us* the earnest of the Spirit in our hearts."—2 Cor. i. 21, 22 (R.V.).

It is not easy to show the precise connexion between these words and those which immediately precede. Possibly it is emotional, rather than logical. The Apostle's heart swells as he contemplates in the Gospel the goodness and faithfulness of God; and though his argument is complete when he has exhibited the Gospel in that light, his mind dwells upon it involuntarily, past the mere point of proof; he lingers over the wonderful experience which Christians have of the rich and sure mercies. Those who try to make out a more precise sequence of thought than this are not very successful. Of course it is apparent that the keynote of the passage is in harmony with that of the previous verses. The ideas of "stablishing," of "sealing," and of an "earnest," are all of one family; they are all, as it were, variations of the one mighty *affirmation* which has been made of God's promises in Christ. From this point of view they have an argumentative value. They suggest that God, in all sorts of ways, makes believers as sure of the Gospel, and as constant to it, as He has made it sure and certain to them; and thus they exclude more decisively than ever the idea that the minister of the Gospel can be a man of Yes and No. But though this is true, it fails to do justice to the word on which the emphasis falls—namely, God. This, according to some interpreters, is done, if we suppose the whole passage to be, in the first instance, a disclaimer of any false inference which might be drawn from the words, "to the glory of God *by us*." "By us," Paul writes; for it was through the apostolic preaching that men were led to receive the Gospel, to look at God's promises, confirmed in Christ, with an appropriating Amen to His glory; but he hastens to add that it was God himself whose grace in its various workings was the beginning, middle, and end both of their faith and of their preaching. This seems to me rather artificial, and I do not think more than a connexion in sentiment, rather than in argument, can be insisted upon.

But setting this question aside, the interpretation of the two verses is of much interest. They contain some of the most peculiar and characteristic words of the New Testament—words to which, it is to be feared, many readers attach no very distinct idea. The simplest plan is to take the assertions one by one, as if God were the subject. Grammatically this is incorrect, for Θεός is certainly the predicate; but for the elucidation of the meaning this may be disregarded.

(1) First of all, then, God confirms us into Christ. "Us," of course, means St. Paul and the preachers whom he associates with himself,—Silas and Timothy. But when he adds "with you," he includes the Corinthians also, and all believers. He does not claim for himself any stedfastness in Christ, or any trustworthiness as dependent upon it, which he would on principle refuse to others. God, who makes His promises sure to those who receive them, gives those who receive them a firm grasp of the promises. Christ is here, with all the wealth of grace in Him, indubitable, unmistakable; and what God has done on that side, He does on the other also. He confirms believers into Christ. He makes their attachment to Christ, their possession of Him, a thing indubitable and irreversible. Salvation, to use the words of St. John, is true *in Him and in them*; in them, so far as God's purpose and work go, as much as in Him. He who is confirmed into Christ is in principle as trustworthy, as absolutely to be depended upon, as Christ Himself. The same character of pure truth is common to them both. Christ's existence as the Saviour, in whom all God's promises are guaranteed, and Paul's existence as a saved man with a sure grasp on all these promises, are alike proofs that God is faithful; the truth of God stands behind them both. It is to this that the appeal of vv. 15-20 is virtually made; it is this in the long-run which is called in question when the trustworthiness of Paul is impeached.

All this, it may be said, is ideal; but in what sense is it so? Not in the sense that it is fanciful or unreal; but in the sense that the divine law of our life, and the divine action upon our life, are represented in it. It is our calling as Christian people to be stedfast in Christ. Such stedfastness God is ever seeking to impart, and in striving to attain to it we can always appeal to Him for help. It is the opposite of instability; in a special sense it is the opposite of untrustworthiness. If we are letting God have His way with us in this respect, we are persons who can always be depended upon, and depended upon for conduct in keeping with the goodness and faithfulness of God, into which we have been confirmed by Him.

(2) From this general truth, with its application to all believers, the Apostle passes to another of more limited range. By including the Corinthians with himself in the first clause, he virtually excludes them in the second—"God anointed us." It is true that the New Testament speaks of an anointing

which is common to all believers—"*Ye* have an anointing from the Holy One; ye all know" (1 John ii. 20): but here, on the contrary, something special is meant. This can only be the consecration of Paul, and of those for whom he speaks, to the apostolic or evangelistic ministry. It is worth noticing that in the New Testament the act of anointing is never ascribed to any one but God. The only unction which qualifies for service in the Christian dispensation, or which confers dignity in the Christian community, is the unction from on high. "God anointed Jesus of Nazareth with the Holy Ghost and with power," and it is the participation in this great anointing which capacitates any one to work in the Gospel.[10] Paul undoubtedly claimed, in virtue of his divine call to apostleship, a peculiar authority in the Church; but we cannot define any peculiarity in his possession of the Spirit. The great gift which must be held in some sense by all Christians—"for if any man have not the Spirit of Christ, he is none of His"—was in him intensified, or specialised, for the work he had to do. But it is one Spirit in him and in us, and that is why we do not find the exercise of his authority alien or galling. It is authority divorced from "unction"—authority without this divine qualification—against which the Christian spirit rebels. And though "unction" cannot be defined; though no material guarantee can be given or taken for the possession of the Spirit; though a merely historical succession is, so far as this spiritual competence and dignity are concerned, a mere irrelevance; though, as Vinet said, we think of unction rather when it is absent than when it is present,—still, the thing itself is recognisable enough. It bears witness to itself, as light does; it carries its own authority, its own dignity, with it; it is the *ultima ratio*, the last court of appeal, in the Christian community. It may be that Paul is preparing already, by this reference to his commission, for the bolder assertion of his authority at a later stage.

(3) These two actions of God, however—the establishing of believers in Christ, which goes on continually (βεβαιῶν), and the consecration of Paul to the apostleship, which was accomplished once for all (χρίσας)—go back to prior actions, in which, again, all believers have an interest. They have a common basis in the great deeds of grace in which the Christian life began. God, he says, is He who also sealed us, and gave the earnest of the Spirit in our hearts.

"He also sealed us." It seems strange that so figurative a word should be used without a hint of explanation, and we must assume that it was so familiar in the Church that the right application could be taken for granted. The middle voice (σφραγισάμενος) makes it certain that the main idea is, "He marked us as His own." This is the sense in which the word is frequently used in the Book of Revelation: the servants of God are sealed on their foreheads, that they may be recognised as His. But what is the seal?

Under the Old Testament, the mark which God set upon His people—the covenant sign by which they were identified as His—was circumcision. Under the New Testament, where everything carnal has passed away, and religious materialism is abolished, the sign is no longer in the body; we are sealed with the Holy Spirit of promise (Eph. i. 13 f.). But the past tense ("He *sealed* us"), and its recurrence in Eph. i. 13 ("ye *were* sealed"), suggest a very definite reference of this word, and beyond doubt it alludes to baptism. In the New Testament, baptism and the giving of the Holy Spirit are regularly connected with each other. Christians are born of water and of the Spirit. "Repent," is the earliest preaching of the Gospel (Acts ii. 38), "and be baptised every one of you, ... and ye shall receive the gift of the Holy Ghost." In early Christian writers the use of the word "seal" (σφραγίς) as a technical term for baptism is practically universal; and when we combine this practice with the New Testament usage in question, the inference is inevitable. God puts His *seal* upon us, He *marks* us as His own, when we are baptised.[11]

But the seal is not baptism as a ceremonial act. It is neither immersion nor sprinkling nor any other mode of lustration which marks us out as God's. The seal by which "the Lord knoweth them that are His" is His Spirit; it is the impress of His Spirit upon them. When that impress can be traced upon our souls, by Him, or by us, or by others, then we have the witness in ourselves; the Spirit bears witness with our spirits that we are children of God.

But of all words "spirit" is the vaguest; and if we had nothing but the word itself to guide us, we should either lapse into superstitious ideas about the virtue of the sacrament, or into fanatical ideas about incommunicable inward experiences in which God marked us for His own. The New Testament provides us with a more excellent way than either; it gives the word "spirit" a rich but definite moral content; it compels us, if we say we have been sealed with the Spirit, and claimed by God as His, to exhibit the distinguishing features of those who are His. "The Lord is the Spirit" (2 Cor. iii. 17). To be sealed with the Spirit is to bear, in however imperfect a degree, in however inconspicuous a style, the image of the heavenly man, the likeness of Jesus Christ. There are many passages in his Epistles in which St. Paul enlarges on the work of the Spirit in the soul; all the various dispositions which it creates, all the fruits of the Spirit, may be conceived as different parts of the impression made by the seal. We must think of these in detail, if we wish to give the word its meaning; we must think of them in contrast with the unspiritual nature, if we wish to give it any edge. Once, say, we walked in the lusts of the flesh: has Christ redeemed us, and set on our souls and our bodies the seal of His purity? Once we were hot and passionate, given to angry words and hasty, intemperate deeds: are we sealed now with the meekness and gentleness of Jesus? Once we were grasping and covetous, even to the verge of dishonesty; we could not let money pass us, and we could not part with it: have we been sealed with the liberality of Him who says, "It is more blessed to give than to receive"? Once a wrong rankled in our hearts; the sun went down upon our wrath, not once or twice, but a thousand times, and found it as implacable as ever: is that deep brand of vindictiveness effaced now, and in its stead imprinted deep the Cross of Christ, where He loved us, and gave Himself for us, and prayed, "Father, forgive them"? Once our conversation was corrupt; it had a taint in it; it startled and betrayed the innocent; it was vile and foolish and unseemly: are these things of the past now? and has Christ set upon our lips the seal of His own grace and truth, of His own purity and love, so that every word we speak is good, and brings blessing to those who hear us? These things, and such as these, are the seal of the Spirit. They are Christ in us. They are the stamp which God sets upon men when He exhibits them as His own.

The seal, however, has another use than that of marking and identifying property. It is a symbol of assurance. It is the answer to a challenge. It is in this sense that it is easiest to apply the figure to baptism. Baptism does not, indeed, carry with it the actual possession of all these spiritual features; it is not even, as an *opus operatum*, the implanting of them in the soul; but it is a divine pledge that they are within our reach; we can appeal to it as an assurance that God has come to us in His grace, has claimed us as His own, and is willing to conform us to the image of His Son. In this sense, it is legitimate and natural to call it God's seal upon His people.

(4) Side by side with "He sealed us," the Apostle writes, "He gave the earnest of the Spirit in our hearts." After what has been said, it is obvious that this is another aspect of the same thing. We are sealed with the Spirit, and we get the earnest of the Spirit. In other words, the Spirit is viewed in two characters: first, as a seal; and then as an earnest. This last word has a very ancient history. It is found in the Book of Genesis (xxxviii. 18: וְעֵרָבֹן), and was carried, no doubt, by Phœnician traders, who had much occasion to use it, both to Greece and Italy. From the classical peoples it has come more or less directly to us. It means properly a small sum of money paid to clench a bargain, or to ratify an engagement. Where there is an earnest, there is more to follow, and more of essentially the same kind—that is what it signifies. Let us apply this now to the expression of St. Paul, "the earnest of the Spirit." It means, we must see, that in the gift of this Spirit, in that measure in which we now possess it, God has not given all He has to give. On the contrary, He has come under an obligation to give more:

what we have now is but "the firstfruits of the Spirit" (Rom. viii. 23). It is an indication and a pledge of what is yet to be, but bears no proportion to it. All we can say on the basis of this text is, that between the present and the future gift—between the earnest and that which it guarantees—there must be some kind of congruity, some affinity which makes the one a natural and not an arbitrary reason for believing in the other.

But the Corinthians were not limited to this text. They had St. Paul's general teaching in their minds to interpret it by; and if we wish to know what it meant even for them, we must fill out this vague idea with what the Apostle tells us elsewhere. Thus in the great text in Ephesians (i. 13 f.), so often referred to, he speaks of the Holy Spirit with which we were sealed as the earnest *of our inheritance*. God has an "inheritance" in store for us. His Spirit makes us sons; and if sons, then heirs; heirs of God, joint-heirs with Christ. This connexion of the Spirit, sonship, and inheritance, is constant in St. Paul; it is one of his most characteristic combinations. What then *is* the inheritance of which the Spirit is the earnest? That no one can tell. "Eye hath not seen, nor ear heard, neither have entered into the heart of man, the things that God hath prepared for them that love Him." But though we cannot tell more precisely, we can say that if the Spirit is the earnest of it, it must be in some sense a development of the Spirit; life in an order of being which matches the Spirit, and for which the Spirit qualifies. If we say it is "glory," then we must remember that only Christ in us (the seal of the Spirit) can be *the hope* of glory.

The application of this can be made very plain. Our whole life in this world looks to some future, however near or bounded it may be; and every power we perfect, every capacity we acquire, every disposition and spirit we foster, is an earnest of something in that future. Here is a man who gives himself to the mastery of a trade. He acquires all its skill, all its methods, all its resources. There is nothing any tradesman can do that he cannot do as well or better. What is that the earnest of? What does it ensure, and as it were put into his hand by anticipation? It is the earnest of constant employment, of good wages, of respect from fellow-workmen, perhaps of wealth. Here, again, is a man with the scientific spirit. He is keenly inquisitive about the facts and laws of the world in which we live. Everything is interesting to him—astronomy, physics, chemistry, biology, history. What is this the earnest of? It is the earnest, probably, of scientific achievements of some kind, of intellectual toils and intellectual victories. This man will enter into the inheritance of science; he will walk through the kingdoms of knowledge in the length of them and the breadth of them, and will claim them as his own. And so it is wherever we choose to take our illustrations. Every spirit that dwells in us, and is cultivated and cherished by us, is an *earnest*, because it fits and furnishes us for some particular thing. *God's* Spirit also is an earnest of an inheritance which is incorruptible, undefiled, imperishable: can we assure ourselves that we have anything in our souls which promises, because it matches with, an inheritance like this? When we come to die, this will be a serious question. The faculties of accumulation, of mechanical skill, of scientific research, of trade on a great or a small scale, of agreeable social intercourse, of comfortable domestic life, may have been brought to perfection in us; but can we console ourselves with the thought that *these* have the earnest of immortality? Do they qualify us for, and by qualifying assure us of, the incorruptible kingdom? Or do we not see at once that a totally different equipment is needed to make men at home there, and that nothing can be the earnest of an eternal life of blessedness with God except that Holy Spirit with which He seals His own, and through which He makes them, even here, partakers of the divine nature?

We cannot study these words without becoming conscious of the immense enlargement which the Christian religion has brought to the human mind, of the vast expansion of hope which is due to the Gospel, and at the same time of the moral soundness and sobriety with which that hope is conceived. The promises of God were first really apprehended in Jesus Christ; in Him as He lived and died and rose again from the dead, in Him especially as He lives in immortal glory, men first saw what God was able and willing to do for them, and they saw this in its true relations. They saw it under its moral and spiritual conditions. It was not a future unconnected with the present, or connected with it in an arbitrary or incalculable way. It was a future which had its earnest in the present, a guarantee not alien to it, but akin—the Spirit of Christ implanted in the heart, the likeness of Christ sealed upon the nature. The glorious inheritance was the inheritance, not of strangers, but of sons; and it still becomes sure as the Spirit of sonship is received, and fades into incredibility when that Spirit is extinguished or depressed. If we could live in the Spirit with the completeness of Christ, or even of St. Paul, we should feel that we really had an earnest of immortality; the glory of heaven would be as certain to us as the faithfulness of God to His promise.

V
A PASTOR'S HEART

"But I call God for a witness upon my soul, that to spare you I forbare to come unto Corinth. Not that we have lordship over your faith, but are helpers of your joy: for by faith ye stand. But I determined this for myself, that I would not come again to you with sorrow. For if I make you sorry, who then is he that maketh me glad, but he that is made sorry by me? And I wrote this very thing, lest, when I came, I should have sorrow from them of whom I ought to rejoice; having confidence in you all, that my joy is *the joy* of you all. For out of much affliction and anguish of heart I wrote unto you with many tears; not that ye should be made sorry, but that ye might know the love which I have more abundantly unto you."—2 Cor. i. 23-ii. 4 (R.V.).

When Paul came to the end of the paragraph in which he defends himself from the charge of levity and untrustworthiness by appealing to the nature of the Gospel which he preached, he seems to have felt that it was hardly sufficient for his purpose. It might be perfectly true that the Gospel was one mighty affirmation, with no dubiety or inconsistency about it; it might be as true that it was a supreme testimony to the faithfulness of God; but bad men, or suspicious men, would not admit that its character covered his. Their own insincerities would keep them from understanding its power to change its loyal ministers into its own likeness, and to stamp them with its own simplicity and truth. The mere invention of the argument in vv. 18-20 is of itself the highest possible testimony to the ideal height at which the Apostle lived; no man conscious of duplicity could ever have had it occur to him. But it had the defect of being too good for his purpose; the foolish and the false could see a triumphant reply to it; and he leaves it for a solemn asseveration of the reason which actually kept him from carrying out his first intention. "I call God to witness against my soul, that sparing you I forbore to come[12] to Corinth." The soul is the seat of life; he stakes his life, as it were, in God's sight, upon the truth of his words. It was not consideration for himself, in any selfish spirit, but consideration for them, which explained his change of purpose. If he had carried out his intention, and gone to Corinth, he would have had to do so, as he says in 1 Cor. iv. 21, with a rod, and this would not have been pleasant either for him or for them.

This is very plain—plain even to the dullest; the Apostle has no sooner set it down than he feels it is too plain. "To spare us," he hears the Corinthians say to themselves as they read: "who is he that he should take this tone in speaking to us?" And so he hastens to anticipate and deprecate their touchy criticism: "Not that we lord it over your faith, but we are helpers of your joy; as far as faith is concerned, your position, of course, is secure."

This is a very interesting aside; the digressions in St. Paul, as in Plato, are sometimes more attractive than the arguments. It shows us, for one thing, the freedom of the Christian faith. Those who have received the Gospel have all the responsibilities of mature men; they have come to their majority as spiritual beings; they are not, in their character and standing as Christians, subject to arbitrary and irresponsible interference on the part of others. Paul himself was the great preacher of this spiritual emancipation: he gloried in the liberty with which Christ made men free. For him the days of bondage were over; there was no subjection for the Christian to any custom or tradition of men, no enslavement of his conscience to the judgment or the will of others, no coercion of the spirit except by itself. He had great confidence in this Gospel and in its power to produce generous and beautiful characters. That it was capable of perversion also he knew very well. It was open to the infusion of self-will; in the intoxication of freedom from arbitrary and unspiritual restraint, men might forget that the believer was bound to be a law to himself, that he was free, not in lawless self-will, but only in the Lord. Nevertheless, the principle of freedom was too sacred to be tampered with; it was necessary both for the education of the conscience and for the enrichment of spiritual life with the most various and independent types of goodness; and the Apostle took all the risks, and all the inconveniences even, rather than limit it in the least.

This passage shows us one of the inconveniences. The newly enfranchised are mightily sensible of their freedom, and it is extremely difficult to tell them of their faults. At the very mention of authority all that is bad in them, as well as all that is good, is on the alert; and spiritual independence and the liberty of the Christian people have been represented and defended again and again, not only by an awful sense of responsibility to Christ, which lifts the lowliest lives into supreme greatness, but by pride, bigotry, moral insolence, and every bad passion. What is to be done in such cases as these, where liberty has forgotten the law of Christ? It is certainly not to be denied in principle: Paul, even with the peculiar position of an apostle, and of the spiritual father of those to whom he writes (1 Cor. iv. 15), does not claim such an authority over their faith—that is, over the people themselves in their character of believers—as a master has over his slaves. Their position as Christians is secure; it is taken for granted by him as by them; and this being so, no arbitrary *ipse dixit* can settle anything in dispute between them; he can issue no orders to the Church such as the Roman Emperor could issue to his soldiers. He may appeal to them on spiritual grounds; he may enlighten their consciences by interpreting to them the law of Christ; he may try to reach them by praise or blame; but simple compulsion is not one of his resources. If St. Paul says this, occupying as he does a position which contains in itself a natural authority which most ministers can never have, ought not all official persons and classes in the Church to beware of the claims they make for themselves? A clerical hierarchy, such as has been developed and perfected in the Church of Rome, does lord it over faith; it *legislates* for the laity, both in faith and practice, without their co-operation, or even their consent; it keeps the *cœtus fidelium*, the mass of believing men, which *is* the Church, in a perpetual minority. All this, in a so-called apostolic succession, is not only anti-apostolic, but anti-Christian. It is the confiscation of Christian freedom; the keeping of believers in leading-strings all their days, lest in their liberty they should go astray. In the Protestant Churches, on the other hand, the danger on the whole is of the opposite kind. We are too jealous of authority. We are too proud of our own competence. We are too unwilling, individually, to be taught and corrected. We resent, I will not say criticism, but the most serious and loving voice which speaks to us to disapprove. Now liberty, when it does not deepen the sense of responsibility to God and to the brotherhood—and it does not always do so—is an anarchic and disintegrating force. In all the Churches it exists, to some extent, in this degraded form; and it is this which makes Christian education difficult, and Church discipline often impossible. These are serious evils, and we can only overcome them if we cultivate the sense of responsibility at the same time that we maintain the principle of liberty, remembering that it is those only of whom he says, "Ye were bought with a price" (and are therefore Christ's slaves), to whom St. Paul also gives the charge: "Be not ye slaves of men."

This passage not only illustrates the freedom of Christian faith, it presents us with an ideal of the Christian ministry. "We are not lords over your faith," says St. Paul, "but we are helpers of your joy." It is implied in this that joy is the very end and element of the Christian life, and that it is the minister's duty to be at war with all that restrains it, and to co-operate in all that leads to it. Here, one would say, is something in which all can agree: all human souls long for joy, however much they may differ about the spheres of law and liberty. But have not most Christian people, and most Christian congregations, something here to accuse themselves of? Do not many of us bear false witness against the Gospel on this very point? Who that came into most churches, and looked at the uninterested faces, and hearkened to the listless singing, would feel that the soul of the religion, so languidly honoured, was mere joy—joy unspeakable, if we trust the Apostles, and full of glory? It is ingratitude which makes us forget this. We begin to grow blind to the great things which lie at the basis of our faith; the love of God in Jesus Christ—that love in which He died for us upon the tree—begins to lose its newness and its wonder; we speak of it without apprehension and without feeling; it does not make our hearts burn within us any more; we have no joy in it. Yet we may be sure of this—that we can have no joy without it. And he is our best friend, the truest minister of God to us, who helps us to the place where the love of God is poured out in our hearts in its omnipotence, and we renew our joy in it. In doing so, it may be necessary for the minister to cause pain by the way. There is no joy, nor any possibility of it, where evil is tolerated. There is no joy where sin has been taken under the patronage of those who call themselves by Christ's name. There is no joy where pride is in arms in the soul, and is reinforced by suspicion, by obstinacy, even by jealousy and hate, all waiting to dispute the authority of the preacher of repentance. When these evil spirits are overcome, and cast out, which may only be after a painful conflict, joy will have its opportunity again,—joy, whose right it is to reign in the Christian soul and the Christian community. Of all evangelistic forces, this joy is the most potent; and for that, above all other reasons, it should be cherished wherever Christian people wish to work the work of their Lord.

After this little digression on the freedom of the faith, and on joy as the element of the Christian life, Paul returns to his defence. "To spare you I forbore to come; for I made up my own mind on this, not to come to you a second time in sorrow." Why was he so determined about this? He explains in the second verse. It is because all his joy is bound up in the Corinthians, so that if he grieves them he has no one left to gladden him except those whom he has grieved—in other words, he has no joy at all. And he not only made up his mind definitely on this; he wrote also in exactly this sense: he did not wish, when he came, to have sorrow from those from whom he ought to have joy. In that desire to spare himself, as well as them, he counted on their sympathy; he was sure that his own joy was the joy of every one of them, and that they would appreciate his motives in not fulfilling a promise, the fulfilment of which in the circumstances would only have brought grief both to them and him. The delay has given them time to put right what was amiss in their Church, and has ensured a joyful time to them all when his visit is actually accomplished.

There are some grammatical and historical difficulties here which claim attention. The most discussed is that of the first verse: what is the precise meaning of τὸ μὴ πάλιν ἐν λύπῃ πρὸς ὑμᾶς ἐλθεῖν? There is no doubt that this is the correct order of the words, and just as little, I think, that the natural meaning is that Paul had once visited Corinth in grief, and was resolved not to repeat such a visit. So the words are taken by Meyer, Hofmann, Schmiedel, and others. The visit in question cannot have been that on occasion of which the Church was founded; and as the connexion between this passage and the last chapter of the First Epistle is as close as can be conceived (see the Introduction), it cannot have fallen between the two: the only other supposition is, that it took place before the First Epistle was written. This is the opinion of Lightfoot, Meyer, and Weiss; and it is not fatal to it that no such visit is mentioned elsewhere—*e.g.*, in the book of Acts. Still, the interpretation is not essential; and if we can get over chap. xiii. 2, it is quite possible to agree with Heinrici that Paul had only been in Corinth once, and that what he means in ver. 1 here is: "I determined not to carry out my purpose of revisiting you, in sorrow."

There is a difficulty of another sort in ver. 2. One's first thought is to read καὶ τίς ὁ εὐφραίνων με κ.τ.λ., as a real singular, with a reference, intelligible though indefinite, to the notorious but penitent sinner of Corinth. "I vex you, I grant it; but where does my joy come from—the joy without which I am resolved not to visit you—except from one who is vexed by me?" The bad man's repentance had made Paul glad, and there is a worthy considerateness in this indefinite way of designating him. This interpretation has commended itself to so sound a judge as Bengel, and though more recent scholars reject it with practical unanimity, it is difficult to be sure that it is wrong. The alternative is to generalise the τίς, and make the question mean: "If I vex you, where can I find joy? All my joy is in you, and to see you grieved leaves me absolutely joyless."

A third difficulty is the reference of ἔγραψα τοῦτο αὐτὸ in ver. 3. Language very similar is found in ver. 9 (εἰς τοῦτο γὰρ καὶ ἔγραψα), and again in chap. vii. 8-12 (ἐλύπησα ὑμᾶς ἐν τῇ ἐπιστολῇ). It is very natural to think here of our First Epistle. It served the purpose contemplated by the letter here described; it told of Paul's change of purpose; it warned the Corinthians to rectify what was amiss, and so to order their affairs that he might come, not with a rod, but in love and in the spirit of meekness; or, as he says here, not to have sorrow, but, what he was entitled to, joy from his visit. All that is alleged against this is that our First Epistle does not suit the description given of the writing in ver. 4: "out of much affliction and anguish of heart I wrote unto you with many tears." But when those parts of the First Epistle are read, in which St. Paul is not answering questions submitted to him by the Church, but writing out of his heart upon its spiritual condition, this will appear a dubious assertion. What a pain must have been at his heart, when such passionate words broke from him as these: "Is Christ divided? Was Paul crucified for you?—What is Apollos, and what is Paul?—With me it is a very little thing to be judged by you.—Though ye have ten thousand instructors in Christ, yet have ye not many fathers: for in Christ Jesus I begot you through the Gospel.—I will know, not the speech of them that are puffed up, but the power." Not to speak of the fifth and sixth chapters, words like these justify us in supposing that the First Epistle may be, and in all probability is, meant.[13]

Putting these details aside, as of mainly historical interest, let us look rather at the spirit of this passage. It reveals, more clearly perhaps than any passage in the New Testament, the essential qualification of the Christian minister—a heart pledged to his brethren in the love of Christ. That is the only possible basis of an authority which can plead its own and its Master's cause against the aberrations of spiritual liberty, and there is always both room and need for it in the Church. Certainly it is the hardest of all authorities to win, and the costliest to maintain, and therefore substitutes for it are innumerable. The poorest are those that are merely official, where a minister appeals to his standing as a member of a separate order, and expects men to reverence that. If this was once possible in Christendom, if it is still possible where men secretly wish to shunt their spiritual responsibilities upon others, it is not possible where emancipation has been grasped either in an anarchic or in a Christian spirit. Let the great idea of liberty, and of all that is cognate with liberty, once dawn upon their souls, and men will never sink again to the recognition of anything as an authority that does not attest itself in a purely spiritual way. "Orders" will mean nothing to them but an arrogant unreality, which in the name of all that is free and Christian they are bound to contemn. It will be the same, too, with any authority which has merely an intellectual basis. A professional education, even in theology, gives no man authority to meddle with another in his character as a Christian. The University and the Divinity Schools can confer no competence here. Nothing that distinguishes a man from his fellows, nothing in virtue of which he takes a place of superiority apart: on the contrary, that love only which makes him entirely one with them in Jesus Christ, can ever entitle him to interpose. If their joy is his joy; if to grieve them, even for their good, is his grief; if the cloud and sunshine of their lives cast their darkness and their light immediately upon him; if he shrinks from the faintest approach to self-assertion, yet would sacrifice anything to perfect their joy in the Lord,—then he is in the true apostolical succession; and whatever authority may rightly be exercised, where the freedom of the spirit is the law, may rightly be exercised by him. What is required of Christian workers in every degree—of ministers and teachers, of parents and friends, of all Christian people with the cause of Christ at heart—is a greater expenditure of soul on their work. Here is a whole paragraph of St. Paul, made up almost entirely of "grief" and "joy"; what depth of feeling lies behind it! If this is alien to us in our work for Christ, we need not wonder that our work does not tell.

And if this is true generally, it is especially true when the work we have to do is that of rebuking sin. There are few things which try men, and show what spirit they are of, more searchingly than this. We like to be on God's side, and to show our zeal for Him, and we are far too ready to put all our bad passions at His service. But these are a gift which He declines. Our wrath does not work His righteousness—a lesson that even good men, of a kind, are very slow to learn. To denounce sin, and to declaim about it, is the easiest and cheapest thing in the world: one could not do less where sin is concerned, unless he did nothing at all. Yet how common denunciation is. It seems almost to be taken for granted as the natural and praiseworthy mode of dealing with evil. People assail the faults of the community, or even of their brethren in the Church, with violence, with temper, with the tone, often, of injured innocence. They think that when they do so they are doing God service; but surely we should have learned by this time that nothing could be so unlike God, so unfaithful and preposterous as a testimony for Him. God Himself overcomes evil with good; Christ vanquishes the sin of the world by taking the burden of it on Himself; and if we wish to have part in the same work, there is only the same method open to us. Depend upon it, we shall not make others weep for that for which we have not wept; we shall not make that touch the hearts of others which has not first touched our own. That is the law which God has established in the world; He submitted to it Himself in the person of His Son, and He requires us to submit to it. Paul was certainly a very fiery man; he could explode, or flame up, with far more effect than most people; yet it was not there that his great strength lay. It was in the passionate tenderness that checked that vehement temper, and made the once haughty spirit say what he says here: "Out of much affliction and anguish of heart, I wrote unto you with many tears, not that you might be grieved, but that you might know the love which I have more abundantly toward you." In words like these the very spirit speaks which is God's power to subdue and save the sinful.

It is worth dwelling upon this, because it is so fundamental, and yet so slowly learned. Even Christian ministers, who ought to know the mind of Christ, almost universally, at least in the beginning of their work, when they preach about evil, lapse into the scolding tone. It is of no use whatever in the pulpit, and of just as little in the Sunday-school class, in the home, or in any relation in which we seek to exercise moral authority. The one basis for that authority is love; and the characteristic of love in the presence of evil is not that it becomes angry, or insolent, or disdainful, but that it takes the burden and the shame of the evil to itself. The hard, proud heart is impotent; the mere official is impotent, whether he call himself priest or pastor; all hope and help lie in those who have learned of the Lamb of God who bore the sin of the world. It is soul-travail like His, attesting love like His; that wins all the victories in which He can rejoice.

VI
CHURCH DISCIPLINE

"But if any hath caused sorrow, he hath caused sorrow, not to me, but in part (that I press not too heavily) to you all. Sufficient to such a one is this punishment which was *inflicted* by the many; so that contrariwise ye should rather forgive him and comfort him, lest by any means such a one should be swallowed up with his overmuch sorrow. Wherefore I beseech you to confirm your love toward him. For to this end also did I write, that I might know the proof of you, whether ye are obedient in all things. But to whom ye forgive anything, I *forgive* also: for what I also have forgiven, if I have forgiven anything, for your sakes *have I forgiven it* in the person of Christ; that no advantage may be gained over us by Satan: for we are not ignorant of his devices."—2 Cor. ii. 5-11 (R.V.).

The foregoing paragraph of the Epistle has said a great deal about sorrow, the sorrow felt by St. Paul on the one hand, and the sorrow he was reluctant to cause the Corinthians on the other. In the passage before us reference is evidently made to the person who was ultimately responsible for all this trouble. If much in it is indefinite to us, and only leaves a doubtful impression, it was clear enough for those to whom it was originally addressed; and that very indefiniteness has its lesson. There are some things to which it is sufficient, and more than sufficient, to allude; least said is best said. And even when plain-speaking has been indispensable, a stage arrives at which there is no more to be gained by it; if the subject *must* be referred to, the utmost generality of reference is best. Here the Apostle discusses the case of a person who had done something extremely bad; but with the sinner's repentance assured, it is both characteristic and worthy of him that neither here nor in chap. vii. does he mention the name either of offender or offence. It is perhaps too much to expect students of his writings, who wish to trace out in detail all the events of his life, and to give the utmost possible definiteness to all its situations, to be content with this obscurity; but students of his spirit—Christian people reading the Bible for practical profit—do not need to perplex themselves as to this penitent man's identity.

He may have been the person mentioned in 1 Cor. v. who had married his stepmother; he may have been some one who had been guilty of a personal insult to the Apostle: the main point is that he was a sinner whom the discipline of the Church had saved.[14]

The Apostle had been expressing himself about his sorrow with great vehemence, and he is careful in his very first words to make it plain that the offence which had caused such sorrow was no personal matter. It concerned the Church as well as him. "If any one hath caused sorrow, he hath not caused sorrow to me, but in part to you all." To say more than this would be to exaggerate (ἐπιβαρεῖν).[15] The Church, in point of fact, had not been moved either as universally or as profoundly as it should have been by the offence of this wicked man. The penalty imposed upon him, whatever it may have been, had not been imposed by a unanimous vote, but only by a majority; there were some who sympathised with him, and would have been less severe.[16] Still, it had brought conviction of his sin to the offender; he could not brazen it out against such consenting condemnation as there was; he was overwhelmed with penitential grief. This is why the Apostle says, "Sufficient to such a one is this punishment which was inflicted by the majority." It has served the purpose of all disciplinary treatment; and having done so, must now be superseded by an opposite line of action. "Contrariwise ye should rather forgive him and comfort him, lest by any means such a one should be swallowed up with his overmuch sorrow." In St. Paul's sentence "such a one" comes last, with the emphasis of compassion upon it. He had been "such a one," to begin with, as it was a pain and a shame even to think about; he is "such a one," now, as the angels in heaven are rejoicing over; "such a one" as the Apostle, having the spirit of Him who received sinners, regards with profoundest pity and yearning; "such a one" as the Church ought to meet with pardoning and restoring love, lest grief sink into despair, and the sinner cut himself off from hope. To prevent such a deplorable result, the Corinthians are by some formal action (κυρῶσαι: cf. Gal. iii. 15) to forgive him, and receive him again as a brother; and in their forgiveness and welcome he is to find the pledge of the great love of God.

This whole passage is of interest from the light which it throws upon the discipline of the Church; or, to use less technical and more correct language, the Christian treatment of the erring.

It shows us, for one thing, the aim of all discipline: it is, in the last resort, the restoration of the fallen. The Church has, of course, an interest of its own to guard; it is bound to protest against all that is inconsistent with its character; it is bound to expel scandals. But the Church's protest, its condemnation, its excommunication even, are not ends in themselves; they are means to that which is really an end in itself, a priceless good which justifies every extreme of moral severity, the winning again of the sinner through repentance. The judgment of the Church is the instrument of God's love, and the moment it is accepted in the sinful soul it begins to work as a redemptive force. The humiliation it inflicts is that which God exalts; the sorrow, that which He comforts. But when a scandal comes to light in a Christian congregation—when one of its members is discovered in a fault gross, palpable, and offensive—what is the significance of that movement of feeling which inevitably takes place? In how many has it the character of goodness and of severity, of condemnation and of compassion, of love and fear, of pity and shame, the only character that has any virtue in it to tell for the sinner's recovery? If you ask nine people out of ten what a scandal is, they will tell you it is something which makes talk; and the talk in nine cases out of ten will be malignant, affected, more interesting to the talkers than any story of virtue or piety—scandal itself, in short, far more truly than its theme. Does anybody imagine that gossip is one of the forces that waken conscience, and work for the redemption of our fallen brethren? If this is all we can do, in the name of all that is Christian let us keep silence. Every word spoken about a brother's sin, that is not prompted by a Christian conscience, that does not vibrate with the love of a Christian heart, is itself a sin against the mercy and the judgment of Christ.

We see here not only the end of Church discipline, but the force of which it disposes for the attainment of its end. That force is neither more nor less than the conscience of the Christian people who constitute the Church: discipline is, in principle, the reaction of that force against all immorality. In special cases, forms may be necessary for its exercise, and in the forms in which it is exercised variations may be found expedient, according to time, place, or degree of moral progress; the congregation as a body, or a representative committee of it, or its ordained ministers, may be its most suitable executors; but that on which all alike have to depend for making their proceedings effective to any Christian intent is the vigour of Christian conscience, and the intensity of Christian love, in the community as a whole. Where these are wanting, or exist only in an insignificant degree, disciplinary proceedings are reduced to a mere form; they are legal, not evangelical; and to be legal in such matters is not only hypocritical, but insolent. Instead of rendering a real Christian service to offenders, which by awakening conscience will lead to penitence and restoration, discipline under such conditions is equally cruel and unjust.

It is plain also, from the nature of the force which it employs, that discipline is a function of the Church which is in incessant exercise, and is not called into action only on special occasions. To limit it to what are technically known as cases of discipline—the formal treatment of offenders by a Church court, or by any person or persons acting in an official character—is to ignore its real nature, and to give its exercise in these cases a significance to which it has no claim. The offences against the Christian standard which can be legally impeached even in Church courts are not one in ten thousand of those against which the Christian conscience ought energetically to protest; and it is the vigour with which the ceaseless reaction against evil in every shape is instinctively maintained which measures the effectiveness of all formal proceedings, and makes them means of grace to the guilty. The officials of a Church may deal in their official place with offences against soberness, purity, or honesty; they are bound to deal with them, whether they like it or not; but their success will depend upon the completeness with which they, and those whom they represent, have renounced not only the vices which they are judging, but all that is out of keeping with the mind and spirit of Christ. The drunkard, the sensualist, the thief, know perfectly well that drunkenness, sensuality, and theft are not the only sins which mar the soul. They know that there are other vices, just as real if not so glaring, which are equally fatal to the life of Christ in man, and as completely disqualify men for acting in Christ's name. They are conscious that it is not a *bona fide* transaction when their sins are impeached by men whose consciences endure with equanimity the reign of meanness, duplicity, pride, hypocrisy, self-complacency. They are aware that God is not present where these are dominant, and that God's power to judge and save can never come through such channels. Hence the exercise of discipline in these legal forms is often resented, and often ineffective; and instead of complaining about what is obviously inevitable, the one thing at which all should aim who wish to protect the Church from scandals is to cultivate the common conscience, and bring it to such a degree of purity and vigour, that its spontaneous resentment of evil will enable the Church practically to dispense with legal forms. This Christian community at Corinth had a thousand faults; in many points we are tempted to find in it rather a warning than an example; but I think we may take this as a signal proof that it was really sound at heart: its condemnation of this guilty man fell upon his conscience as the sentence of God, and brought him in tears to the feet of Christ. No legal proceedings could have done that: nothing could have done it but a real and passionate sympathy with the holiness and the love of Christ. Such sympathy is the one subduing, reconciling, redeeming power in our hands; and Paul might well rejoice, after all his affliction and anguish of heart, when he found it so unmistakably at work in Corinth. Not so much formal as instinctive, though not shrinking on occasion from formal proceedings; not malignant, yet closing itself inexorably against evil; not indulgent to badness, but with goodness like Christ's, waiting to be gracious,—this Christian virtue really holds the keys of the kingdom of heaven, and opens and shuts with the authority of Christ Himself. We need it in all our Churches to-day, as much as it was needed in Corinth; we need it that special acts of discipline may be effective; we need it still more that they may be unnecessary. Pray for it as for a gift that comprehends every other—the power to represent Christ, and work His work, in the recovery and restoration of the fallen.

In vv. 9-11, the same subject is continued, but with a slightly different aspect exposed. Paul had obviously taken the initiative in this matter, though the bulk of the Church, at his prompting, had acted in a right spirit. Their conduct was in harmony with his motive in writing to them,[17] which had really been to make proof of their obedience in all points. But he has already disclaimed either the right or the wish to lord it over them in their liberty as believers; and here, again, he represents himself rather as following them in their treatment of the offender, than as pointing out the way. "Now to whom ye forgive anything, I also forgive"—so great is my confidence in you: "for what I also have forgiven, if I have forgiven anything, for your sakes have I forgiven it in the presence of Christ." When he says "if I *have* forgiven anything," he does not mean that his forgiveness is dubious, or in suspense; what he does is to deprecate the thought that his forgiveness is the main thing, or that he had been the person principally offended. When he says *"for your sakes* have I forgiven it," the words are explained by what follows: to have refused his forgiveness in the circumstances would have been to perpetuate a state of matters which could only have injured the Church. When he adds that his forgiveness is bestowed "in the presence of Christ," he gives the assurance that it is no complaisance or formality, but a real acceptance of the offender to peace and friendship again.[18] And we should not overlook the fact that in this association of Christ, of the Corinthians, and of himself, in the work of forgiveness and restoration, Paul is really encompassing a desponding soul with all the grace of earth and heaven. Surely he will not let his grief become despair, when all around him and above him there is a present and convincing witness that, though God is intolerant of sin, He is the refuge of the penitent.

The gracious and conciliatory tone of these verses seems to me worthy of special admiration; and I can only express my astonishment that to some they have appeared insincere, a vain attempt to cover a defeat with the semblance of victory, a surrender to the opposition at Corinth, the painfulness of which is ill-disguised by the pretence of agreement with them. The exposition just given renders the refutation of such a view unnecessary. We ought rather to regard with reverence and affection the man who knew how to combine, so strikingly, unflinching principle and the deepest tenderness and consideration for others; we ought to propose his modesty, his sensitiveness to the feelings even of opponents, his sympathy with those who had no sympathy with him, as examples for our imitation. Paul had been deeply moved by what had taken place at Corinth, possibly he had been deeply injured; but even so his personal interest is kept in the background; for the obedient loyalty which he wishes to prove is not so much *his* interest as theirs to whom he writes. He cares only for others. He cares for the poor soul who has forfeited his place in the community; he cares for the good name of the Church; he cares for the honour of Jesus Christ; and he exerts all his power with these interests in view. If it needs rigour, he can be rigorous; if it needs passion, he can be passionate; if it needs consideration, graciousness, a conciliatory temper, a willingness to keep out of sight, he can be depended upon for all these virtues. If they were only affected, Paul would deserve the praise of a great diplomatist; but it is far easier to believe them real, and see in them the signs of a great minister of Christ.

The last verse puts the aim of his proceedings in another light: all this, he says, I do, "that no advantage may be gained over us by Satan: for we are not ignorant of his devices." The important words in the last clause are of the same root; it is as if Paul had said: "Satan is very knowing, and is always on the alert to get the better of us; but we are not without knowledge of his knowing ways." It was the Apostle's acquaintance with the wiles of the devil which made him eager to see the restoration of the penitent sinner duly carried through. This implies one or two practical truths, with which, by way of application, this exposition may close.

(1) A scandal in the Church gives the devil an opportunity. When one who has named the name of Jesus, and vowed loyal obedience to Him, falls into open sin, it is a chance offered to the enemy which he is not slow to improve. He uses it to discredit the very name of Christ: to turn that which ought to be to the world the symbol of the purest goodness into a synonym of hypocrisy. Christ has committed His honour, if not His character, to our keeping; and every lapse into vice gives Satan an advantage over Him.

(2) The devil finds his gain in the incompetence of the Church to deal with evil in the Spirit of Christ. It is a fine thing for him if he can drive the convicted sinner to despair, and persuade him that there is no more forgiveness with God. It is a fine thing if he can prompt those who love little, because they know little of God's love, to show themselves rigid, implacable, irreconcilable, even to the penitent. If he can deform the likeness of Christ into a morose Pharisaism, what an incalculable gain it is! If the disciples of Him who received sinners look askance on those who have lapsed, and chill the hope of restoration with cold suspicion and reserve, there will be joy over it, not in heaven, but in hell. And not only this, but the opposite is a device of the devil, of which we ought not to be ignorant. There is hardly

a sin that some one has not an interest in extenuating. Even the incestuous person in Corinth had his defenders: there were some who were puffed up, and gloried in what he had done as an assertion of Christian liberty. The devil takes advantage of the scandals that occur in the Church to bribe and debauch men's consciences; indulgent words are spoken, which are not the voice of Christ's awful mercy, but of a miserable self-pity; the strongest and holiest thing in the world, the redeeming love of God, is adulterated and even confounded with the weakest and basest thing, the bad man's immoral forgiveness of himself. And not to mention anything else under this head, could any one imagine what would please and suit the devil better than the absolutely unfeeling but extremely interesting gossip which resounds over every exposure of sin?

(3) But, lastly, the devil finds his advantage in the dissensions of Christians. What an opportunity he would have had in Corinth, had strained relations continued between the Apostle and the Church! What opportunities he has everywhere, when tempers are on edge, and every movement means friction, and every proposal rouses suspicion! The last prayer Christ prayed for His Church was that they might all be one: to be one in Him is the final security against the devices of Satan. What a frightful commentary the history of the Church is on this prayer! What frightful illustrations it furnishes of the devil's gain out of the saints' quarrels! There are plenty of subjects, of course, even in Church life, on which we may naturally and legitimately differ; but we ought to know better than to let the differences enter into our souls. At bottom, we should be all one; it is giving ourselves away to the enemy, if we do not, at all costs, "keep the unity of the Spirit in the bond of peace."

VII
CHRIST'S CAPTIVE

"Now when I came to Troas for the Gospel of Christ, and when a door was opened unto me in the Lord, I had no relief for my spirit, because I found not Titus my brother: but taking my leave of them, I went forth into Macedonia. But thanks be unto God, which always leadeth us in triumph in Christ, and maketh manifest through us the savour of His knowledge in every place. For we are a sweet savour of Christ unto God, in them that are being saved, and in them that are perishing; to the one a savour from death unto death; to the other a savour from life unto life. And who is sufficient for these things? For we are not as the many, corrupting the Word of God: but as of sincerity, but as of God, in the sight of God, speak we in Christ."—2 Cor. ii. 12-17 (R.V.).

In this passage the Apostle returns from what is virtually, if not formally, a digression, to the narrative which begins in chap. i. 8 f., and is continued in i. 15 f. At the same time he makes a transition to a new subject, really though not very explicitly connected with what goes before—namely, his independent and divinely granted authority as an apostle. In the last verses of chap, ii., and in chap. iii. 1-4, this is treated generally, but with reference in particular to the success of his ministry. He then goes on to contrast the older and the Christian dispensation, and the character of their respective ministries, and terminates the section with a noble statement of the spirit and principles with which he fulfilled his apostolic calling (chap. iv. 1-6).

Before leaving Ephesus, Paul had apparently made an appointment to meet Titus, on his return from Corinth, at Troas. He went thither himself to preach the Gospel, and found an excellent opportunity for doing so; but the non-arrival of his brother kept him in such a state of unrest[19] that he was unable to make that use of it which he would otherwise have done. This seems a singular confession, but there is no reason to suppose that it was made with a bad conscience. Paul was probably grieved that he had not the heart to go in at the door which had been opened to him in the Lord, but he did not feel guilty. It was not selfishness which made him turn away, but the anxiety of a true pastor about other souls which God had committed to his care. "I had no relief *for my spirit*," he says; and the spirit, in his language, even though it be a constituent of man's nature, is that in him which is akin to the divine, and receptive of it. That very element in the Apostle, in virtue of which he could act for God at all, was already preoccupied, and though the people were there, ready to be evangelised, it was beyond his power to evangelise them. His spirit was absorbed and possessed by hopes and fears and prayers for the Corinthians; and as the human spirit, even when in contact with the divine, is finite, and only capable of so much and no more, he was obliged to let slip an occasion which he would otherwise have gladly seized. He probably felt with all missionaries that it is as important to secure as to win converts; and if the Corinthians were capable of reflection, they might reflect with shame on the loss which their sin had entailed on the people of Troas. The disorders of their wilful community had engrossed the Apostle's spirit, and robbed their fellow-men across the sea of an apostolic ministry. They could not but feel how genuine was the Apostle's love, when he had made such a sacrifice to it; but such a sacrifice ought never to have been required.

When Paul could bear the suspense no longer, he said good-bye to the people of Troas, crossed the Thracian Sea, and advanced into Macedonia to meet Titus. He did meet him, and heard from him a full report of the state of matters at Corinth (chap. vii. 5 ff.); but here he does not take time to say so. He breaks out into a jubilant thanksgiving, occasioned primarily no doubt by the joyful tidings he had just received, but widening characteristically, and instantaneously, to cover all his apostolic work. It is as though he felt God's goodness to him to be all of a piece, and could not be sensitive to it in any particular instance without having the consciousness rise within him that he lived and moved and had his being in it. "Now to God be thanks, who always leadeth us in triumph in Christ."

The peculiar and difficult word in this thanksgiving is θριαμβεύοντι. The sense which first strikes one as suitable is that which is given in the Authorised Version: "God which always *causeth us to triumph*." Practically Paul had been engaged in a conflict with the Corinthians, and for a time it had seemed not improbable that he might be beaten; but God had caused him to triumph in Christ—that is, acting in Christ's interests, in matters in which Christ's name and honour were at stake, the victory (as always) had remained with him; and for this he thanks God. This interpretation is still maintained by so excellent a scholar as Schmiedel, and the use of θριαμβεύειν in this transitive sense is defended by the analogy of μαθητεύειν in Matt. xxviii. 19.

But appropriate as this interpretation is, there is one apparently fatal objection to it. There is no doubt that θριαμβεύειν is here used transitively, but we have not to guess, by analogy, what it must mean when so used; there are other examples which fix this unambiguously. One is found elsewhere in St. Paul himself (Col. ii. 15), where θριαμβεύσας αὐτοὺς indubitably means "having triumphed over them." In accordance with this, which is only one out of many instances,[20] the Revisers have displaced the old rendering here, and substituted for it, "Thanks be to God, which always *leadeth us in triumph*." The triumph here is God's, not the Apostle's; Paul is not the soldier who wins the battle, and shouts for victory, as he marches in the triumphal procession; he is the captive who is led in the Conqueror's train, and in whom men see the trophy of the Conqueror's power. When he says that God always leads him in triumph *in Christ*, the meaning is not perfectly obvious. He may intend to define, as it were, the area over which God's victory extends. In everything which is covered by the name and authority of Christ, God triumphantly asserts His power over the Apostle. Or, again, the words may signify that it is through Christ that God's victorious power is put forth. These two meanings, of course, are not inconsistent; and practically they coincide.

It cannot be denied, I think, if this is taken quite rigorously, that there is a certain air of irrelevance about it. It does not seem to be to the purpose of the passage to say that God always triumphs over Paul and those for whom He speaks, or even that He always leads them in triumph. It is this feeling, indeed, which mainly influences those who keep to the rendering of the Authorised Version, and regard Paul as the victor. But the meaning of θριαμβεύοντι is not really open to doubt, and the semblance of irrelevance disappears if we remember that we are dealing with a figure, and a figure which the Apostle himself does not press. Of course in an ordinary triumph, such as the triumph of Claudius over Caractacus, of which St. Paul may easily have heard, the captives had no share in the victory; it was not only a victory over them, but a victory against them. But when God wins a victory over man, and leads his captive in triumph, the captive too has an interest in what happens; it is the beginning of all triumphs, in any true sense, for him. If we apply this to the case before us, we shall see that the true meaning is not irrelevant. Paul had once been the enemy of God in Christ; he had fought against Him in his own soul, and in the Church which he persecuted and wasted. The battle had been long and strong; but not far from Damascus it had terminated in a decisive victory for God. There the mighty man fell, and the weapons of his warfare perished. His pride, his self-righteousness, his sense of superiority to others and of competence to attain to the righteousness of God, collapsed for ever, and he rose from the earth to be the slave of Jesus Christ. That was the beginning of God's triumph over him; from that hour God led him in triumph in Christ. But it was the beginning also of all that made the Apostle's life itself a triumph, not a career of hopeless internal strife, such as it had been, but of unbroken Christian victory. This, indeed, is not involved *in the mere word* θριαμβεύοντι, but it is the real *thing* which was present to the Apostle's mind when he used the word. When we recognise this, we see that the charge of irrelevance does not really apply; while nothing could be more characteristic of the Apostle than to hide himself and his success in this way behind God's triumph over him and through him.

Further, the true meaning of the word, and the true connexion of ideas just explained, remind us that the only triumphs we can ever have, deserving the name, must begin with God's triumph over us. This is the one possible source of joy untroubled. We may be as selfish as we please, and as successful in our selfishness; we may distance all our rivals in the race for the world's prizes; we may appropriate and engross pleasure, wealth, knowledge, influence; and after all there will be one thing we must do without—the power and the happiness of thanking God. No one will ever be able to thank God because he has succeeded in pleasing himself, be the mode of his self-pleasing as respectable as you will; and he who has not thanked God with a whole heart, without misgiving and without reserve, does not know what joy is. Such thanksgiving and its joy have one condition: they rise up spontaneously in the soul when it allows God to triumph over it. When God appears to us in Jesus Christ, when in the omnipotence of His love and purity and truth He makes war upon our pride and falsehood and lusts, and prevails against them, and brings us low, then we are admitted to the secret of this apparently perplexing passage; we know how natural it is to cry, "Thanks be unto God who in His victory over us giveth us the victory! Thanks be to Him who always leadeth us in triumph!" It is out of an experience like this that Paul speaks; it is the key to his whole life, and it has been illustrated anew by what has just happened at Corinth.

But to return to the Epistle. God is described by the Apostle not only as triumphing over them (*i.e.*, himself and his colleagues) in Christ, but as making manifest through them the savour of His knowledge in every place. It has been questioned whether "His" knowledge is the knowledge of God or of Christ. Grammatically, the question can hardly be answered; but, as we see from chap. iv. 6, the two things which it proposes to distinguish are really one; what is manifested in the apostolic ministry is the knowledge of God as He is revealed in Christ. But why does Paul use the expression "*the savour* of His knowledge"? It was suggested probably by the figure of the triumph, which was present to his mind in all the detail of its circumstances.

Incense smoked on every altar as the victor passed through the streets of Rome; the fragrant steam floated over the procession, a silent proclamation of victory and joy. But Paul would not have appropriated this feature of the triumph, and applied it to his ministry, unless he had felt that there was a real point of comparison, that the knowledge of Christ which he diffused among men, wherever he went, was in very truth a fragrant thing.[21] True, he was not a free man; he had been subdued by God, and made the slave of Jesus Christ; as the Lord of glory went forth conquering and to conquer, over Syria and Asia and Macedonia and Greece, He led him as a captive in the triumphal march of His grace; he was the trophy of Christ's victory; every one who saw him saw that necessity was laid upon Him; but what a gracious necessity it was! "The *love* of Christ constraineth us." The captives who were dragged in chains behind a Roman chariot also made manifest the knowledge of their conqueror; they declared to all the spectators his power and his pitilessness; there was nothing in that knowledge to suggest the idea of a fragrance like incense. But as Paul moved through the world, all who had eyes to see saw in him not only the power but the sweetness of God's redeeming love. The mighty Victor made manifest through Him, not only His might, but His charm, not only His greatness, but His grace. It was a good thing, men felt, to be subdued and led in triumph like Paul; it was to move in an atmosphere perfumed by the love of Christ, as the air around the Roman triumph was perfumed with incense. The Apostle is so sensible of this that he weaves it into his sentence as an indispensable part of his thought; it is not merely the knowledge of God which is made manifest through him as he is led in triumph, but that knowledge as a fragrant, gracious thing, speaking to every one of victory and goodness and joy.

The very word "savour," in connexion with the "knowledge" of God in Christ, is full of meaning. It has its most direct application, of course, to preaching. When we proclaim the Gospel, do we always succeed in manifesting it as a savour? Or is not the savour—the sweetness, the winsomeness, the charm and attractiveness of it—the very thing that is most easily left out? Do we not catch it sometimes in the words of others, and wonder that it eludes our own? We miss what is most characteristic in the knowledge of God if we miss this. We leave out that very element in the Evangel which makes it evangelic, and gives it its power to subdue and enchain the souls of men. But it is not to preachers only that the word "savour" speaks; it is of the widest possible application. Whereever Christ is leading a single soul in triumph, the fragrance of the Gospel should go forth; rather, it does go forth, in proportion as His triumph is complete. There is sure to be that in the life which will reveal the graciousness as well as the omnipotence of the Saviour. And it is this virtue which God uses as His main witness, as His chief instrument, to evangelise the world. In every relation of life it should tell. Nothing is so insuppressible, nothing so pervasive, as a fragrance. The lowliest life which Christ is really leading in triumph will speak infallibly and persuasively for Him. In a Christian brother or sister, brothers and sisters will find a new strength and tenderness, something that goes deeper than natural affection, and can stand severer shocks; they will catch the fragrance which declares that the Lord in His triumphant grace is there. And so in all situations, or, as the Apostle has it, "in every place." And if we are conscious that we fall in this matter, and that the fragrance of the knowledge of Christ is something to which our life gives no testimony, let us be sure that the explanation of it is to be found in self-will. There is something in us which has not yet made complete surrender to Him, and not till He leads us unresistingly in triumph will the sweet savour go forth.

At this point the Apostle's thought is arrested by the issues of his ministry, though he carries the figure of the fragrance, with a little pressure, through to the end. In God's sight, he says, or so far as God is concerned, we are a sweet savour of Christ, a perfume redolent of Christ, in which He cannot but take pleasure. In other words, Christ proclaimed in the Gospel, and the ministries and lives which proclaim Him, are always a joy to God. They are a joy to Him, whatever men may think of them, alike in them that are being saved and in them that are perishing. To those who are being saved, they are a savour "from life to life"; to those who are perishing, a savour "from death to death." Here, as everywhere, St. Paul contemplates these exclusive opposites as the sole issues of man's life, and of the Gospel ministry. He makes no attempt to subordinate one to the other, no suggestion that the way of death may ultimately lead to life, much less that it must do so. The whole solemnity of the situation, which is faced in the cry "And who is sufficient for these things?" depends on the finality of the contrast between life and death. These are the goals set before men, and those who are being saved and those who are perishing are respectively on their way to one or the other. Who *is* sufficient for the calling of the Gospel ministry, when such are the alternatives involved in it? Who is sufficient, in love, in wisdom, in humility, in awful earnestness, for the duties of a calling the issues of which are life or death for ever?

There is considerable difficulty in the sixteenth verse, partly dogmatic, partly textual. Commentators so opposite in their bias as Chrysostom and Calvin have pondered and remarked upon the opposite effects here ascribed to the Gospel. It is easy to find analogies to these in nature. The same heat which hardens clay melts iron. The same sunlight which gladdens the healthy eye tortures that which is diseased. The same honey which is sweet to the sound palate is nauseous to the sick; and so on. But such analogies do not explain anything, and one can hardly see what is meant by calling them illustrations. It remains finally inexplicable that the Gospel, which appeals to some with winning irresistible power, subduing and leading them in triumph, should excite in others a passion of antipathy which nothing else could provoke. This remains inexplicable, because it is irrational. Nothing that can be pointed to in the universe is the least like a bad heart closing itself against the love of Christ, like a bad man's will stiffening into absolute rigidity against the will of God. The preaching of the Gospel may be the occasion of such awful results, but it is not their cause. The God whom it proclaims is the God of grace; it is never His will that any should perish— always that all should be saved. But He can save only by subduing; His grace must exercise a sovereign power in us, which through righteousness will lead to life everlasting (Rom. v. 21). And when this exercise of power is resisted, when we match our self-will against the gracious saving will of God, our pride, our passions, our mere sloth, against the soul-constraining love of Christ; when we prevail in the war which God's mercy wages with our wickedness,—then the Gospel itself may be said to have ministered to our ruin; it was ordained to life, and we have made it a sentence of death. Yet even so, it is the joy and glory of God; it is a sweet savour to Him, fragrant of Christ and His love.

The textual difficulty is in the words ἐκ θανάτου εἰς θάνατον, and ἐκ ζωῆς εἰς ζωήν. These words are rendered in the Revised Version *"from* death to death," and *"from* life to life." The Authorised Version, following the *Textus Receptus*, which omits ἐκ in both clauses, renders "a savour *of* death unto death," and *"of* life unto life." In spite of the inferior MS. support, the *Textus Receptus* is preferred by many modern scholars—*e.g.*, Heinrici, Schmiedel, and Hofmann. They find it impossible to give any precise interpretation to the better attested reading, and an examination of any exposition which accepts it goes far to justify them. Thus Professor Beet comments: *"From death for death* (comp. Rom. i. 17): a scent proceeding *from*, and thus revealing the presence of, *death*; and, like malaria from a putrefying corpse, causing *death*. Paul's labours among some men revealed the eternal death which day by day cast an ever-deepening shadow upon them [this answers to ὀσμὴ ἐκ θανάτου]; and by arousing in them increased opposition to God, promoted the spiritual mortification which had already begun" [this answers to εἰς θάνατον]. Surely it is safe to say that nobody in Corinth could ever have guessed this from the words. Yet this is a favourable specimen of the interpretations given. If it were possible to take ἐκ θανάτου εἰς θάνατον, and ἐκ ζωῆς εἰς ζωήν, as Baur took ἐκ πίστεως εἰς πίστιν in Rom. i. 17, that would be the simplest way out of the difficulty, and quite satisfactory. What the Apostle said would then be this: that the Gospel which he preached, ever good as it was to God, had the most opposite characters and effects among men,—in some it was death *from beginning to end*, absolutely and unmitigatedly deadly in its nature and workings; in others, again, it was life from beginning to end—life was the uniform sign of its presence, and its invariable issue. This also is the meaning which we get by omitting ἐκ: the genitives ζωῆς and θανάτου are then adjectival,—a vital fragrance, with life as its element and end; a fatal fragrance, the end of which is death. This has the advantage of being the meaning which occurs to an ordinary reader; and if the critically approved text, with the repeated ἐκ, cannot bear this interpretation, I think there is a fair case for defending the received text on exegetical grounds. Certainly nothing but the broad impression of the received text will ever enter the general mind.

The question that rises to the Apostle's lips as he confronts the solemn situation created by the Gospel is not directly answered. "Who is sufficient for these things? Who? I say. For we are not as the many,[22] who corrupt the Word of God: but as of sincerity, but as of God, in the sight of God, we speak in Christ." Paul is conscious as he writes that his awful sense of responsibility as a preacher of the Gospel is not shared by all who exercise the same vocation. To be the bearer and the representative of a power with issues so tremendous ought surely to annihilate every thought of self; to let personal interest intrude is to declare oneself faithless and unworthy. We are startled to hear from Paul's lips what at first sight seems to be a charge of just such base self-seeking laid against the majority of preachers. "We are not as the many, corrupting the Word of God." The expressive word rendered here "corrupting" has the idea of self-interest, and especially of petty gain, at its basis. It means literally to sell in small quantities, to retail for profit. But it was specially applied to tavern-keeping, and extended to cover all the devices by which the wine-sellers in ancient times deceived their customers. Then it was used figuratively, as here; and Lucian, *e.g.*, speaks of philosophers as selling the sciences, and in most cases (οἱ πολλοί: a curious parallel to St. Paul), like tavern keepers, "blending, adulterating, and giving bad measure." It is plain that there are two separable ideas here. One is that of men qualifying the Gospel, infiltrating their own ideas into the Word of God, tempering its severity, or perhaps its goodness, veiling its inexorableness, dealing in compromise. The other is that all such proceedings are faithless and dishonest, because some private interest underlies them. It need not be avarice, though it is as likely to be this as anything else. A man corrupts the Word of God, makes it the stock-in-trade of a paltry business of his own, in many other ways than by subordinating it to the need of a livelihood. When he exercises his calling as a minister for the gratification of his vanity, he does so. When he preaches not that awful message in which life and death are bound up, but himself, his cleverness, his learning, his humour, his fine voice even or fine gestures, he does so. He makes the Word minister to him, instead of being a minister of the Word; and that is the essence of the sin. It is the same if ambition be his motive, if he preaches to win disciples to himself, to gain an ascendency over souls, to become the head of a party which will bear the impress of his mind. There was something of this at Corinth; and not only there, but wherever it is found, such a spirit and such interests will change the character of the Gospel. It will not be preserved in that integrity, in that simple, uncompromising, absolute character which it has as revealed in Christ. Have another interest in it than that of God, and that interest will inevitably colour it. You will make it what it was not, and the virtue will depart from it.

In contrast with all such dishonest ministers, the Apostle represents himself and his friends speaking "as of sincerity." They have no mixture of motives in their work as evangelists; they have indeed no independent motives at all: God is leading them in triumph, and proclaiming His grace through them. It is He who prompts every word (ὡς ἐκ Θεοῦ). Yet their responsibility and their freedom are intact. They feel themselves in His presence as they speak, and in that presence they speak "in Christ." "In Christ" is the Apostle's mark. Not in himself apart from Christ, where any mixture of motives, any process of adulteration, would have been possible, but only in that union with Christ which was the very life of his life, did he carry on his evangelistic work. This was his final security, and it is still the only security, that the Gospel can have fair play in the world.

VIII
LIVING EPISTLES

"Are we beginning again to commend ourselves? or need we, as do some, epistles of commendation to you or from you? Ye are our epistle, written in our hearts, known and read of all men; being made manifest that ye are an epistle of Christ, ministered by us, written not with ink, but with the Spirit of the living God; not in tables of stone, but in tables *that are* hearts of flesh."—2 Cor. iii. 1-3 (R.V.).

"Are we beginning again to commend ourselves?" Paul does not mean by these words to admit that he had been commending himself before: he means that he has been accused already of doing so, and that there are those at Corinth who, when they hear such passages of this letter as that which has just preceded, will be ready to repeat the accusation. In the First Epistle he had found it necessary to vindicate his apostolic authority, and especially his interest in the Corinthian Church as its spiritual father (1 Cor. ix. 1-27, iv. 6-21), and obviously his enemies at Corinth had tried to turn these personal passages against him. They did so on the principle *Qui s'excuse s'accuse*. "He is commending himself," they said, "and self-commendation is an argument which discredits, instead of supporting, a cause." The Apostle had heard of these malicious speeches, and in this Epistle makes repeated reference to them (see chaps, v. 12, x. 18, xiii. 6). He entirely agreed with his opponents that self-praise was no honour. "Not he who commendeth himself is approved, but he whom the Lord commendeth." But he denied point-blank that he was commending himself. In distinguishing as he had done in chap. ii. 14-17 between himself and his colleagues, who spoke the Word "as of sincerity, as of God, in the sight of God," and "the many" who corrupted it, nothing was further from his mind than to plead his cause, as a suspected person, with the Corinthians. Only malignity could suppose any such thing, and the indignant question with which the chapter opens tacitly accuses his adversaries of this hateful vice. It is pitiful to see a great and generous spirit like Paul compelled thus to stand upon guard, and watch against the possible misconstruction of every lightest word. What needless pain it inflicts upon him, what needless humiliation! How it checks all effusion of feeling, and robs what should be brotherly intercourse of everything that can make it free and glad! Further on in the Epistle there will be abundant opportunity of speaking on this subject at greater length; but it is proper to remark here that a minister's character is the whole capital he has for carrying on his business, and that nothing can be more cruel and wicked than to cast suspicion on it without cause. In most other callings a man may go on, no matter what his character, provided his balance at the bank is on the right side; but an evangelist or a pastor who has lost his character has lost everything. It is humiliating to be subject to suspicion, painful to be silent under it, degrading to speak. At a later stage Paul was compelled to go further than he goes here; but let the indignant emotion of this abrupt question remind us that candour is to be met with candour, and that the suspicious temper which would fain malign the good eats like a canker the very heart of those who cherish it.

From the serious tone the Apostle passes suddenly to the ironical. "Or need we, as do some, epistles of commendation to you or from you?" The "some" of this verse are probably the same as "the many" of chap. ii. 17. Persons had come to Corinth in the character of Christian teachers, bringing with them recommendatory letters which secured their standing when they arrived. An example of what is meant can be seen in Acts xvii. 27. There we are told that when Apollos, who had been working in Ephesus, was minded to pass over into Achaia, the Ephesian brethren encouraged him, and wrote to the disciples to receive him—that is, they gave him an epistle of commendation, which secured him recognition and welcome in Corinth. A similar case is found in Rom. xvi. 1, where the Apostle uses the very word which we have here: "I commend unto you Phœbe our sister, who is a servant of the Church that is at Cenchreæ: that ye receive her in the Lord, worthily of the saints, and that ye assist her in whatsoever matter she may have need of you: for she herself also hath been a succourer of many, and of mine own self." This was Phœbe's introduction, or epistle of commendation, to the Church of Rome. The Corinthians were evidently in the habit both of receiving such letters from other Churches, and of granting them on their own account; and Paul asks them ironically if they think he ought to bring one, or when he leaves them to apply for one. Is *that* the relation which ought to obtain between him and them? The "some," to whom he refers, had no doubt come from Jerusalem: it is they who are referred to in chap. xi. 22 ff. But it does not follow that their recommendatory letters had been signed by Peter, James, and John; and just as little that those letters justified them in their hostility to Paul. No doubt there were many—many myriads, the Book of Acts says—at Jerusalem, whose conception of the Gospel was very different from his, and who were glad to counteract him whenever they could; but there were many also, including the three who seemed to be pillars, who had a thoroughly good understanding with him, and who had no responsibility for the "some" and their doings. The epistles which the "some" brought were plainly such as the Corinthians themselves could grant, and it is a complete misinterpretation to suppose that they were a commission granted by the Twelve for the persecution of Paul.

The giving of recommendatory letters is a subject of considerable practical interest. When they are merely formal, as in our certificates of Church membership, they come to mean very little. It is an unhappy state of affairs perhaps, but no one would take a certificate of Church membership by itself as a satisfactory recommendation. And when we go past the merely formal, difficult questions arise. Many people have an estimate of their own character and competence, in which it is impossible for others to share, and yet they apply without misgiving to their friends, and especially to their minister or their employer, to grant them "epistles of commendation." We are bound to be generous in these things, but we are bound also to be honest. The rule which ought to guide us, especially in all that belongs to the Church and its work, is the interest of the cause, and not of the worker. To flatter is to do a wrong, not only to the person flattered, but to the cause in which you are trying to employ him. There is no more ludicrous reading in the world than a bundle of certificates, or testimonials, as they are called. As a rule, they certify nothing but the total absence of judgment and conscience in the people who have granted them. If you do not know whether a person is qualified for any given situation or not, you do not need to say anything about it. If you know he is not, and he asks you to say that he is, no personal consideration must keep you from kindly but firmly declining. I am not preaching suspicion, or reserve, or anything ungenerous, but justice and truth. It is wicked to betray a great interest by bespeaking it for incompetent hands; it is cruel to put any one into a place for which he is unfit. Where you are confident that the man and the work will be well matched, be as generous as you please; but never forget that the work is to be considered in the first place, and the man only in the second.

Paul has been serious, and ironical, in the first verse; in ver. 2 he becomes serious again, and remains so. "*You*," he says, answering his ironical question, "*you* are our epistle." Epistle, of course, is to be taken in the sense of the preceding verse. "*You* are the commendatory letter which *I* show, when I am asked for my credentials." But to whom does he show it? In the first instance, to the captious Corinthians themselves. The tone of chap. ix. in the First Epistle is struck here again: "Wherever I may need recommendations, it is certainly not at Corinth." "If I be not an apostle to others, yet doubtless I am to you: the seal of mine apostleship are ye in the Lord." Had they been a Christian community when he first visited them, they might have asked who he was; but they owed their Christianity to him; he was their father in Christ; to put him to the question in this superior, suspicious style was unnatural, unfilial ingratitude. They themselves were the living evidence of the very thing which they threw doubt upon—the apostleship of Paul.

This bold utterance may well excite misgivings in those who preach constantly, yet see no result of their work. It is common to disparage success, the success of visible acknowledged conversions, of bad men openly renouncing badness, bearing witness against themselves, and embracing a new life. It is common to glorify the ministry which works on, patient and uncomplaining, in one monotonous round, ever sowing, but never reaping, ever casting the net, but never drawing in the fish, ever marking time, but never advancing. Paul frankly and repeatedly appeals to his success in evangelistic work as the final and sufficient proof that God had called him, and had given him authority as an apostle; and search as we will, we shall not find any test so good and unequivocal as this success. Paul had seen the Lord; he was qualified to be a witness of the Resurrection; but these, at the very most, were his own affair, till the witness he bore had proved its power in the hearts and consciences of others. How to provide, to train, and to test the men who are to be the ministers of the Christian Church is a matter of the very utmost consequence, to which sufficient attention has not yet been given. Congregations which choose their own pastor are often compelled to take a man quite untried, and to judge him more or less on superficial grounds. They can easily find out whether he is a competent scholar; they can see for themselves what are his gifts of speech, his virtues or defects of manner; they can get such an impression as sensible people always get, by seeing and hearing a man, of the general earnestness or lack of earnestness in his character. But often they feel that more is wanted. It is not exactly more in the way of character; the members of a Church have no right to expect that their minister will be a truer Christian than they themselves are. A special inquisition into his conversion, or his religious experience, is mere hypocrisy; if the Church is not sufficiently in earnest to guard herself against insincere members, she must take the risk of insincere ministers. What is wanted is what the Apostle indicates here—that intimation of God's concurrence which is given through success in evangelistic work. No other intimation of God's concurrence is infallible—no call by a congregation, no ordination by a presbytery or by a bishop. Theological education is easily provided, and easily tested; but it will not be so easy to introduce the reforms which are needed in this direction. Great masses of Christian people, however, are becoming alive to the necessity for them; and when the pressure is more strongly felt, the way for action will be discovered.

Only those who can appeal to what they have done in the Gospel can be known to have the qualifications of Gospel ministers; and in due time the fact will be frankly recognised.

The conversion and new life of the Corinthians were Paul's certificate as an apostle. They were a certificate known, he says, and read by all men. Often there is a certain awkwardness in the presenting of credentials. It embarrasses a man when he has to put his hand into his breast pocket, and take out his character, and submit it for inspection. Paul was saved this embarrassment. There was a fine unsought publicity about his testimonials. Everybody knew what the Corinthians had been, everybody knew what they were; and the man to whom the change was due needed no other recommendation to a Christian society. Whoever looked at them saw plainly that they were an epistle of Christ; the mind of Christ could be read upon them, and it had been written by the intervention of Paul's hand. This is an interesting though a well-worn conception of the Christian character. Every life has a meaning, we say; every face is a record; but the text goes further. The life of the Christian is an epistle; it has not only a meaning, but an address; it is a message from Christ to the world. Is Christ's message to men legible on our lives? When those who are without look at us, do they see the hand of Christ quite unmistakably? Does it ever occur to anybody that there is something in our life which is not of the world, but which is a message to the world from Christ? Did you ever, startled by the unusual brightness of a true Christian's life, ask as it were involuntarily, "Whose image and superscription is this?" and feel as you asked it that these features, these characters, could only have been traced by one hand, and that they proclaimed to all the grace and power of Jesus Christ? Christ wishes so to write upon us that men may see what He does for man. He wishes to engrave His image on our nature, that all spectators may feel that it has a message for them, and may crave the same favour. A congregation which is not in its very existence and in all its works and ways a legible epistle, an unmistakable message from Christ to man, does not answer to this New Testament ideal.

Paul claims no part here but that of Christ's instrument. The Lord, so to speak, dictated the letter, and he wrote it. The contents of it were prescribed by Christ, and through the Apostle's ministry became visible and legible in the Corinthians. More important is it to notice with what the writing was done: "not with ink," says St. Paul, "but with the Spirit of the living God." At first sight this contrast seems formal and fantastic; nobody, we think, could ever dream of making either of these things do the work of the other, so that it seems perfectly gratuitous in Paul to say, "not with ink, but with the Spirit." Yet ink is sometimes made to bear a great deal of responsibility. The characters of the τινὲς ("some") in ver. i, were only written in ink; they had nothing, Paul implies, to recommend them but these documents in black and white. That was hardly sufficient to guarantee their authority, or their competence as ministers in the Christian dispensation. But do not Churches yet accept their ministers with the same inadequate testimonials? A distinguished career at the University, or in the Divinity Schools, proves that a man can write with ink, under favourable circumstances; it does not prove more than that; it does not prove that he will be spiritually effective, and everything else is irrelevant. I do not say this to disparage the professional training of ministers; on the contrary, the standard of training ought to be higher than it is in all the Churches: I only wish to insist that nothing which can be represented in ink, no learning, no literary gifts, no critical acquaintance with the Scriptures even, can write upon human nature the Epistle of Christ. To do that needs "the Spirit of the living God." We feel, the moment we come upon those words, that the Apostle is anticipating; he has in view already the contrast he is going to develop between the old dispensation and the new, and the irresistible inward power by which the new is characterised. Others might boast of qualifications to preach which could be certified in due documentary form, but he carried in him wherever he went a power which was its own witness, and which overruled and dispensed with every other. Let all of us who teach or preach concentrate our interest here. It is in "the Spirit of the living God," not in any acquirements of our own, still less in any recommendations of others, that our serviceableness as ministers of Christ lies. We cannot write His epistle without it. We cannot see, let us be as diligent and indefatigable in our work as we please, the image of Christ gradually come out in those to whom we minister. Parents, teachers, preachers, this is the one thing needful for us all. "Tarry," said Jesus to the first evangelists, "tarry in the city of Jerusalem, until ye be endued with power from on high"; it is of no use to begin without that.

This idea of the "epistle" has taken such a hold of the Apostle's mind, and he finds it so suggestive whichever way he turns it, that he really tries to say too much about it in one sentence. The crowding of his ideas is confusing. One learned critic enumerates three points in which the figure becomes inconsistent with itself, and another can only defend the Apostle by saying that this figurative letter might well have qualities which would be self-contradictory in a real one. This kind of criticism smells a little of ink, and the only real difficulty in the sentence has never misled any one who read it with sympathy. It is this—that St. Paul speaks of the letter as written in two different places. "Ye are our epistle," he says at the beginning, "written *in our hearts*"; but at the end he says, "written not on tables of stone, but on tables that are hearts of flesh"—meaning evidently *on the hearts of the Corinthians*. Of course this last is the sense which coheres with the figure. Paul's ministry wrote the Epistle of Christ upon the Corinthians, or, if we prefer it, wrought such a change in their hearts that they became an epistle of Christ, an epistle to which he appealed in proof of his apostolic calling. In expressing himself as he does about this, he is again anticipating the coming contrast of Law and Gospel. Nobody would think of writing a *letter* on tables of stone, and he only says "not on stone tables" because he has in his mind the difference between the Mosaic and the Christian dispensation. It is quite out of place to refer to Ezek. xi. 19, xxxvi. 26, and to drag in the contrast between hard and tender hearts. What Paul means is that the Epistle of Christ is not written on dead matter, but on human nature, and that too at its finest and deepest. When we remember the sense of depth and inwardness which attaches to the heart in Scripture, it is not forcing the words to find in them the suggestion that the Gospel works no merely outward change. It is not written on the surface, but in the soul. The Spirit of the living God finds access for itself to the secret places of the human spirit; the most hidden recesses of our nature are open to it, and the very heart is made new. To be able to write *there* for Christ, to point not to anything dead, but to living men and women, not to anything superficial, but to a change that has reached the very core of man's being, and works its way out from thence, is the testimonial which guarantees the evangelist; it is the divine attestation that he is in the true apostolical succession.[23]

What, then, does Paul mean by the other clause, "ye are our epistle, written on *our* hearts?" I do not think we can get much more than an emotional certainty about this expression. When a man has been an intensely interested spectator, still more an intensely interested actor, in any great affair, he might say afterwards that the whole thing and all its circumstances were engraved upon his heart. I imagine that is what St. Paul means here. The conversion of the Corinthians made them an epistle of Christ; in making them believers through St. Paul's ministry, Christ wrote on *their* hearts what was really an epistle to the world; and the whole transaction, in which Paul's feelings had been deeply engaged, stood written on *his* heart for ever. Interpretations that go beyond this do not seem to me to be justified by the words. Thus Heinrici and Meyer say, "We have in our own consciousness the certainty of being recommended to you by yourselves and to others by you"; and they elucidate this by saying, "The Apostle's *own good consciousness* was, as it were, *the tablet* on which this living epistle of the Corinthians stood, and *that* had to be left unassailed even by the most malevolent." A sense so pragmatical and pedantic, even if one can grasp it at all, is surely out of place, and many readers will fail to discover it in the text. What the words do convey is the warm love of the Apostle, who had exercised his ministry among the Corinthians with all the passion of his nature, and who still bore on his ardent heart the fresh impression of his work and its results.

Amid all these details let us take care not to lose the one great lesson of the passage. Christian people owe a testimony to Christ. His name has been pronounced over them, and all who look at them ought to see His nature. We should discern in the heart and in the behaviour of Christians the handwriting, let us say the characters, not of avarice, of suspicion, of envy, of lust, of falsehood, of pride, but of Christ. It is to us He has committed Himself; we are the certification to men of what He does for man; His character is in our care. The true epistles of Christ to the world are not those which are expounded in pulpits; they are not even the gospels in which Christ Himself lives and moves before us; they are living men and women, on the tables of whose hearts the Spirit of the living God, ministered by a true evangelist, has engraved the likeness of Christ Himself. It is not the written Word on which Christianity ultimately depends; it is not the sacraments, nor so-called necessary institutions: it is this inward, spiritual, Divine writing which is the guarantee of all else.

IX
THE TWO COVENANTS

"And such confidence have we through Christ to God-ward: not that we are sufficient of ourselves, to account anything as from ourselves; but our sufficiency is from God; who also made us sufficient as ministers of a new covenant; not of the letter, but of the spirit: for the letter killeth, but the spirit giveth life. But if the ministration of death, written, *and* engraven on stones, came with glory, so that the children of Israel could not look stedfastly upon the face of Moses for the glory of his face; which *glory* was passing away: how shall not rather the ministration of the spirit be with glory? For if the ministration of condemnation is glory, much rather doth the ministration of righteousness exceed in glory. For verily that which hath been made glorious hath not been made glorious in this respect, by reason of the glory that surpasseth. For if that which passeth away *was* with glory, much more that which remaineth *is* in glory."—2 Cor. iii. 4-11 (R.V.).

The confidence referred to in the opening of this passage is that which underlies the triumphant sentences at the end of the second chapter. The tone of those sentences was open to misinterpretation, and Paul guards himself against this on two sides. To begin with, his motive in so expressing himself was quite pure: he had no thought of commending himself to the Corinthians. And, again, the ground of his confidence was not in himself. The courage which he had to speak as he did he had through Jesus Christ, and that, too, in relation to God. It was virtually confidence in God, and therefore inspired by God.

It is this last aspect of his confidence which is expanded in the fifth verse: "not that we are sufficient of ourselves, to account anything as from ourselves; but our sufficiency is from God." This vehement disclaimer of any self-sufficiency has naturally been taken in the widest sense, and theologians from Augustine downward have found in it one of the most decisive proofs of the inability of man for any spiritual good accompanying salvation. No one, we may be sure, would have ascribed salvation, and all spiritual good accompanying it, entirely to God with more hearty sincerity than the Apostle; but it does seem better here to give his words a narrower and more relevant interpretation. The "sufficiency to account anything," of which he speaks, must have a definite meaning for the context; and this meaning is suggested by the words of chap. ii. 14-17. Paul would never have dared, he tells us—indeed, he would never have been able—on his own motion, and out of his own resources, either to form conclusions, or to express them, on the subjects there in view. It is not for any man at random to say what the true Gospel is, what are its issues, what the responsibilities of its hearers or preachers, what is the spirit requisite in the evangelist, or what are the methods legitimate for him. The Gospel is God's concern, and only those who have been capacitated by Him are entitled to speak as Paul has spoken. If this is a narrower sense than that which is expounded so vigorously by Calvin, it is more pertinent, and some will find it quite as pungent. Of all things that are done hastily and inconsiderately, by people calling themselves Christian, the criticism of evangelists is one of the most conspicuous. At his own prompting, out of his own wise head, any man almost will both make up his mind and speak his mind about any preacher with no sense of responsibility whatever. Paul certainly did form opinions about preachers, opinions which were anything but flattering; but he did it through Jesus Christ and in relation to God; he did it because, as he writes, God had made him sufficient, *i.e.* had given him capacity to be, and the capacity of, a true evangelist, so that he knew both what the Gospel was, and how it ought to be proclaimed. It would silence much incompetent, because self-sufficient, criticism, if no one "thought anything" who had not this qualification.

The qualification having been mentioned, the Apostle proceeds, as usual, to enlarge upon it. "Our sufficiency is of God; who also made us sufficient as ministers of a new covenant; not of letter, but of spirit: for the letter killeth, but the spirit giveth life." At the first glance, we see no reason why his thought should take this direction, and it can only be because those whom he is opposing, and with whom he has contrasted himself in chap. ii. 17, are in some sense representatives of the old covenant, ministers of the letter in spite of their claim to be evangelists, and appealing not to a competency which came from God, but to one which rested on "the flesh." They based their title to preach on certain advantages of birth, or on having known Jesus when He lived in the world, or perhaps on certification by others who had known Him; at all events, not on that spiritual competence which Paul's ministry at Corinth had shown him to possess. That this was really the case will be seen more fully at a later stage (especially in chaps. x. ff.).

With the words "ministers of a new covenant" we enter upon one of the great passages in St. Paul's writings, and are allowed to see one of the inspiring and governing ideas in his mind. "Covenant," even to people familiar with the Bible, is beginning to be a remote and technical term; it needs to be translated or explained. If no more than another word is to be used, perhaps "dispensation" or "constitution" would suggest something. God's covenant with Israel was the whole constitution under which God was the God of Israel, and Israel the people of God. The new covenant of which Paul speaks necessarily implies an old one; and the old one is this covenant with Israel. It was a national covenant, and for that, among other reasons, it was represented and embodied in legal forms. There was a legal constitution under which the nation lived, and according to which all God's dealings with it, and all its dealings with God, were regulated. Without entering more deeply, in the meantime, into the nature of this constitution, or the religious experiences which were possible to those who lived under it, it is sufficient to notice that the best spirits in the nation became conscious of its inadequacy, and eventually of its failure. Jeremiah, who lived through the long agony of his country's dissolution, and saw the final collapse of the ancient order, felt this failure most deeply, and was consoled by the vision of a brighter future. That future rested for him on a more intimate relation of God to His people, on a constitution, as we may fairly paraphrase his words, less legal and more spiritual. "Behold, the days come, saith the Lord, that I will make a new covenant with the house of Israel, and with the house of Judah: not according to the covenant that I made with their fathers in the day that I took them by the hand to bring them out of the land of Egypt; which My covenant they brake, although I was an husband unto them, saith the Lord. But this is the covenant that I will make with the house of Israel after those days, saith the Lord; I will put my law in their inward parts, and in their heart will I write it; and I will be their God, and they shall be My people: and they shall teach no more every man his neighbour, and every man his brother, saying, Know the Lord: for they shall all know Me, from the least of them unto the greatest of them, saith the Lord: for I will forgive their iniquity, and their sin will I remember no more." This wonderful passage, so profound, so spiritual, so evangelical, is the utmost reach of prophecy; it is a sort of stepping-stone between the Old Testament and the New. Jeremiah has cried to God out of the depths, and God has heard his cry, and raised him to a spiritual height from which his eye ranges over the land of promise, and rests with yearning on all its grandest features. We do not know whether many of his contemporaries or successors were able to climb the mount which offered this glorious prospect; but we know that the promise remained a promise—a rainbow light across the dark cloud of national disaster—till Christ claimed its fulfilment as His work. It was His to make good all that the prophets had spoken; and when in the last hours of His life He said to His disciples, "This is My blood of the covenant,[24] which is shed for many, for the remission of sins," it was exactly as if He had laid His hand on that passage of Jeremiah, and said, "This day is this scripture fulfilled before your eyes." By the death of Jesus a new spiritual order was established; it rested on the forgiveness of sins, it made God accessible to all, it made obedience an instinct and a joy; all the intercourse of God and man was carried on upon a new footing, under a new constitution; to use the words of the prophet and the apostle, God made a new covenant with His people.

Among the Christians of the first age, no one so thoroughly appreciated the newness of Christianity, or was so immensely impressed by it, as St. Paul. The difference between the earlier dispensation and the later, between the religion of Moses' disciples and the religion of believers in Jesus Christ, was one that could hardly be exaggerated; he himself had been a zealot of the old, he was now a zealot of the new; and the gulf between his former and his present self was one that no geometry could measure. He had lived, after the straitest sect of the old religion, a Pharisee; touching the righteousness which is in the law he could call himself blameless; he had tasted the whole bitterness of the legalism, the formality, the bondage, in which the old covenant entangled those who were devoted to it in his days. It is with this in his memory that he here sets the old and the new in unrelieved opposition to each other. His feeling is like that of a man who has just been liberated from prison, and whose whole mind is possessed and filled up with the single sensation that it is one thing to be chained, and another thing to be free. In the passage before us, this is all the Apostle has in view. He speaks as if the old covenant and the new had nothing in common, as if the new, to borrow Baur's expression, had merely a negative relation to the old, as if it could only be contrasted with it, and not compared to it, or illustrated by it. And with this restricted view he characterises the old dispensation as one of letter, and the new as one of spirit.[25] Speaking out of his own experience, which was not solitary, but typical, he could truly speak thus. The essence of the old, to a Pharisee born and bred, was its documentary, statutory character: the law, written in letters, on stone tablets or parchment sheets, simply confronted men with its uninspiring imperative; it had never yet given any one a good conscience or enabled him to attain to the righteousness of God. The essence of the new, on the other hand, was spirit; the Christian was one in whom, through Christ, the Holy Spirit of God dwelt, putting the righteousness of God within his reach, enabling him to perfect holiness in God's fear. The contrast is made absolute, *pro tem.* There is no "spirit" in the old at all; there is no "letter" in the new. This last assertion was more natural then than now; for at the time when Paul wrote this Epistle, there was no "New Testament of our Lord and Saviour Jesus Christ" consigned in documents and collected for the use of the Church. The Gospel existed in the world, not at all in books, but only in men; all the epistles were living epistles; there was literally no letter, but only spirit.

This, doubtless, is the explanation of the blank antithesis of the old covenant and the new in the passage before us. But it is obvious, when we think of it, that this antithesis does not exhaust the relations of the two. It is not the whole truth about the earlier dispensation to say that, while the new is spiritual, it is not. The religion of the Old Testament was not mere legalism; if it had been, the Old Testament would be for us an unprofitable and almost an unintelligible book. That religion had its spiritual side, as all but utterly corrupt religions always have; God administered His grace to His people through it, and in psalms and prophecies we have records of their experiences, which are not legal, but spiritual, and priceless even to Christian men. Nor would Paul, under other circumstances, have refused to admit this; on the contrary, it is a prominent element in his teaching. He knows that the old bears in its bosom the promise of the new, a sum of promises that has been confirmed and made good in Jesus Christ (chap. i. 20). He knows that the righteousness of God, which is proclaimed in the Gospel, is witnessed to by the law and the prophets (Rom. iii. 21). He knows that "the law," even, is "spiritual" (Rom. vii. 14). He knows that the righteousness of faith was a secret revealed to David (Rom. iv. 6 f.). He would probably have agreed with Stephen that the oracles received and delivered by Moses in the wilderness were "living" oracles; and his profound mind would have thrilled to hear that great word of Jesus, "I am not come to destroy, but to fulfil." Had he lived to a time like ours, when the Gospel also has been embodied in a book, instead of using "letter" and "spirit" as mutually exclusive, he would have admitted, as we do, that both ideas apply, in some sense, to both dispensations, and that it is possible to take the old and the new alike either in the letter or in the spirit. Nevertheless, he would have been entitled to say that, if they were to be characterised in their differences, they must be characterised as he has done it: the mark of the old, as opposed to the new, is literalism, or legalism; the mark of the new, as opposed to the old, is spirituality, or freedom. They differ as law differs from life, as compulsion from inspiration. Taken thus, no one can have any difficulty in agreeing with him.

But the Apostle does not rest in generalities: he goes on to a more particular comparison of the old and the new dispensations, and especially to a demonstration that the new is the more glorious. He starts with a statement of their working, as dependent on their nature just described. One is letter; the other, spirit. Well, the letter kills, but the spirit gives life. A sentence so pregnant as this, and so capable of various applications, must have been very perplexing to the Corinthians, had they not been fairly acquainted beforehand with the Apostle's "form of doctrine" (Rom. vi. 17). It condenses in itself a whole cycle of his characteristic thoughts. All that he says in the Epistles to the Romans and the Galatians about the working of the law, in its relation to the flesh, is represented in "the letter killeth." The power of the law to create the consciousness of sin and to intensify it; to stimulate transgression, and so make sin exceeding sinful, and shut men up in despair; to pass sentence upon the guilty, the hopeless sentence of death,—all this is involved in the words. The fulness of meaning is as ample in "the spirit giveth life." The Spirit of Christ, given to those who receive Christ in the Gospel, is an infinite power and an infinite promise. It includes the reversal of all that the letter has wrought. The sentence of death is reversed; the impotence to good is counteracted and overcome; the soul looks out to, and anticipates, not the blackness of darkness for ever, but the everlasting glory of Christ.[26] When the Apostle has written these two little sentences—when he has supplied "letter" and "spirit" with the predicates "kill" and "make alive," in the sense which they bear in the Christian revelation—he has gone as far as the mind of man can go in stating an effective contrast. But he works it out with reference to some special points in which the superiority of the new to the old is to be observed.

(1) In the first place, the ministry of the old was a ministry of death. Even as such it had a glory, or splendour, of its own. The face of Moses, its great minister, shone after he had been in the presence of God; and though that brightness was passing away even as men caught sight of it (τὴν καταργουμένην is partic. impf.), it was so resplendent as to dazzle the beholders. But the ministry of the new is a ministry of spirit: and who would not argue *a fortiori* that it should appear in glory greater still? Both the μᾶλλον ("rather"), and the future (ἔσται), in ver. 8, are logical. Paul speaks, to use Bengel's expression, looking forward as it were from the Old Testament into the New. He does not say in what the glory of the new consists. He does not say that it is veiled at present, and will be manifested when Christ comes to transfigure His own. Even the use of "hope" in ver. 12 does not prove this. He leaves it quite indefinite; and arguing from the nature of the two ministries, which has just been explained, simply concludes that in glory the new must far transcend the old.

(2) In vv. 9 and 10 he puts a new point upon this. "Death" and "life" are here replaced by "condemnation" and "righteousness." It is through condemnation that man becomes the prey of death; and the grace which reigns in him to eternal life reigns through righteousness (Rom. v. 21). The contrast of these two words is very significant for Paul's conception of the Gospel: it shows how essential to his idea of righteousness, how fundamental in it, is the thought of acquittal or acceptance with God. Men are bad men, sinful men, under God's condemnation; and he cannot conceive a Gospel at all which does not announce, at the very outset, the removal of that condemnation, and a declaration in the sinner's favour. Perhaps there are other ways of conceiving men, and other aspects in which God can come to them as their Saviour; but the Pauline Gospel has proved itself, and will always prove itself anew, the Gospel for the sinful, who know the misery of condemnation and despair. Mere pardon, as it has been called, may be a meagre conception, but it is that without which no other Christian conception can exist for a moment. That which lies at the bottom of the new covenant, and supports all its magnificent promises and hopes, is this: "I will forgive their iniquities, and I will remember their sins no more." If we could imagine this taken away, what were left? Of course the righteousness which the Gospel proclaims *is* more than pardon; it is not exhausted when we say it is the opposite of condemnation; but unless we feel that the very nerve of it lies in the removal of condemnation, we shall never understand the New Testament tone in speaking of it. It is this which explains the joyous rebound of the Apostle's spirit whenever he encounters the subject; he remembers the black cloud, and now there is clear shining; he was under sentence then, but now he is justified by faith, and has peace with God. He cannot exaggerate the contrast, nor the greater glory of the new state. Granting that the ministry of condemnation had its glory—that the revelation of law "had an austere majesty of its own"—does not the ministry of righteousness, the Gospel which annulled the condemnation and restored man to peace with God, overflow with glory? When he thinks of it, he is tempted to withdraw the concession he has made. We may call the old dispensation and its ministry glorious if we like; they are glorious when they stand alone; but when comparison is made with the new,[27] they are not glorious at all. The stars are bright till the moon rises; the moon herself reigns in heaven till her splendour pales before the sun; but when the sun shines in his strength, there is no other glory in the sky. All the glories of the old covenant have vanished for Paul in the light which shines from the Cross and from the Throne of Christ.

(3) A final superiority belongs to the new dispensation and its ministry as compared with the old—the superiority of permanence to transiency. "If

that which passeth away *was* with glory, much more that which remaineth *is* in glory." The verbs here are supplied by the translators, but one may question whether the contrast of past and present was so definite in the Apostle's mind. I think not, and the reference to Moses' face does not prove that it was. All through these comparisons St. Paul expresses himself with the utmost generality; logical and ideal, not temporal, relations, dominate his thoughts. The law *was* given in glory (ἐγενήθη ἐν δόξῃ, ver. 7)—there is no dispute about that; but what the eleventh verse makes prominent is that while glory is the attendant or accompaniment of the transient, it is the element of the permanent. The law is indeed of God; it has a function in the economy of God; it is at the very lowest a negative preparation for the Gospel; it shuts men up to the acceptance of God's mercy. In this respect the glory on Moses' face represents the real greatness which belongs to the law as a power used by God in the working out of His loving purpose. But at the best the law only shuts men up to Christ, and then its work is done. The true greatness of God is revealed, and with it His true glory, once for all, in the Gospel. There is nothing beyond the righteousness of God, manifested in Christ Jesus, for the acceptance of faith. That is God's last word to the world: it has absorbed in it even the glory of the law; and it is bright for ever with a glory above all other. It is God's chief end to reveal this glory in the Gospel, and to make men partakers of it; it has been so always, is so still, and ever shall be; and in the consciousness that he has seen and been saved by the eternal love of God, and is now a minister of it, the Apostle claims this finality of the new covenant as its crowning glory. The law, like the lower gifts of the Christian life, passes away; but the new covenant abides, for it is the revelation of love—that love which is the being and the glory of God Himself.

These qualities of the Christian dispensation, which constitute its newness, are too readily lost sight of. It is hard to appreciate and to live up to them, and hence they are always lapsing out of view, and requiring to be rediscovered. In the first age of Christianity there were many myriads of Jews, the Book of Acts tells us, who had very little sense of the newness of the Gospel; they were exceedingly zealous for the law, even for the letter of all its ritual prescriptions: Paul and his spiritual conception of Christianity were their bugbear. In the first half of the second century the religion even of the Gentile Churches had already become more legal than evangelical; there was wanting any sufficient apprehension of the spirituality, the freedom, and the newness of Christianity as opposed to Judaism; and though the reaction of Marcion, who denied that there was any connexion whatever between the Old Testament and the New, went to a false and perverse extreme, it was the natural, and in its motives the legitimate, protest of spirit and life against letter and law. The Reformation in the sixteenth century was essentially a movement of similar character: it was the rediscovery of the Pauline Gospel, or of the Gospel in those characteristics of it which made Paul's heart leap for joy—its justifying righteousness, its spirituality, its liberty. In a Protestant scholasticism this glorious Gospel has again been lost oftener than once; it is lost when "a learned ministry" deals with the New Testament writings as the scribes dealt with the Old; it is lost also—for extremes meet—when an unlearned piety swears by verbal, even by literal, inspiration, and takes up to mere documents an attitude which in principle is fatal to Christianity. It is in the life of the Church—especially in that life which communicates itself, and makes the Christian community what the Jewish never was, essential a missionary community—that the safeguard of all these high characteristics lies. A Church devoted to learning, or to the maintenance of a social or political position, or even merely to the cultivation of a type of character among its own members, may easily cease to be spiritual, and lapse into legal religion: a Church actively engaged propagating itself never can. It is not with the "letter" one can hopefully address unbelieving men; it is only with the power of the Holy Spirit at work in the heart; and where the Spirit is, there is liberty. None are so "sound" on the essentials of the faith as men with the truly missionary spirit; but at the same time none are so completely emancipated, and that by the self-same Spirit, from all that is not itself spiritual.

X
THE TRANSFIGURING SPIRIT

"Having therefore such a hope, we use great boldness of speech, and *are* not as Moses, *who* put a veil upon his face, that the children of Israel should not look stedfastly on the end of that which was passing away: but their minds were hardened: for until this very day at the reading of the old covenant the same veil remaineth unlifted; which veil is done away in Christ. But unto this day, whensoever Moses is read, a veil lieth upon their heart. But whensoever it shall turn to the Lord, the veil is taken away. Now the Lord is the Spirit: and where the Spirit of the Lord is, *there* is liberty. But we all, with unveiled face reflecting as a mirror the glory of the Lord, are transformed into the same image from glory to glory, even as from the Lord the Spirit."—2 Cor. iii. 12-18 (R.V.).

The "hope" which here explains the Apostle's freedom of speech is to all intents and purposes the same as the "confidence" in ver. 4.[28] It is much easier to suppose that the word is thus used, with a certain latitude, as it might be in English, than to force upon it a reference to the glory to be revealed when Christ comes again, and to give the same future reference to "glory" all through this passage. The new covenant is present, and present in its glory; and though it has a future, with which the Apostle's hope is bound up, it is not in view of its future only, it is because of what it is even now, that he is so grandly confident, and uses such boldness of speech. It is quite fair to infer from chap. iv. 3—"if our Gospel is veiled, it is veiled in those that are perishing"—that Paul's opponents at Corinth had charged him with behaviour of another kind. They had accused him of making a mystery of his Gospel—preaching it in such a fashion that no one could really see it, or understand what he meant. If there is any charge which the true preacher will feel keenly, and resent vehemently, it is this. It is his first duty to deliver his message with a plainness that defies misunderstanding. He is sent to all men on an errand of life or death; and to leave any man wondering, after the message has been delivered, what it is about, is the worst sort of treachery. It belies the Gospel, and God who is its author. It may be due to pride, or to a misguided intention to commend the Gospel to the wisdom or the prejudices of men; but it is never anything else than a fatal mistake.

Paul not only resents the charge; he feels it so acutely that he finds an ingenious way of retorting it. "We," he says, "the ministers of the new covenant, we who preach life, righteousness, and everlasting glory, have nothing to hide; we wish every one to know everything about the dispensation which we serve. It is the representatives of the old who are really open to the charge of using concealment; the first and the greatest of them all, Moses himself, put a veil on his face, that[29] the children of Israel should not look stedfastly on the end of that which was passing away. The glory on his face was a fading glory, because it was the glory of a temporary dispensation; but he did not wish the Israelites to see clearly that it was destined to disappear; so he veiled his face, and left them to think the law a permanent divine institution."

Perhaps the best thing to do with this singular interpretation is not to take it too seriously. Even sober expositors like Chrysostom and Calvin have thought it necessary to argue gravely that the Apostle is not accusing the law, or saying anything insulting of Moses; while Schmiedel, on the other hand, insists that a grave moral charge *is* made against Moses, and that Paul most unjustly uses the Old Testament, in its own despite, to prove its own transitoriness. I believe it would be far truer to say that the character of Moses never crossed Paul's mind in the whole passage, for better or worse; he only remembered, as he smarted under the accusation of veiling his Gospel of the new covenant, a certain transaction under the old covenant in which a veil did figure—a transaction which a Rabbinical interpretation, whimsical indeed to us, but provoking if not convincing to his adversaries, enabled him to turn against them. As for proving the transitoriness of the Old Testament by a forced and illegitimate argument, that transitoriness was abundantly established to Paul, as it is to us, on real grounds; nothing whatever depends on what is here said of Moses and the veil. It is not necessary, if we take this view, to go into the historical interpretation of the passage in Exod. xxxiv. 29-35. The comparison of the Apostle with the Old Testament writer has been made more difficult for the English reader by the serious error in the Authorised Version of Exod. xxxiv. 33. Instead of "*till* Moses had done speaking with them," we ought to read, as in the Revised Version, "*when* Moses had done speaking." This exactly reverses the meaning. Moses spoke to the people with face bare and radiant; the glory was to be visible at least in his official intercourse with them, or *whenever he spoke for God*. At other times he wore the veil, putting it off, however, when he went into the tabernacle—that is, *whenever he spoke with*

God. In all divine relations, then, we should naturally infer, there was to be the open and shining face; in other words, so far as he acted as mediator of the old covenant, Moses really acted in the spirit of Paul. It would therefore have been unjust in the Apostle to charge him with hiding anything, if the charge had really meant more than this—that Paul saw in his use of the veil a symbol of the fact that the children of Israel did not see that the old covenant was transitory, and that its glory was to be lost in that of the new. No one can deny that this *was* the fact, and no one therefore need be exercised if Paul pictured it in the manner of his own time and race, and not in the manner of ours. To suppose that he means to charge Moses with a deliberate act of dishonesty is to suppose what no sensible person will ever credit; and we may return, without more ado, to the painful situation which he contemplates.

Their minds were hardened. This is stated historically, and seems to refer in the first instance to those who watched Moses put on the veil, and became insensible, as he did so, to the nature of the old covenant. But it is applicable to the Jewish race at all periods of their history; they never discovered the secret which Moses hid from their forefathers beneath the veil. The only result that followed the labours even of great prophets like Isaiah had been the deepening of the darkness; having eyes the people saw not, having ears they heard not; their heart was fat and heavy, so that they did not apprehend the ways of God nor turn to Him. All around him the Apostle saw the melancholy evidence that there had been no change for the better. Until this day the same veil remains, when the Old Testament is read,[30] not taken away; for it is only undone in Christ, and of Christ they will know nothing. He repeats the sad statement, varying it slightly to indicate that the responsibility for a condition so blind and dreary rests not with the old covenant itself, but with those who live under it. "Until this day, I say, whensoever Moses is read, a veil lies upon their heart."

This witness, we must acknowledge, is almost as true in the nineteenth century as in the first. The Jews still exist as a race and a sect, acknowledging the Old Testament as a revelation from God, basing their religion upon it, keeping their ancient law so far as circumstances enable them to keep it, not convinced that as a religious constitution it has been superseded by a new one. Many of them, indeed, have abandoned it without becoming Christians. But in so doing they have become secularists; they have not appreciated the old covenant to the full, and then outgrown it; they have been led for various reasons to deny that there ever was anything divine in it, and have renounced together its discipline and its hopes. Only where the knowledge of the Christ has been received is the veil which lies upon their hearts taken away; they can then appreciate both all the virtues of the ancient dispensation and all its defects; they can glorify God for what it was and for what it shut them up to; they can see that in all its parts it had a reference to something lying beyond itself—to a "new thing" that God would do for His people; and in welcoming the new covenant, and its Mediator Jesus Christ, they can feel that they are not making void, but establishing, the law.

This is their hope, and to this the Apostle looks in ver. 16: "But whensoever it shall turn to the Lord, the veil is taken away." The Greek expression of this passage is so closely modelled on that of Exod. xxxiv. 34, that Westcott and Hort print it as a quotation. Moses evidently is still in the Apostle's mind. The veiling of his face symbolised the nation's blindness; the nation's hope is to be seen in that action in which Moses was unveiled. He uncovered his face when he turned from the people to speak to God. "Even so," says the Apostle, "when *they* turn to the Lord, the veil of which we have been speaking is taken away,[31] and they see clearly."[32] One can hardly avoid feeling in this a reminiscence of the Apostle's own conversion. He is thinking not only of the unveiling of Moses, but of the scales which fell from his own eyes when he was baptised in the name of Jesus, and was filled with the Holy Ghost, and saw the old covenant and its glory lost and fulfilled in the new. He knew how stupendous was the change involved here; it meant a revolution in the whole constitution of the Jews' spiritual world as vast as that which was wrought in the natural world when the sun supplanted the earth as the centre of our system. But the gain was corresponding. The soul was delivered from an *impasse*. Under the old covenant, as bitter experience had shown him, the religious life had come to a dead-lock; the conscience was confronted with a torturing, and in its very nature insoluble, problem: man, burdened and enslaved by sin, was required to attain to a righteousness which should please God. The contradictions of this position were solved, its mystery was abolished, when the soul turned to the Lord, and appropriated by faith the righteousness and life of God in him. The old covenant found its place, an intelligible and worthy though subordinate place, in the grand programme of redemption; the strife between the soul and God, between the soul and the conditions of existence, ceased; life opened out again; there was a large room to move in, an inspiring power within; in one word, there was spiritual life and liberty, and Christ was the author of it all.

This is the force of the seventeenth verse: "Now the Lord is the Spirit: and where the Spirit of the Lord is, there is liberty." The Lord, of course, is Christ, and the Spirit is that of which Paul has already spoken in the sixth verse. It is the Holy Spirit, the Lord and Giver of life under the new covenant. He who turns to Christ receives this Spirit; it is through it that

Christ dwells in His people; what are called "fruits of the Spirit" are traits of Christ's own character which the Spirit produces in the saints; practically, therefore, the two may be identified, and hence the expression "the Lord is the Spirit," though startling at first sight, is not improper, and ought not to mislead.[33] It is a mistake to connect it with such passages as Rom. i. 4, and to draw inferences from it as to Paul's conception of the person of Christ. He does not say "the Lord is spirit," but "the Lord is the Spirit"; what is in view is not the person of Christ so much as His power. To identify the Lord and the Spirit without qualification, in the face of the benediction in chap. xiii. 14, is out of the question. The truth of the passage is the same as that of Rom. viii. 9 ff.: "If any man have not *the Spirit of Christ,* he is none of His. And if *Christ is in you,*" etc. Here, so far as the practical experience of Christians goes, no distinction is made between the Spirit of Christ and Christ Himself; Christ dwells in Christians through His Spirit. The very same truth, as is well known, pervades the chapters in the Fourth Gospel in which Christ consoles His disciples for His departure from this world; He will not leave them orphans—He will come to them, and remain with them in the other Comforter. To turn to Christ, the Apostle wishes to assert with the utmost emphasis, is not to do a thing which has no virtue and no consequences; it is to turn to one who has received of the Father the gift of the Holy Ghost, and who immediately sets up the new spiritual life, which is nothing less than His own life, by that Spirit, in the believing soul. And summing up in one word the grand characteristic and distinction of the new covenant, as realised by this indwelling of Christ through His Spirit, he concludes: "And where the Spirit of the Lord is, there is liberty."

In the interpretation of the last word, we must have respect to the context; liberty has its meaning in contrast with that state to which the old covenant had reduced those who adhered to it. It means freedom from the law; freedom, fundamentally, from its condemnation, thanks to the gift of righteousness in Christ; freedom, also, from its letter, as something simply without us and over against us. No written word, as such, can ever be pleaded against the voice of the Spirit within. Even the words we call in an eminent sense "inspired," words of the Spirit, are subject to this law: they do not put a limit to the liberty of the spiritual man. He can overrule the letter of them when the literal interpretation or application would contravene the spirit which is common both to them and him. This principle is capable of being abused, no doubt, and by bad men and fanatics has been abused; but its worst abuses can hardly have done more harm than the pedantic word-worship which has often lost the soul even of the New Testament, and read the words of the Lord and His Apostles with a veil upon its face through which nothing could be seen. There is such a thing as an unspiritual scrupulosity in dealing with the New Testament, now that we have it in documentary form, just as there used to be in dealing with the Old; and we ought to remind ourselves continually that the documentary form is an accident, not an essential, of the new covenant. That covenant existed, and men lived under it and enjoyed its blessings, before it had any written documents at all; and we shall not appreciate its characteristics, and especially this one of its spiritual freedom, unless we put ourselves occasionally, in imagination, in their place. It is far easier to make Paul mean too little than too much; and the liberty of the Spirit in which he exults here covers, we may be sure, not only liberty from condemnation, and liberty from the unspiritual yoke of the ritual law, but liberty from all that is in its nature statutory, liberty to organise the new life, and to legislate for it, from within.

The bearing of this passage on the religious blindness of the Jews ought not to hide from us its permanent application. The religious insensibility of his countrymen will cease, Paul says; their religious perplexities will be solved, when they turn to Christ. This is the beginning of all intelligence, of all freedom, of all hope, in things spiritual. Much of the religious doubt and confusion of our own times is due to the preoccupation of men's minds with religion at points from which Christ is invisible. But it is He who is the key to *all* human experiences as well as to the Old Testament; it is He who answers the questions of the world as well as the questions of the Jews; it is He who takes *our* feet out of the net, opens the gate of righteousness before us, and gives us spiritual freedom. It is like finding a pearl of great price when the soul discovers this, and to point it out to others is to do them a priceless service. Disregard everything else in the meantime, if you are bewildered, baffled, in bonds which you cannot break; turn to Jesus Christ, as Moses turned to God, with face uncovered; put down prejudice, preconceptions, pride, the disposition to make demands; only look stedfastly till you see what He is, and all that perplexes you will pass away, or appear in a new light, and serve a new and spiritual purpose.

Something like this larger application of his words passed, we may suppose, before the Apostle's mind when he wrote the eighteenth verse. In the grandeur of the truth which rises upon him he forgets his controversy and becomes a poet. We breathe the ampler ether, the diviner air, as we read: "But we all, with unveiled face beholding as in a glass the glory of the Lord, are transformed into the same image from glory to glory, even as from the Lord the Spirit." I have kept here for κατοπτριζόμενοι the rendering of the Authorised Version, which in the Revised has been relegated to the margin, and replaced by "reflecting as a mirror." There do not seem to be sufficient grounds for the change, and the old translation is defended in Grimm's Lexicon, in Winer's Grammar, and by Meyer, Heinrici, and Beet.

The active voice of the verb κατοπτρίζω means "to exhibit in a mirror"; and the middle, "to mirror oneself"—*i.e.*, "to look at oneself in a mirror." This, at least, is the sense of most of the examples of the middle which are found in Greek writers; but as it is quite inapplicable here, the question of interpretation becomes rather difficult. It is, however, in accordance with analogy to say that if the active means "to show in a mirror," the middle means "to get shown to one in a mirror," or, as the Authorised Version puts it, "to behold in a mirror." I cannot make out that any analogy favours the new rendering, "reflecting as a mirror"; and the authority of Chrysostom, which would otherwise be considerable on this side, is lessened by the fact that he seems never to have raised the question, and in point of fact combines both renderings.[34] His illustration of the polished silver lying in the sunshine, and sending back the rays which strike it, is in favour of the change; but when he writes, "We not only *look upon* the glory of God, but also catch thence a kind of radiance," he may fairly be claimed for the other side. There are two reasons also which seem to me to have great weight in favour of the old rendering: first, the expression "with unveiled face," which, as Meyer remarks, is naturally of a piece with "beholding"; and, second, an unequivocal example of the middle voice of κατοπτρίζομαι in the sense of "seeing," while no unequivocal example can be produced for "reflecting." This example is found in Philo i. 107 (*Leg. Alleg.*, iii. 33), where Moses prays to God: "Show not Thyself to me through heaven or earth, or water or air, or anything at all that comes into being; nor let me see Thy form mirrored in any other thing than in Thee, even in God" (Μηδὲ κατοπτρισαίμην ἐν ἄλλῳ τινὶ τὴν σὴν ἰδέαν ἢ ἐν σοὶ τῷ Θεῷ). This seems to me decisive, and there is the less reason to reject it on other than linguistic grounds, when we consider that the idea of "reflecting," if it is given up in κατοπτριζόμενοι, is conserved in μεταμορφούμεθα. The transformation has the reflection of Christ's glory for its effect, not for its cause; but the reflection, eventually, is there.

Assuming, then, that "beholding as in a glass" is the right interpretation of this hard word, let us go on to what the Apostle says. "We all" probably means "all Christians," and not only "all Christian teachers." If there is a comparison implied, it is between the two dispensations, and the experiences open to those who lived under them, not between the mediator of the old and the heralds of the new. Under the old covenant one only saw the glory; now the beatific vision is open to all. We all behold it "with unveiled face." There is nothing on Christ's part that leads to disguise, and nothing on ours that comes between us and Him. The darkness is past, the true light already shines, and Christian souls cannot look on it too fixedly, or drink it in to excess. But what is meant by "the glory of the Lord" on which we gaze with face unveiled?

It will not be questioned, by those who are at home in St. Paul's thoughts, that "the Lord" means the exalted Saviour, and that the glory must be something which belongs to Him. Indeed, if we remember that in the First Epistle, chap. ii. 8, He is characteristically described by the Apostle as "the Lord of glory," we shall not feel it too much to say that the glory is *everything* which belongs to Him. There is not any aspect of the exalted Christ, there is not any representation of Him in the Gospel, there is not any function which He exercises, that does not come under this head. "In His temple everything saith Glory!" There is a glory even in the mode of His existence: St. Paul's conception of Him is dominated always by that appearance on the way to Damascus, when he saw the Christ through a light above the brightness of the sun. It is His glory that He shares the Father's throne,[35] that He is head of the Church, possessor and bestower of all the fulness of divine grace, the coming Judge of the world, conqueror of every hostile power, intercessor for His own, and, in short, bearer of all the majesty which belongs to His kingly office. The essential thing in all this—essential to the understanding of the Apostle, and to the existence of the apostolic *"Gospel of the glory of Christ"* (chap. iv. 4)—is that the glory in question is the glory of a Living Person. When Paul thinks of it, he does not look back, he looks up; he does not remember, he beholds in a glass; the glory of the Lord has no meaning for him apart from the present exaltation of the Risen Christ. "The Lord reigneth; He is apparelled with majesty"—that is the anthem of His praise.

I have insisted on this, because, in a certain reaction from what was perhaps an exaggerated Paulinism, there is a tendency to misapply even the most characteristic and vital passages in St. Paul's Gospel, and pre-eminently to misapply passages like this. Nothing could be more misleading than to substitute here for the glory of the exalted Christ as mirrored in the apostolic Gospel that moral beauty which was seen in Jesus of Nazareth. Of course I do not mean to deny that the moral loveliness of Jesus is glorious; nor do I question that in the contemplation of it in the pages of our Gospels—*subject to one grand condition*—a transforming power is exercised through it; but I do deny that any such thing was in the mind of St. Paul. The subject of the Apostle's Gospel was not Jesus the carpenter of Nazareth, but Christ the Lord of glory; men, as he understood the matter, were saved, not by dwelling on the wonderful words and deeds of One who had lived some time ago, and reviving these in their imagination, but by receiving the almighty, emancipating, quickening Spirit of One who lived and reigned for evermore. The transformation here spoken of is not the work of a powerful imagination, which can make the figure in the pages of the Gospels live again, and suffuse the soul with feeling as it gazes upon it; preach this as gospel who will, it was never preached by an apostle of Jesus Christ. It is the work of the Spirit, and the Spirit is given, not to the memory or imagination which can vivify the past, but to the faith which sees Christ upon His throne. *And it is subject to the condition of faith in the living Christ that contemplation of Jesus in the Gospels changes us into the same image.* There can be no doubt that at the present time many are falling back upon this contemplation in a despairing rather than a believing mood; what they seek and find in it is rather a poetic consolation than religious inspiration; their faith in the living Christ is gone, or is so uncertain as to be practically of no saving power, and they have recourse to the memory of what Jesus was as at least something to cling to. "We thought that it had been He which should have delivered Israel." But surely it is as clear as day that in religion—in the matter of redemption—we must deal, not with the dead, but with the living. Paul may have known less or more of the contents of our first three Gospels; he may have valued them more or less adequately; but just because he had been saved by Christ, and was preaching Christ as a Saviour, the centre of his thoughts and affections was not Galilee, but "the heavenlies." *There* the Lord of glory reigned; and from that world He sent the Spirit which changed His people into His image. And so it must always be, if Christianity is to be a living religion. Leave out this, and not only is the Pauline Gospel lost, but everything is lost which could be called Gospel in the New Testament.

The Lord of glory, Paul teaches here, is the pattern and prophecy of a glory to be revealed in us; and as we contemplate Him in the mirror of the Gospel,[36] we are gradually transformed into the same image, even as by the Lord the Spirit. The transformation, these last words again teach, is not accomplished by beholding, but while we behold; it does not depend on the vividness with which we can imagine the past, but on the present power of Christ working in us. The result is such as befits the operation of such a power. We are changed into the image of Him from whom it proceeds. We are made like Himself. It may seem far more natural to say that the believer is made like Jesus of Nazareth, than that he is made like the Lord of glory; but that does not entitle us to shift the centre of gravity in the Apostle's teaching, and it only tempts us to ignore one of the most prominent and enviable characteristics of the New Testament religious life. Christ is on His throne, and His people are *exalted and victorious* in Him. When we forget Christ's exaltation in our study of His earthly life—when we are so preoccupied, it may even be so fascinated, with what He was, that we forget what He is—when, in other words, a pious historical imagination takes the place of a living religious faith—*that victorious consciousness is lost*, and in a most essential point the image of the Lord is not reproduced in the believer.

This is why the Pauline point of view—if indeed it is to be called Pauline, and not simply Christian—is essential. Christianity is a religion, not merely a history, though it should be the history told by Matthew, Mark, and Luke; and the chance of having the history itself appreciated for religion is that He who is its subject shall be contemplated, not in the dim distance of the past, but in the glory of His heavenly reign, and that He shall be recognised, not merely as one who lived a perfect life in His own generation, but as the Giver of life eternal by His Spirit to all who turn to Him. The Church will always be justified, while recognising that Christianity is a historical religion, in giving prominence, not to its historicity, but to what makes it a religion at all—namely, the present exaltation of Christ. This involves everything, and determines, as St. Paul tells us here, the very form and spirit of her own life.

XI
THE GOSPEL DEFINED

> "Therefore seeing we have this ministry, even as we obtained mercy, we faint not: but we have renounced the hidden things of shame, not walking in craftiness, nor handling the Word of God deceitfully; but by the manifestation of the truth commending ourselves to every man's conscience in the sight of God. But and if our Gospel is veiled, it is veiled in them that are perishing: in whom the god of this world hath blinded the minds of the unbelieving, that the light of the Gospel of the glory of Christ, who is the image of God, should not dawn *upon them*. For we preach not ourselves, but Christ Jesus as Lord, and ourselves as your servants for Jesus' sake. Seeing it is God, that said, Light shall shine out of darkness, who shined in our hearts, to give the light of the knowledge of the glory of God in the face of Jesus Christ."—2 Cor. iv. 1-6 (R.V.).

In this paragraph Paul resumes for the last time the line of thought on which he had set out at chap. iii. 4, and again at chap. iii. 12. Twice he has allowed himself to be carried away into digressions, not less interesting than his argument; but now he proceeds without further interruption. His subject is the New Testament ministry, and his own conduct as a minister.

"Seeing we have this ministry," he writes, "even as we obtained mercy, we faint not." The whole tone of the passage is to be triumphant; above the common joy of the New Testament it rises, at the close (ver. 16 ff.), into a kind of solemn rapture; and it is characteristic of the Apostle that before he abandons himself to the swelling tide of exultation, he guards it all with the words, "even as we obtained mercy." There was nothing so deep down in Paul's soul, nothing so constantly present to his thoughts, as this great experience. No flood of emotion, no pressure of trial, no necessity of conflict, ever drove him from his moorings here. The mercy of God underlay his whole being; it kept him humble even when he boasted; even when engaged in defending his character against false accusations—a peculiarly trying situation—it kept him truly Christian in spirit.

The words may be connected equally well, so far as either meaning or grammar is concerned, with what precedes, or with what follows. It was a signal proof of God's mercy that He had entrusted Paul with the ministry of the Gospel; and it was only what we should expect, when one who had obtained such mercy turned out a good soldier of Jesus Christ, able to endure hardship and not faint. Those to whom little is forgiven, Jesus Himself tells us, love little; it is not in them for Jesus' sake to bear all things, believe all things, hope all things, endure all things. They faint easily, and are overborne by petty trials, because they have not in them that fountain of brave patience—a deep abiding sense of what they owe to Christ, and can never, by any length or ardour of service, repay. It accuses us, not so much of human weakness, as of ingratitude, and insensibility to the mercy of God, when we faint in the exercise of our ministry.

"We faint not," says Paul: "we show no weakness. On the contrary, we have renounced the hidden things of shame, not walking in craftiness, nor handling the Word of God deceitfully." The contrast marked by ἀλλὰ is very instructive: it shows, in the things which Paul had renounced, whither weakness leads. It betrays men. It compels them to have recourse to arts which shame bids them conceal; they become diplomatists and strategists, rather than heralds; they manipulate their message; they adapt it to the spirit of the time, or the prejudices of their auditors; they make liberal use of the principle of accommodation. When these arts are looked at closely, they come to this: the minister has contrived to put something of his own between his hearers and the Gospel; the message has really not been declared. His intention, of course, with all this artifice, is to recommend himself to men; but the method is radically vicious. The Apostle shows us a more excellent way. "We have renounced," he says, "all these weak ingenuities; and by manifestation of the truth commend ourselves to every man's conscience in the sight of God."[37]

This is probably the simplest and most complete directory for the preaching of the Gospel. The preacher is to make the truth manifest. It is implied in what has just been said, that one great hindrance to its manifestation may easily be its treatment by the preacher himself. If he wishes to do anything else at the same time, the manifestation will not take effect. If he wishes, in the very act of preaching, to conciliate a class, or an interest; to create an opinion in favour of his own learning, ability, or eloquence; to enlist sympathy for a cause or an institution which is only accidentally connected with the Gospel,—the truth will not be seen, and it will not tell. The truth, we are further taught here, makes its appeal to the conscience; it is there that God's witness in its favour resides. Now, the conscience is the moral nature of man, or the moral element in his nature; it is this, therefore, which the preacher has to address. Does not this involve a certain directness and simplicity of method, a certain plainness and urgency also, which it is far easier to miss than to find? Conscience is not the abstract logical faculty in man, and the preacher's business is therefore not to prove, but to proclaim, the Gospel. All he has to do is to let it be seen, and the more nakedly visible it is the better. His object is not to frame an irrefragable argument, but to produce an irresistible impression. There is no such thing as an argument to which it is impossible for a wilful man to make objections; at least there is no such thing in the sphere of Christian truth. Even if there were, men would object to it on that very ground. They would say that, in matters of this description, when logic went too far, it amounted to moral intimidation, and that in the interests of liberty they were entitled to protest against it. Practically, this is what Voltaire said of Pascal.[38] But there is such a thing as an irresistible impression,—an impression made upon the moral nature against which it is vain to attempt any protest; an impression, which subdues and holds the soul for ever. When the truth is manifested, and men see it, this is the effect to be looked for; this, consequently, is the preacher's aim. In the sight of God—that is, acting with absolute sincerity— Paul trusted to this simple method to recommend himself to men. He brought no letters of introduction from others; he had no artifices of his own; he held up the truth in its unadorned integrity till it told upon the conscience of his hearers; and after that, he needed no other witness. The same conversions which accredited the power of the message accredited the character of him who bore it.

To this line of argument there is a very obvious reply. What, it may be asked, of those on whom "the manifestation of the truth" produces no effect? What of those who in spite of all this plain appeal to conscience neither see nor feel anything? It is sadly obvious that this is no mere supposition; the Gospel remains a secret, an impotent ineffective secret, to many who hear it again and again. Paul faces the difficulty without flinching, though the answer is appalling. "If our Gospel *is* veiled (and the melancholy fact cannot be denied), it is veiled in the case of the perishing." The fact that it remains hidden from some men is their condemnation; it marks them out as persons on the way to destruction. The Apostle proceeds to explain himself further. As far as the rationale can be given of what is finally irrational, he interprets the moral situation for us. The perishing people in question are unbelievers, whose thoughts, or minds, the god of this world has blinded. [39] The intention of this blinding is conveyed in the last words of ver. 4: "that the illumination which proceeds from the Gospel, the Gospel of the glory of Christ, who is the image of God, may not dawn upon them."

Let these solemn words appeal to our hearts and consciences, before we attempt to criticise them. Let us have a due impression of the stupendous facts to which they refer, before we raise difficulties about them, or say rashly that the expression is disproportioned to the truth. To St. Paul the Gospel was a very great thing. A light issued from it so dazzling, so overwhelming, in its splendour and illuminative power, that it might well appear incredible that men should not see it. The powers counteracting it, "the world-rulers of this darkness," must surely, to judge by their success, have an immense influence. Even more than an immense influence, they must have an immense malignity. For what a blessedness it meant for men, that that light should dawn upon them! What a deprivation and loss, that its brightness should be obscured! Paul's whole sense of the might and malignity of the powers of darkness is condensed in the title which he here gives to their head—"*the god* of this world." It is literally "of this age," the period of time which extends to Christ's coming again. The dominion of evil is not unlimited, in duration; but while it lasts it is awful in its intensity and range. It does not seem an extravagance to the Apostle to describe Satan as the god of the present æon; and if it seems extravagant to us, we may remind ourselves that our Saviour also twice speaks of him as "*the prince* of this world." Who but Christ Himself, or a soul like St. Paul in complete sympathy with the mind and work of Christ, is capable of seeing and feeling the incalculable mass of the forces which are at work in the world to defeat the Gospel? What sleepy conscience, what moral mediocrity, itself purblind, only dimly conscious of the height of the Christian calling, and vexed by no aspirations toward it, has any right to say that it is too much to call Satan "the god of this world"? Such sleepy consciences have no idea of the omnipresence, the steady persistent pressure, the sleepless malignity, of the evil forces which beset man's life. They have no idea of the extent to which these forces frustrate the love of God in the Gospel, and rob men of their inheritance in Christ. To ask why men *should* be exposed to such forces is another, and here an irrelevant, question. What St. Paul saw, and what becomes apparent to every one in proportion as his interest in evangelising becomes intense, is that evil has a power and dominion in the world, which are betrayed, by their counteracting of the Gospel, to be purely malignant— in other words, Satanic—and the dimensions of which no description can exaggerate. Call such powers Satan, or what you please, but do not imagine that they are inconsiderable. During this age they *reign*; they have virtually taken what should be God's place in the world.

It is the necessary complement of this assertion of the malign dominion of evil, when St. Paul tells us that it is exercised in the case of unbelievers. It is their minds which the god of this world has blinded. We need not try to investigate more narrowly the relations of these two aspects of the facts. We need not say that the dominion of evil produces unbelief, though this is true (John iii. 18, 19); or that unbelief gives Satan his opportunity; or even that unbelief and the blindness here referred to are reciprocally cause and effect of each other. The moral interests involved are protected by the fact that blindness is only predicated in the case in which the Gospel has been rejected by individual unbelief; and the mere individualism, which is the source of so many heresies, doctrinal and practical, is excluded by the recognition of spiritual forces as operative among men which are far more wide-reaching than any individual knows. Nor ought we to overlook the suggestion of pity, and even of hope, for the perishing, in the contrast between their darkness and the illumination which the Gospel of the glory of Christ lights up. The perishing are not the lost; the unbelievers may yet believe: "in our deepest darkness, we know the direction of the light" (Beet). Final unbelief would mean final ruin; but we are not entitled to make sense the measure of spiritual things, and to argue that because we see men blind and unbelieving now they are bound for ever to remain so. In preaching the Gospel we must preach with hope that the light is stronger than the darkness, and able, even at the deepest, to drive it away. Only, when we see, as we sometimes will, how dense and impenetrable the darkness is, we cannot but cry with the Apostle, "Who is sufficient for these things?"

This passage is one of those in which the subject of the Gospel is distinctly enunciated: it is the Gospel of the glory of Christ, who is the image of God. The glory of Christ, or, which is the same thing, Christ in His glory, is the sum and substance of it, that which gives it both its contents and its character. Paul's conception of the Gospel is inspired and controlled from beginning to end by the appearance of the Lord which resulted in his conversion. In the First Epistle to the Corinthians (i. 18, 23), and in the Epistle to the Galatians (vi. 14), he seems to find what is essential and distinguishing in the Cross rather than the Throne; but this is probably due to the fact that the significance of the Cross had been virtually denied by those for whom His words are meant. The Christ whom he preached had died, and died, as the next chapter will make very prominent, to reconcile the world to God; but Paul preached Him as he had seen Him on that ever-memorable day; with all the virtue of His atoning death in it, the Gospel was yet the Gospel of *His glory*. It is in the combination of these two that the supreme power of the Gospel lies. In the distaste for the supernatural which has prevailed so widely, many have tried to ignore this, and to get out of the Cross alone an inspiration which it cannot yield if severed from the Throne. Had the story of Jesus ended with the words "suffered under Pontius Pilate, was crucified, dead, and buried," it is very certain that these words would never have formed part of a Creed—there would never have been such a thing as the Christian religion. But when these words are combined with what follows—"He rose again from the dead on the third day, He ascended into heaven, and sitteth at the right hand of God the Father"—we have the basis which religion requires; we have a living Lord, in whom all the redemptive virtue of a sinless life and death is treasured up, and who is able to save to the uttermost all that trust Him. It is not the emotions excited by the spectacle of the Passion, any more than the admiration evoked by the contemplation of Christ's life, that save; it is the Lord of glory, who lived that life of love, and in love endured that agony, and who is now enthroned at God's right hand. The life and death in one sense form part of His glory, in another they are a foil to it; He could not have been our Saviour but for them; He would not be our Saviour unless He had triumphed over them, and entered into a glory beyond.

When the Apostle speaks of Christ as the image of God, we must not let extraneous associations with this title deflect us from the true line of his thought. It is still the Exalted One of whom he is speaking: there is no other Christ for him. In that face which flashed upon him by Damascus twenty years before, he had seen, and always saw, all that man could see of the invisible God. It represented for him, and for all to whom he preached, the Sovereignty and the Redeeming Love of God, as completely as man could understand them. It evoked those ascriptions of praise which a Jew was accustomed to offer to God alone. It inspired doxologies. When it passed before the inward eye of the Apostle, he worshipped: "to Him," he said, "be the glory and the dominion for ever and ever." Whether the pre-incarnate Son was also the image of God, and whether the same title is applicable to Jesus of Nazareth, are separate questions. If they are raised, they must be answered in the affirmative, with the necessary qualifications; but they are quite irrelevant here. Much misunderstanding of the Pauline Gospel would have been prevented if men could have remembered that what was only of secondary importance to them, and even of doubtful certainty—namely, the exaltation of Christ—was itself the foundation of the Apostle's Christianity, the one indubitable fact from which his whole knowledge of Christ, and his whole conception of the Gospel, set forth. Christ on the throne was, if one may say so, a more immediate certainty to Paul, than Jesus on the banks of the lake, or even Jesus on the cross. It may not be natural or easy for *us* to start thus; but if we do not make the effort, we shall involuntarily dislocate and distort the whole system of his thoughts.

In the fourth verse the stress is logically, if not grammatically, on Christ. "The Gospel of the glory of *Christ*," I say. "For we preach not ourselves, but Christ Jesus as Lord, and ourselves as your servants for Jesus' sake." Perhaps ambition had been laid to Paul's charge; "the necessity of being first" is one of the last infirmities of noble minds. But the Gospel is too magnificent to have any room for thoughts of self. A proud man may make a nation, or even a Church, the instrument or the arena of his pride; he may find in it the field of his ambition, and make it subservient to his own exaltation. But the defence which Paul has offered of his truthfulness in chap. i. is as capable of application here. No one whom Christ has seized, subdued, and made wholly His own for ever, can practise the arts of self-advancement in Christ's service. The two are mutually exclusive. Paul preaches Christ Jesus as Lord—the absolute character in which he knows Him; as for himself, he is every man's servant for Jesus' sake. He obtained mercy, that he might be found faithful in service: the very name of Jesus kills pride in his heart, and makes him ready to minister even to the unthankful and evil.

This is the force of the "for" with which the sixth verse begins. It is as if he had written, "With our experience, no other course is possible to us; for it is God, who said, Light shall shine out of darkness, who shined in our hearts to give the light of the knowledge of the glory of God in the face of Jesus Christ." But the connexion here is of little importance in comparison with the grandeur of the contents. In this verse we have the first glimpse of the Pauline doctrine, explicitly stated in the next chapter—"that if any man be in Christ, he is a new creature." The Apostle finds the only adequate parallel to his own conversion in that grand creative act in which God brought light, by a word, out of the darkness of chaos. It is not forcing the figure unduly, nor losing its poetic virtue, to think of gloom and disorder as the condition of the soul on which the Sun of Righteousness has not risen. Neither is it putting any strain upon it to make it suggest that only the creative word of God can dispel the darkness, and give the beauty of life and order to what was waste and void. There is one point, indeed, in which the miracle of grace is more wonderful than that of creation. God only commanded the light to shine out of darkness when time began; but He shone Himself in the Apostle's heart: *Ipse lux nostra* (Bengel). He shone "to give the light of the knowledge of the glory of God in the face of Jesus Christ." In that light which God flashed into his heart, he saw the face of Jesus Christ, and knew that the glory which shone there was the glory of God. What these words mean has already been explained. In the face of Jesus Christ, the Lord of Glory, Paul saw God's Redeeming Love upon the throne of the universe; it had descended deeper than sin and death; it was exalted now above all heavens; it filled all things. That sight he carried with him everywhere; it was his salvation and his Gospel, the inspiration of his inmost life, and the motive of all his labours. One who owed all this to Christ was not likely to make Christ's service the theatre of his own ambitions; he could not do anything but take the servant's place, and proclaim Jesus Christ as Lord.

There is a difficulty in the last half of ver. 6: it is not clear what precisely meant by πρὸς φωτισμὸν τῆς γνώσεως τῆς δόξης τοῦ Θεοῦ κ.τ.λ. By some the passage is rendered: God shined in our hearts, "that *He* might bring into the light (for *us* to see it) the knowledge of His glory," etc. This is certainly legitimate, and strikes me as the most natural interpretation. It would answer then to what Paul says in Gal. i. 15 f., referring to the same event: "It pleased God to reveal His Son in me." But others think all this is covered by the words "God shined in our hearts," and they take πρὸς φωτισμὸν κ.τ.λ., as a description of the apostolic vocation: God shined in our hearts, "that *we* might bring into the light (for *others* to see) the knowledge of His glory," etc. The words would then answer to what follows in Gal. i. 16: God revealed His Son in me, "that I might preach Him among the heathen." This construction is possible, but I think forced. In Paul's experience his conversion and vocation were indissolubly connected; but πρὸς φωτισμὸν κ.τ.λ., can only mean one, and the conversion is the likelier.

XII
THE VICTORY OF FAITH

"But we have this treasure in earthen vessels, that the exceeding greatness of the power may be of God, and not from ourselves; *we are* pressed on every side, yet not straitened; perplexed, yet not unto despair; pursued, yet not forsaken; smitten down, yet not destroyed; always bearing about in the body the dying of Jesus, that the life also of Jesus may be manifested in our body. For we which live are alway delivered unto death for Jesus' sake, that the life also of Jesus may be manifested in our mortal flesh. So then death worketh in us, but life in you. But having the same spirit of faith, according to that which is written, I believed, and therefore did I speak; we also believe, and therefore also we speak; knowing that He which raised up the Lord Jesus shall raise up us also with Jesus, and shall present us with you. For all things *are* for your sakes, that the grace, being multiplied through the many, may cause the thanksgiving to abound unto the glory of God.

"Wherefore we faint not; but though our outward man is decaying, yet our inward man is renewed day by day. For our light affliction, which is for the moment, worketh for us more and more exceedingly an eternal weight of glory; while we look not at the things which are seen, but at the things which are not seen: for the things which are seen are temporal; but the things which are not seen are eternal."—2 Cor. iv. 7-18 (R.V.).

In the opening verses of this chapter Paul has magnified his office, and his equipment for it. He has risen to a great height, poetic and spiritual, in speaking of the Lord of glory, and of the light which shines from His face for the illumining and redemption of men. The disproportion between his own nature and powers, and the high calling to which he has been called, flashes across his mind. It is quite possible that this disproportion, viewed with a malignant eye, had been made matter of reproach by his adversaries. "Who," they may have said, "is this man, who soars to such heights, and makes such extraordinary claims? The part does not suit him; he is quite unequal to it; his bodily presence is weak, and his speech contemptible." It is possible, further, though I hardly think it probable, that the very sufferings Paul endured in his apostolic work were cast in his teeth by Jewish teachers at Corinth; they were read by these spiteful interpreters as signs of God's wrath, the judgment of the Almighty on a wanton subverter of His law. But surely it is not too much to suppose that Paul could sometimes think unchallenged. A soul as great and as sensitive as his might well be struck by the contrast which pervades this passage without requiring to have it suggested by the malice of his foes. The interpretation which he puts upon the contrast is not merely a happy artifice (so Calvin), and still less a *tour de force*; it is a profound truth, a favourite, if one may say so, in the New Testament, and of universal application.

"We have this treasure," he writes—the treasure of the knowledge of the glory of God in the face of Jesus Christ, including the apostolic vocation to diffuse that knowledge—"we have this treasure in earthen vessels, that the exceeding greatness of the power [which it exercises, and which is exhibited in sustaining us in our function] may be seen to be God's, and not from us." Earthen vessels are fragile, and what the word immediately suggests is no doubt bodily weakness, and especially mortality; but the nature of some of the trials referred to in vv. 8 and 9 (ἀπορούμενοι, ἀλλ' οὐκ ἐξαπορούμενοι) shows that it would be a mistake to confine the meaning to the body. The earthen vessel which holds the priceless treasure of the knowledge of God—the lamp of frail ware in which the light of Christ's glory shines for the illumination of the world—is human nature as it is; man's body in its weakness, and liability to death; his mind with its limitations and confusions; his moral nature with its distortions and misconceptions, and its insight not yet half restored. It was not merely in his physique that Paul felt the disparity between himself and his calling to preach the Gospel of the glory of Christ; it was in his whole being. But instead of finding in this disparity reason to doubt his vocation, he saw in it an illustration of a great law of God. It served to protect the truth that *salvation is of the Lord*. No one who saw the exceeding greatness of the power which the Gospel exercised—not only in sustaining its preachers under persecution, but in transforming human nature, and making bad men good—no one who saw this, and looked at a preacher like Paul, could dream that the explanation lay in *him*. Not in an ugly little Jew, without presence, without eloquence, without the means to bribe or to compel, could the source of such courage, the cause of such transformations, be found; it must be sought, not in him, but in God. "God hath chosen the foolish things of the world to confound the wise; and God hath chosen the weak things of the world to confound the things which are mighty; and base things of the world, and things which are despised, hath God chosen, yea, and things which are not, to bring to nought things which are." And the end of it all is that he which glorieth should glory *in the Lord*.

This verse is never without its application; and though the contempt of the world did not suggest it to St. Paul, it may naturally enough recall it to us. One would sometimes think, from the tone of current literature, that no person with gifts above contempt is any longer identified with the Gospel. Clever men, we are told, do not become preachers now—still less do they go to church. They find it impossible to have real or sincere intellectual intercourse with Christian ministers. Perhaps this is not so alarming as the clever people think. There always have been men in the world so clever that God could make no use of them; they could never do His work, because they were so lost in admiration of their own. But God's work never depended on them, and it does not depend on them now. It depends on those who, when they see Jesus Christ, become unconscious, once and for ever, of all that they have been used to call their wisdom and their strength—on those who are but earthen vessels in which another's jewel is kept, lamps of clay in which another's light shines. The kingdom of God has not changed its administration since the first century; its supreme law is still the glory of God, and not the glory of the clever men; and we may be quite sure it will not change. God will always have his work done by instruments who are willing to have it clear that the exceeding greatness of the power is His, and not theirs.

The eighth and ninth verses illustrate the contrast between Paul's weakness and God's power. In the series of participles which the Apostle uses, the earthen vessel is represented by the first in each pair, the divine power by the second. "We are pressed on every side, but not straitened"— *i.e.*, not brought into a narrow place from which there is no escape. "We are perplexed, but not unto despair," or, preserving the relation between the words of the original, "put to it, but not utterly put out." This distinctly suggests inward rather than merely bodily trials, or at least the inward aspect of these: constantly at a loss, the Apostle nevertheless constantly finds the solution of his problems. "Pursued, but not abandoned"—*i.e.*, not left in the enemy's hands. "Smitten down, but not destroyed": even when trouble has done its worst, when the persecuted man has been overtaken and struck to the ground, the blow is not fatal, and he rises again. All these partial contrasts of human weakness and Divine power are condensed and concentrated in the tenth verse in one great contrast, the two sides of which are presented in their divinely intended relation to each other: "always bearing about in the body the dying of Jesus, that the life also of Jesus may be manifested in our body." And this again, with its mystical poetic aspect, especially in the first clause, is reaffirmed and rendered into prose in ver. 11: "For we, alive as we are, are ever being delivered unto death for Jesus' sake, that the life also of Jesus may be manifested in our mortal flesh."

Paul does not say that he bears about in his body the death of Jesus (θάνατος), but his dying (νέκρωσις, *mortificatio*), the process which produces death. The sufferings which come upon him daily in his work for Jesus are gradually killing him; the pains, the perils, the spiritual pressure, the excitement of danger and the excitement of deliverance, are wearing out his strength, and soon he must die. In the very same way Jesus Himself had spent His strength and died, and in that life of weakness and suffering which was always bringing him nearer the grave, Paul felt himself in intimate sympathetic communion with his Master: it was "the dying *of Jesus*" that he carried about in his body. But that was not all. In spite of the dying, he was not dead. Perpetually in peril, he had a perpetual series of escapes; perpetually at his wits end, his way perpetually opened before him. What was the explanation of that? It was *the life of Jesus* manifesting itself in his body. The life of Jesus can only mean the life which Jesus lives now at God's right hand; and these repeated escapes of the Apostle, these restorations of his courage, are manifestations of that life; they are, so to speak, a series of resurrections. Paul's communion with Jesus is not only in His dying, but in His rising again; he has the evidence of the Resurrection, because he has its power, present with him, in these constant deliverances and renewals. Nay, the very purpose of his sufferings and perils is to provide occasion for the manifestation of this resurrection life. Unless he were exposed to death, God could not deliver him from it; unless he were pressed in the spirit, God could not give him relief; there could be no setting off of the exceeding greatness of His power in contrast with the exceeding frailty of the earthen vessel. The use of body and of mortal flesh in these verses has been appealed to in support of an interpretation which would limit the meaning to what is merely physical: "I am in daily danger of death, God daily delivers me from it, and thus the life of Jesus is manifested in me." This is of course included in the interpretation given above; but I cannot suppose it is all the Apostle meant. The truth is, there is no such thing in the passage, or indeed in human life, as a merely physical experience. To be delivered to death *for Jesus' sake* is an experience which is at once and indissolubly physical and spiritual; it could not be, unless the soul had its part, and that the chief part, in it. To be delivered *from* such death is also an experience as much spiritual as physical. And in both aspects, and not least in the first, is the life of Jesus manifested. Nor can I see that it is in the least degree unnatural for one who feels this to speak of that life as being manifested in his "body," or in his "mortal flesh"; it is a way which all men understand of describing the human nature, which is the scene of the manifestation, as a frail and powerless thing.

The moral of the passage is similar to that of chap. i. 3-11. Suffering, for the Christian, is not an accident; it is a divine appointment and a divine opportunity. To wear life out in the service of Jesus is to open it to the entrance of Jesus' life; it is to receive, in all its alleviations, in all its renewals, in all its deliverances, a witness to His resurrection. Perhaps it is only by accepting this service, with the daily dying it demands, that that witness can be given to us; and "the life of Jesus" on His throne may become inapprehensible and unreal in proportion as we decline to bear about in our bodies His dying. All who have commented on this passage have noticed the iteration of the name of Jesus. *Singulariter sensit Paulus dulcedinem ejus.* Schmiedel explains the repetition as partly accidental, and partly indicative of the fact that Christ's death is here regarded as a purely human occurrence, and not as a redemptive deed of the Messiah. This points in the right direction, though it may fairly be doubted whether Paul would have drawn this distinction, or could even have been made to understand it. The analytic tendency of the modern mind often disintegrates what depends for its virtue on being kept whole and entire, and this seems to me a case in point. The use of the name Jesus rather indicates that, in recalling the actual events of his own career, Paul saw them run continually parallel to events in the career of Another; they were one in kind with that painful series of incidents which ended in the death of the historical Saviour. People have often sought in the Epistles of Paul for traces of a knowledge of Christ like that which is conserved in the first three Gospels; in this expression, τὴν νέκρωσιν τοῦ Ἰησοῦ, and in the repetition of the historical proper name, there is an indirect but quite convincing proof that the general character of Christ's life was known to the Apostle. And though he does not dwell on Christ's sympathy with the fulness and power of the writer to the Hebrews, it is evident from this passage that he was in sympathetic fellowship with One who had suffered as he suffered, and that even to name His human name was consolation.

In ver. 12 an abrupt conclusion is drawn from all that precedes: "So then death worketh in us, but life in you." *Ironice dictum,* is Calvin's comment, and the words are at least intelligible if so taken. The stinging passage beginning at chap. iv. 8 of the First Epistle is ironical in precisely this sense—"We are fools for Christ's sake, but ye are wise in Christ; we are weak, but ye are strong; ye have glory, but we have dishonour": this is as it were a variation on the theme "death worketh in us, but life in you." Still, the irony does not seem in place here: Paul writes in all seriousness that the sufferings which he endures as a preacher of the Gospel, and which eventually bring death to him—which are the approaches of death, or death itself at work—are the means by which life, in the most unqualified sense, comes to be at work in the Corinthians. If the death and life which are in view wherever the Gospel appears are to be distributed among them, the death is his, and the life theirs; the dying of Jesus is borne about by the Evangelist, while those who accept the message he brings at this cost are made partakers in Jesus' life.

Not indeed that the contrast can be thus absolute: the thirteenth verse corrects this hasty inference. If death alone were at work in St. Paul, it would frustrate his vocation; he would not be able to preach at all. But he is able to preach. In spite of all the discouragement which his sufferings might beget, his faith remains vigorous; he is conscious of possessing that same confidence toward God which animated the ancient Psalmist to sing, "I believed, therefore I spoke." "We also," he says, "believe, and therefore also we speak." What he believes, and what prompts his utterance, we read in the thirteenth verse: "We speak; knowing that He who raised Jesus shall raise us also like[40] Jesus, and shall present us with you. With you, I say: for the whole thing is for your sakes, that the grace, having become abundant, may by means of many[41] cause the thanksgiving to abound to the glory of God."

What an interesting illustration this is of the communion of the saints! Paul recognises a spiritual kinsman in the writer of the Psalm;[42] faith in God, the power which faith confers, the obligations which faith imposes, are the same in all ages. He recognises spiritual kinsmen in the Corinthians also. All his sufferings have their interest in view, and it is part of his joy, as he looks on to the future, that when God raises him from the dead, as He raised His own Son, He will present him *along with them*. Their unity will not be dissolved by death. The word here rendered "present" has often a technical sense in Paul's Epistles; it is almost appropriated to the presenting of men before the judgment-seat of Christ. Good scholars insist on that meaning here; but even with the proviso that acceptance in the judgment is taken for granted, I cannot feel that it is quite congruous. There is such a thing as presentation to a sovereign as well as to a judge—the presenting of the bride to the bridegroom on the wedding day as well as of the criminal to the justice—and it is the great and glad occasion which answers to the feeling in the Apostle's mind. The communion of the saints, in virtue of which his sufferings bring blessing to the Corinthians, has its issue in the joyful union of all before the throne. As Paul thinks of that, he sees an end in the Gospel lying beyond the blessing it brings to men. That end is God's glory. The more he toils and suffers, the more God's grace is made known and received; and the more it is received, the more does it cause thanksgiving to abound to the glory of God.

Two practical reflections present themselves here, nearly related to each other. The first is that faith naturally speaks; the second, that grace merits thanksgiving. Put the two into one, and we may say that grace received by faith merits articulate thanksgiving. Much modern faith is inarticulate, and it is far too soothing to be true if we say, Better so. Of course the utterance of faith is not prescribed to it; to be of any value it must be spontaneous. Not all the believing are to be teachers and preachers, but all are to be confessors. Every one who has faith has a witness to bear to God. Every one who has accepted God's grace by faith has a thankful acknowledgment of it to make, and at some time or other to make in words. It is not the faculty of speech that is wanting where this is not done; it is courage and gratitude; it is the same Spirit of faith which prompted the Psalmist and St. Paul. It is true that hypocrites sometimes speak, and that testimonies and thanksgivings are apt to be discredited on their account; but bad money would never be put in circulation unless good money was indisputably valuable. It is not the dumb, but the confessing Christian, not the taciturn, but the outspokenly thankful, who glorifies God, and helps on the Gospel. Calvin is properly severe on our "pseudo-nicodemi," who make a merit of their silence, and boast that they have never by a syllable betrayed their faith. Faith is betrayed in another and more serious sense when it is kept secret.

But to return to the Apostle, who himself, at ver. 16, returns to the beginning of the chapter, and resumes the οὐκ ἐγκακοῦμεν of ver. 1: "Wherefore we faint not." "Wherefore" means "With all that has been said in view"; not only the glorious future in which Paul and his disciples are to be raised and presented together to Christ, but his daily experience of the life of Jesus manifested in his mortal flesh. This kept him brave and strong. "We faint not; but though our outward man is decaying, yet our inward man is renewed day by day." The outward man covers the same area as "our body," or "our mortal flesh." It is human nature as it is constituted in this world—a weak, fragile, perishable thing. Paul could not mistake, and did not hide from himself, the effect which his apostolic work had upon him. He saw it was killing him. He was old long before the time. He was a sorely broken man at an age when many are in the fulness of their strength.

The earthen vessel was visibly crumbling. Still, that was not the *whole* of his experience. "The inward man is renewed day by day." The meaning of these words must be fixed mainly by the opposition in which they stand to οὐκ ἐγκακοῦμεν ("we faint not"). The same word (ἀνακαινοῦσθαι) is used of the renewal of the soul in the Creator's image (Col. iii. 10)—*i.e.*, of the work of sanctification; but the opposition in question proves that this is not contemplated here. We must rather think of the daily supply of spiritual power for apostolic service—of the new strength and joy which were given to St. Paul every morning, in spite of the toils and sufferings which every day exhausted him. Of course we can say of all people, bad as well as good, "The outward man is decaying." Time tires the stoutest runner, crumbles the compactest wall. But we cannot say of all, "The inward man is renewed day by day." That is not the compensation of every one; it is the compensation of those whose outward man has decayed in Jesus' service, who have been worn out in labours for His sake. It is they, and they only, who have a life within which is independent of outward conditions, which sufferings and deaths cannot crush, and which never grows old. The decay of the outward man in the godless is a melancholy spectacle, for it is the decay of everything; in the Christian it does not touch that life which is hid with Christ in God, and which is in the soul itself a well of water springing up to life eternal.

But who shall speak of the two great verses in which the Apostle, leaving controversy out of sight, solemnly weighs against each other time and eternity, the seen and the unseen, and claims his inheritance beyond? "Our light affliction, which is for the moment, worketh for us more and more exceedingly an eternal weight of glory; while we look not at the things which are seen, but at the things which are not seen: for the things which are seen are temporal; but the things which are not seen are eternal." One can imagine that he was dictating quick and eagerly as he began the sentence; he "crowds and hurries and precipitates" the grand contrasts of which his mind is full. Affliction in any case is outweighed by glory, but the affliction in question is a light matter, the glory a great weight: the light affliction is but momentary—it ends with death at the latest, it may end in the coming of Jesus to anticipate death; the weight of glory is eternal; and as if this were not enough, the light affliction which is but for a moment works out for us the weight of glory which endures for ever, "in excess and to excess," in a way above conception, to a degree above conception: it works out for us the things which eye hath not seen, nor ear heard, nor man's heart conceived, "all that God has prepared for them that love Him" (1 Cor. ii. 9). If Paul spoke fast and with beating heart as he crowded all this into two brief lines, we can well believe that the pressure was relaxed, and that the pen moved more steadily and slowly over the contemplative words that follow: "while we look not to the things which are seen, but to the things which are not seen: for the things which are seen are temporal, but the things which are not seen are eternal." This sentence is sometimes translated conditionally: "provided we look," etc. This is legitimate, but unnecessary. The Apostle is speaking, in the first instance, of himself, and the looking is taken for granted. The look is not merely equivalent to vision; it means that the unseen is the goal of him who looks. The eye is to be directed to it, not as an indifferent object, but as a mark to aim at, an end to attain. This observation goes some way to limit the application of the whole passage. The contrast of things seen and things unseen is sometimes taken in a latitude which deprives it of much of its force: psychology and metaphysics are dragged in to define and to confuse the Apostle's thought. But everything here is practical. The things seen are to all intents and purposes that tempest-tossed life of which St. Paul has been speaking, that daily dying, that pressure, perplexity, persecution, and downcasting, which are for the present his lot. To these he does not look: in comparison with that to which he does look, these are a light and momentary affliction which is not worth a thought. Similarly, the things unseen are not everything, indefinitely, which is invisible; to all intents and purposes they are the glory of Christ. It is on this the Apostle's eye is fixed, this which is his goal. The stormy life, even when most is made of its storms, passes; but Christ's glory can never pass. It is infinite, inconceivable, eternal. There is an inheritance in it for all who keep their eyes upon it, and, sustained by a hope so high, bear the daily death of a life like Paul's as a light and momentary affliction. The connexion between the two is so close that the one is said to work for us the other. By divine appointment they are united; fellowship with Jesus is fellowship all through—in the daily dying, which soon has done its worst, and then in the endless life. We may say, if we please, that the glory is the reward of the suffering; it would be truer to say that it was its compensation, truer still that it was its fruit. There is a vital connexion between them, but no one can imagine he is reading Paul's thought who should find here the idea that the trivial service of man can make God his debtor for so vast a sum. The excellency of the power which raises the earthen vessel to this height of faith, hope, and inspiration is itself God's, and God's alone.

Distrust of the supernatural, insistence on the present and the practical, and the pride of a self-styled common sense, have done much to rob modern Christianity of this vast horizon, to blind it to this heavenly vision. But wherever the life of Jesus is being manifested in mortal flesh—wherever in

His service and for His sake men and women die daily, wearing out nature, but with spirit ceaselessly renewed—there the unseen becomes real again. Such people know that what they do is not for one dead, but for One who lives; they know that the daily inspirations they receive, the hopes, the deliverances, are wrought in them, not by themselves, but by One who has all power in heaven and on earth. The things that are unseen and eternal stand out as what they are in relation to lives like these; to other lives, they have no relation at all. A worldly and selfish career does not work out an exceeding and eternal weight of glory, and therefore to the worldly and selfish man heaven is for ever an unpractical, incredible thing. But it not only comes out in its brightness, it comes out as a mighty inspiration and support, to every one who bears about in his body the dying of Jesus; as he fastens his eye upon it, he takes heart anew, and in spite of daily dying "faints not."

XIII
THE CHRISTIAN HOPE

"For we know that if the earthly house of our tabernacle be dissolved, we have a building from God, a house not made with hands, eternal, in the heavens. For verily in this we groan, longing to be clothed upon with our habitation which is from heaven: if so be that being clothed we shall not be found naked. For indeed we that are in this tabernacle do groan, being burdened; not for that we would be unclothed, but that we would be clothed upon, that what is mortal may be swallowed up of life. Now He that wrought us for this very thing is God, who gave unto us the earnest of the Spirit. Being therefore always of good courage, and knowing that, whilst we are at home in the body, we are absent from the Lord (for we walk by faith, not by sight); we are of good courage, I say, and are willing rather to be absent from the body, and to be at home with the Lord. Wherefore also we make it our aim, whether at home or absent, to be well-pleasing unto Him. For we must all be made manifest before the judgment-seat of Christ; that each one may receive the things *done* in the body, according to what he hath done, whether *it be* good or bad."—2 Cor. v. 1-10 (R.V.).

That outlook on the future, which at the close of chap. iv. is presented in the most general terms, is here carried out by the Apostle into more definite detail. The passage is one of the most difficult in his writings, and has received the most various interpretations; yet the first impression it leaves on a simple reader is probably as near the truth as the subtlest ingenuity of exegesis. It is indeed to such first impressions that one often returns when the mind has ceased to sway this way and that under the impact of conflicting arguments.

The Apostle has been speaking about his life as a daily dying, and in the first verse of this chapter he looks at the possibility that this dying may be consummated in death. It is only a possibility, for to the end of his life it was always conceivable that Christ might come, and forestall the last enemy.

Still, it *is* a possibility; the earthly house of our tabernacle may be dissolved; the tent in which we live may be taken down. With what hope does the Apostle confront such a contingency? "If this befall us," he says, "we have a building from God, a house not made with hands, eternal, in the heavens." Every word here points the contrast between this new house and the old one, and points it in favour of the new. The old was a tent; the new is a building: the old, though not literally made with hands, had many of the qualities and defects of manufactured articles; the new is God's work and God's gift: the old was perishable; the new is eternal. When Paul says we have this house *in the heavens*, it is plain that it is not heaven itself; it is a new body which replaces and surpasses the old. It is in the heavens in the sense that it is God's gift; it is something which He has for us where He is, and which we shall wear there. "We have it" means "it is ours"; any more precise definition must be justified on grounds extraneous to the text.

The second verse brings us to one of the ambiguities of the passage. "For verily," our R.V. reads, "in this we groan, longing to be clothed upon with our habitation which is from heaven." The meaning which the English reader finds in the words "in this we groan" is in all probability "in our present body we groan." This is also the meaning defended by Meyer, and by many scholars. But it cannot be denied that ἐν τούτῳ does not naturally refer to ἡ ἐπίγειος ἡμῶν οἰκία τοῦ σκήνους. If it means "in this body," it must be attached specially to σκήνους, and σκήνους is only a subordinate word in the clause. Elsewhere in the New Testament ἐν τούτῳ means "on this account," or "for this reason" (see 1 Cor. iv. 4; John xvi. 30: Ἐν τούτῳ πιστεύομεν ὅτι ἀπὸ Θεοῦ ἐξῆλθες), and I prefer to take it in this sense here: "For this cause—*i.e.*, because we are the heirs of such a hope—we groan, longing to be clothed upon with our habitation which is from heaven." If Paul had no hope, he would not sigh for the future; but the very longing which pressed the sighs from his bosom became itself a witness to the glory which awaited him. The same argument, it has often been pointed out, is found in Rom. viii. 19 ff. The earnest expectation of the creation, waiting for the manifestation of the sons of God, is evidence that this manifestation will in due time take place. The spiritual instincts are prophetic. They have not been implanted in the soul by God only to be disappointed. It is of the longing hope of immortality—that very hope which is in question here— that Jesus says: "If it were not so, I would have told you."

The third verse states the great gain which lies in the fulfilment of this hope: "Since, of course, being clothed [with this new body], we shall not be found naked [*i.e.*, without any body]." I cannot think, especially looking on to ver. 4, that these two verses (2 and 3) mean anything else than that Paul longs for Christ to come before death. If Christ comes first, the Apostle will receive the new body by the transformation, instead of the putting off, of the old; he will, so to speak, put it on *above* the old ἐπενδύσασθαι; he will be spared the shuddering fear of dying; he will not know what it is to have the old tent taken down, and to be left houseless and naked. We do not need to investigate the opinions of the Hebrews or the Greeks about the condition of souls in Hades in order to understand these words; the conception, figurative as it is, carries its own meaning and impression to every one. It is reiterated, rather than proved, in the fourth verse:[43] "For we who are in the tabernacle groan also, being burdened, in that our will is not to be unclothed, but to be clothed upon, that what is mortal may be swallowed up of life." It is natural to take βαρούμενοι ("being burdened") as referring to the weight of care and suffering by which men are oppressed while in the body; but here also, as in the similar case of ver. 2, the proper reference of the word is forward. What oppresses Paul, and makes him sigh, is the intensity of his desire to escape "being unclothed," his immense longing to see Jesus come, and, instead of passing through the terrific experience of death, to have the corruptible put on incorruption, and the mortal put on immortality, without that trial.

This seems plain enough, but we must remember that the confidence which Paul has been expressing in the first verse is meant to meet the very case in which this desire is *not* gratified, the case in which death *has* to be encountered, and the tabernacle taken down. "*If* this should befall us," he says, "we have another body awaiting us, far better than that which we leave, and hence we are confident." The confidence which this hope inspires would naturally, we think, be most perfect, if in the very act of dissolution the new body were assumed; if death were the initial stage in the transformation scene in which an that is mortal is swallowed up by life; if it were, not the ushering of the Christian into a condition of "nakedness," which, temporary though it be, is a mere blank to the mind and imagination, but his admission to celestial life; if "to be absent from the body" were immediately, and in the fullest sense of the words, the same thing as "to be at home with the Lord." This is, in point of fact, the sense in which the passage is understood by a good many scholars, and those who read it so find in it a decisive turning-point in the Apostle's teaching on the last things. In the First Epistle to the Thessalonians, they say, and indeed in the First to the Corinthians also, Paul's eschatology was still essentially Jewish. The Christian dead are οἱ κοιμώμενοι, or οἱ κοιμηθέντες ("those that sleep"); nothing definite is said of their condition; only it is implied that they do not get the incorruptible body till Jesus comes again and raises them from the dead. In other words, those who die before the Parousia have the soul-chilling prospect of an unknown term of "nakedness." Here this terror is dispelled by the new revelation made to the Apostle, or the new insight to which he has attained: there is no longer any such interval between death and glory; the heavenly body is assumed at once; the state called κοιμᾶσθαι ("being asleep") vanishes from the future. Sabatier and Schmiedel, who adopt this view, draw extreme consequences from it. It marks an advance, according to Schmiedel, of the highest importance. The religious postulate of an uninterrupted communion of life with Christ, violated by the conception of a κοιμᾶσθαι, or falling asleep, is satisfied; Christ's descent from heaven, and a simultaneous resurrection and judgment, become superfluous; judgment is transferred to the moment of death, or rather to the process of development during life on earth; and, finally, the place of eternal blessedness passes from earth (the Jewish and early Christian opinion, probably shared by Paul, as he gives no indication of the contrary) to heaven. All this, it is further pointed out, is an approximation, more or less close, to the Greek doctrine of the immortality of the soul, and may even have been excogitated in part under its influence; and it is at the same time a half-way house between the Pharisaic eschatology of First Thessalonians and the perfected Christian doctrine of a passage like John v. 24: "Verily, verily, I say unto you, He that heareth My word, and believeth Him that sent Me, hath eternal life, and cometh not into judgment, but hath passed out of death into life."

There is no objection to be made in principle to the idea that the Apostle's outlook on the future was subject to modification—that he was capable of attaining, or even did attain, a deeper insight, with experience, into the connexion between that which is and that which is to come. But it is surely somewhat against the above estimate of the alleged change here that Paul himself seems to have been quite unconscious of it. He was not a man whose mind wrought at unawares, and who passed unwittingly from one standpoint to another. He was nothing if not reflective. According to Sabatier and Schmiedel, he had made a revolutionary change in his opinions—a change so vast that on account of it Sabatier reckons this Epistle, and especially this passage, the most important in all his writings for the comprehension of his theological development; and yet, side by side with the new revolutionary ideas, uttered literally in the same breath with them, we find the old standing undisturbed. The simultaneous resurrection and judgment, according to Schmiedel, should be impossible now; but in chap. iv. 14 the resurrection appears precisely as in Thessalonians and in chap. v. 10 the judgment, precisely as in all his Epistles from the first to the last. As for the inconsistency between going to be at home with the Lord and the Lord's coming, it also recurs in later years: Paul writes to the Philippians that he has a desire to depart and to be with Christ; and in the same letter, that the Lord is at hand, and that we wait for the Saviour from heaven. Probably the misleading idea in the study of the whole subject has been the assumption that the κοιμώμενοι—the dead *in Christ*—were in some dismal, dreary condition which could fairly be described as "nakedness." There is not a word in the New Testament which favours this idea. Where we see men die in faith, we see something quite different. "*To-day* shalt thou be with Me in Paradise." "Lord Jesus, receive my spirit." "I saw the souls of them which had been slain for the Word of God ... and there was given them, to each one, a white robe." When Paul speaks of those who have fallen asleep, in First Thessalonians, it is with the express intention of showing that those who survive to the Parousia have no advantage over them. "Jesus Christ died for us," he writes (1 Thess. v. 10), "that, whether we wake or sleep, we may live together with Him." And he uses one most expressive word in a similar connexion (1 Thess. iv. 14): "Them also that sleep in Jesus will God *bring* [ἄξει] with Him." *Suave verbum*, says Bengel: *dicitur de viventibus*. May we not say with equal cogency, not only "de viventibus," but "de viventibus *cum Iesu*"? Those who are asleep are with Him; they are in blessedness with Him; what their mode of existence is it may be impossible for us to conceive, but it is certainly not a thing to shrink from with horror. The taking down of the old tent in which we live here *is* a thing from which one cannot but shrink, and that is why Paul would rather have Christ come, and be saved the pain and fear of dying. With death in view he mentions the new body as the ground of his confidence, because it is the final realisation of the Christian hope, the crown of redemption (Rom. viii. 23). But he does not mean to say that, unless the new body were granted in the very instant of dying, death would usher him into an appalling void, and separate him from Christ. This assumption, on which the interpretation of Sabatier and Schmiedel rests, is entirely groundless, and therefore that interpretation, in spite of a superficial plausibility, is to be decidedly rejected. It is to be rejected all the more when we are invited to see the occasion which produced Paul's supposed change of opinion in the danger which he had lately incurred in Asia (chap. i. 8-10). Paul, we are to imagine, who had always been confident that he would live to see the Parousia, had come to very close quarters with death, and this experience constrained him to seek in his religion a hope and consolation more adequate to the terribleness of death than any he had yet conceived. Hence the mighty advance explained above. But is it not absurd to say that a man, whose life was constantly in peril, had never thought of death till this time? Can any one seriously believe that, as Sabatier puts it, "the image of death, with which the Apostle had not hitherto concerned himself, [here] enters for the first time within the scope of his doctrine"? Can any one who knows the kind of man Paul was deliberately suggest that fear and self-pity conferred on him an enlargement of spiritual vision which no sympathy for bereaved disciples, and no sense of fellowship with those who had fallen asleep in Jesus, availed to bestow? Believe this who will, it seems utterly incredible to me. The passage says nothing inconsistent with Thessalonians, or First Corinthians, or Philippians, or Second Timothy, about the last things: it expresses in a special situation the constant Christian faith and hope—"the redemption of the body"; *that* is the possession of the believer ἔχομεν; it is ours; and the Apostle is not concerned to fix the moment of time at which hope becomes sight. "Come what will," he says, "come death itself, *this* is ours; and because it is ours, though we dread the possible necessity of having to strip off the old body, and would fain escape it, we do not allow it to dismay us."

The Apostle cannot look to the end of the Christian hope without referring to its condition and guarantee. "He that wrought us for this very thing is God, who gave us the earnest of the Spirit." The future is never considered in the New Testament in a speculative fashion; nothing could be less like an apostle than to discuss the immortality of the soul. The question of life beyond death is for Paul not a metaphysical but a Christian question; the pledge of anything worth the name of life is not the inherent constitution of human nature, but the possession of the Divine Spirit. Without the Spirit, Paul could have had no such certainty, no such triumphant hope, as he had; without the Spirit there can be no such certainty yet. Hence it is idle to criticise the Christian hope on purely speculative grounds, and as idle to try on such grounds to establish it. That hope is of a piece with the experience which comes when the Spirit of Him who raised up Christ from the dead dwells in us, and apart from this experience it cannot even be understood. But to say that there is no eternal life except in Christ is not to accept what is called "conditional immortality"; it is only to accept conditional glory.

The fifth verse marks a pause: in the three which follow Paul describes the mood in which, possessed of the Christian hope, he confronts all the conditions of the present and the alternatives of the future. "We are of good courage at all times," he says. "We know that while we are at home in the body we are away from home as far as the Lord is concerned—at a distance from Him." This does not mean that fellowship is broken, or that the soul is separated from the love of Christ; it only means that earth is not heaven, and that Paul is painfully conscious of the fact. This is what is proved by ver. 7: We are absent from the Lord, our true home, "for in this world we are walking through the realm of faith, not through that of actual appearance."[44] There *is* a world, a mode of existence, to which Paul looks forward, which is one of actual appearance; he will be in Christ's presence there, and see Him face to face (1 Cor. xiii. 12). But the world through which his course lies meanwhile is *not* that world of immediate presence and manifestation; on the contrary, it is a world of faith, which realises that future world of manifestation only by a strong spiritual conviction; it is through a faith-land that Paul's journey leads him. All along the way his faith keeps him in good heart; nay, when he thinks of all that it ensures, of all that is guaranteed by the Spirit, he is willing rather to be absent from the body, and to be at home with the Lord.

> "For, ah! the Master is so fair,
> His smile so sweet on banished men,
> That they who meet it unaware
> Can never turn to earth again;
> And they who see Him risen afar,
> At God's right hand to welcome them,
> Forgetful stand of home and land,
> Desiring fair Jerusalem."

If he had to make his choice, it would incline this way, rather than the other; but it is not his to make a choice, and so he does not express himself unconditionally. The whole tone of the passage anticipates that of Phil. i. 21 ff.: "For to me to live is Christ, and to die is gain. But if to live in the flesh,—*if* this is the fruit of my work, then what I shall choose I wot not. But I am in a strait betwixt the two, having the desire to depart and to be with Christ; for it is very far better: yet to abide in the flesh is more needful for your sake." Nothing could be less like the Apostle than a monkish, unmanly wish to die. He exulted in his calling. It was a joy to him above all joys to speak to men of the love of God in Jesus Christ. But nothing, on the other hand, could be less like him than to lose sight of the future in the present, and to forget amid the service of men the glory which is to be revealed. He stood between two worlds; he felt the whole attraction of both; in the earnest of the Spirit he knew that he had an inheritance there as well as here. It is this consciousness of the dimensions of life that makes him so immensely interesting; he never wrote a dull word; his soul was stirred incessantly by impulses from earth and from heaven, swept by breezes from the dark and troubled sea of man's life, touched by inspirations from the radiant heights where Christ dwelt. We do not need to be afraid of the reproach of "other worldliness" if we seek to live in this same spirit; the reproach is as false as it is threadbare. It would be an incalculable gain if we could recover the primitive hope in something like its primitive strength. It would not make us false to our duties in the world, but it would give us the victory over the world.

In bringing this subject to a close, the Apostle strikes a graver note. A certain moral, as well as a certain emotional temper, is evoked by the Christian hope. It fills men with courage, and with spiritual yearnings;

it braces them also to moral earnestness and vigour. "Wherefore also we make it our aim"—literally, we are ambitious, the only lawful ambition—"whether at home or absent, to be well-pleasing unto Him." Modes of being are not of so much consequence. It may agree with a man's feelings better to live till Christ comes, or to die before He comes, and go at once to be with Him; but the main thing is, in whatever mode of being, to be accepted in His sight. "For we must all be manifested before the judgment-seat of Christ, that each one may receive the things done in the body, according to what he hath done, whether it be good or bad." The Christian hope is not clouded by the judgment-seat of Christ; it is sustained at the holy height which befits it. We are forbidden to count upon it lightly. "Every man," we are reminded, "that hath this hope set on Him purifieth himself even as He is pure." It is not necessary for us to seek a formal reconciliation of this verse with Paul's teaching that the faithful are accepted in Christ Jesus; we can feel that both must be true. And if the doctrine of justification freely, by God's grace, is that which has to be preached to sinful men, the doctrine of exact retribution, taught in this passage, has its main interest and importance for Christians. It is Christians only who are in view here, and the law of requital is so exact that every one is said to get back, to carry on for himself, the very things done in the body. In this world, we have not seen the last of anything. We shall all be manifested before the judgment-seat of Christ; all that we have hidden shall be revealed. The books are shut now, but they will be opened then. The things we have done in the body will come back to us, whether good or bad. Every pious thought, and every thought of sin; every secret prayer, and every secret curse; every unknown deed of charity, and every hidden deed of selfishness: we will see them all again, and though we have not remembered them for years, and perhaps have forgotten them altogether, we shall have to acknowledge that they are our own, and take them to ourselves. Is not that a solemn thing to stand at the end of life? Is it not a true thing? Even those who can say with the Apostle, "Being justified by faith, we have peace with God through our Lord Jesus Christ, and rejoice in hope of His glory," know how true it is. Nay, they most of all know, for they understand better than others the holiness of God, and they are especially addressed here. The moral consciousness is not maintained in its vigour and integrity if this doctrine of retribution disappears; and if we are called by a passage like this to encourage ourselves in the Lord, and in the hope which He has revealed, we are warned also that evil cannot dwell with God, and that He will by no means clear the guilty.

XIV
THE MEASURE OF CHRIST'S LOVE

"Knowing therefore the fear of the Lord, we persuade men, but we are made manifest unto God; and I hope that we are made manliest also in your consciences. We are not again commending ourselves unto you, but *speak* as giving you occasion of glorying on our behalf, that ye may have wherewith to answer them that glory in appearance and not in heart. For whether we are beside ourselves, it is unto God; or whether we are of sober mind, it is unto you. For the love of Christ constraineth us; because we thus judge, that One died for all, therefore all died; and He died for all, that they which live should no longer live unto themselves, but unto Him who for their sakes died and rose again."—2 Cor. v. 11-15 (R.V.).

The Christian hope of immortality is elevated and solemnised by the thought of the judgment-seat of Christ. This is no strange thought to St. Paul; many a time he has set himself in imagination in that great presence, and let the awe of it descend upon his heart. This is what he means when he writes, "Knowing the fear of the Lord." Like the pastors addressed in the Epistle to the Hebrews, he exercises his office as one who must render an account. In this spirit, he says, he persuades men. A motive so high, and so stern in its purifying power, no minister of Christ can afford to dispense with. We need something to suppress self-seeking, to keep conscience vigorous, to preserve the message of reconciliation itself from degenerating into good-natured indifference, to prohibit immoral compromises and superficial healing of the soul's hurts. Let us familiarise our minds, by meditation, with the fear due to Christ the judge, and a new element of power will enter into our service, making it at once more urgent and more wholesome than it could otherwise be.

The meaning of the words "we persuade men" is not at once clear. Interpreters generally find in them a combination of two ideas—we try to win men for the Gospel, and we try to convince them of our own purity of motive in our evangelistic work. The word is suitable enough to express either idea; and though it is straining it to make it carry both, the first is suggested by the general tenor of the passage, and the second seems to be demanded by what follows. "We try to convince men of our disinterestedness, but we do not need to try to convince God; we have been manifested to Him already;[45] and we trust also that we have been manifested in your consciences." Paul was well aware of the hostility with which he was regarded by some of the Corinthians, but he is confident that, when his appeal is tried in the proper court, decision must be given in his favour, and he hopes that this has really been done at Corinth. Often we do not give people in his position the benefit of a fair trial. It is not in our consciences they are arraigned—*i.e.*, in God's sight, and according to God's law—but at the bar of our prejudices, our likes and dislikes, sometimes even our whims and caprices. It is not their *character* which is taken into account, but something quite irrelevant to character. Paul did not care for such estimates as these. It was nothing to him whether his appearance made a favourable impression on those who heard him—whether they liked his voice, his gestures, his manners, or even his message. What he did care for was to be able to appeal to their consciences, as he could appeal to God, to whom all things were naked and opened, that in the discharge of his functions as an evangelist he had been absolutely simple and sincere. In speaking thus, he has no intention of again recommending himself. Rather, as he says with a touch of irony, it is for their convenience he writes; he is giving them occasion to boast on his behalf, that when they encounter people who boast in face and not in heart they may not be speechless, but may have something to say for themselves—and for him. It is easy to read between the lines here. The Corinthians had persons among them—Jewish and Judaising teachers evidently—who boasted "in face"; in other words, who prided themselves on outward and visible distinctions, though as Paul asserts, they had nothing within to be proud of. There are suggestions of these distinctions elsewhere, and we can imagine the claims men made, the airs they gave themselves, or at least the recognition they consented to accept, on the ground of them. Their eloquence, their knowledge of the Scriptures, their Jewish descent, their acquaintance with the Twelve, above all acquaintance with Jesus Himself—these were their credentials, and of these their followers made much. Perhaps even on their own ground Paul could have met and routed most of them, but meanwhile he leaves them in undisturbed possession of their advantages, such as they are. He only sums up these advantages in the disparaging word "face," or "appearance"; they are all on the outside; they amount to "a fair show in the flesh," but no more. He would not like if *his* disciples could make no better boast of their master, and all the high things he has written, from chap. ii. 14 on to chap. v. 10, especially his vindication of the absolute purity of his motives, furnish them, if they choose to take it so, with grounds of counter-boasting, far deeper and more spiritual than those of his adversaries. For *he* boasts, not "in appearance, but in heart." The ironical tone in this is unmistakable, yet it is not merely ironical. From the beginning of Christianity to this day, Churches have gathered round men, and made their boast in them. Too often it has been a boast "in face," and not "in heart"—in gifts, accomplishments, and distinctions, which may have given an outward splendour to the individual, but which were entirely irrelevant to the possession of the Christian spirit. Often even the imperfections of the natural man have been gloried in, simply because they were his; and the Lutheran and Calvinistic Churches, for example, owe some of their most distinctive features to an exaggerated appreciation of those very characteristics of Luther and Calvin which had no Christian value. The same thing is seen every day, on a smaller scale, in congregations. People are proud of their minister, not for what he is in heart, but because he is more learned, more eloquent, more naturally capable, than other preachers in the same town. It is a pity when ministers themselves, like the Judaists in Corinth, are content to have it so. The true evangelist or pastor will choose rather, with St. Paul, to be taken for what he is as a Christian, and for nothing else; and if he *must* be spoken about, he will be spoken of in this character, and in no other. Nay, if it really comes to glorying "in face," he will glory in his weaknesses and incapacities; he will magnify the very earthenness of the earthen vessel, the very coarseness of the clay, as a foil to the power and life of Christ which dwell in it.

The connexion of ver. 13 with what precedes is very obscure. Perhaps as fair a paraphrase as any would run thus: "And well may you boast of our complete sincerity; for whether we are beside ourselves, it is to God; or whether we are of sober mind, it is unto you; that is, in no case is self-interest the motive or rule of our conduct." Connexion apart, there is a further difficulty about εἴτε ἐξέστημεν. The Revised Version renders it "whether we *are* beside ourselves," but in the margin gives "*were*" for "are." It makes a very great difference which tense we accept. If the proper meaning is given by "are," the application must be to some constant characteristic of the Apostle s ministry. His enthusiasm, his absolute superiority to common selfish considerations such as are ordinarily supreme in human life, his resolute assertion of truths lying beyond the reach of sense, the unearthly flame which burned unceasingly in his bosom, and never more brightly than when he wrote the fourth and fifth chapters of the Second Epistle to the Corinthians—all these constitute the temper which is described as being "beside oneself," a kind of sacred madness. It was in this sense that the accusation of being beside himself was brought on a memorable occasion against Jesus (Mark iii. 21, ἐξέστη). The disciple and the Master alike seemed to those who did not understand them to be in an overstrained, too highly wrought condition of spirit; in the ardour of their devotion they allowed themselves to be carried beyond all natural limits, and it was not improper to speak of applying some kindly restraint. At first sight this interpretation seems very appropriate, and I do not think that the tense of ἐξέστημεν is decisive against it.[46] Those who think it is point to the change to the present tense in the next clause, εἴτε σωφρονοῦμεν, and allege that this would have no motive unless ἐξέστημεν were a true past. But this may be doubted. On the one hand, ἐξέστη in Mark iii. 21 can hardly mean anything but "He is beside Himself"—*i.e.*, it is virtually a present; on the other, the grammatical present ἐξιστάμεθα would not unambiguously convey the idea of madness, and would therefore be inappropriate here. But assuming that the change of tense has the effect of making ἐξέστημεν a real past, and that the proper rendering is "whether we *were* beside ourselves," what is the application then? We must suppose that some definite occasion is before the Apostle and his readers, on which he had been in an ecstasy (cf. ἐν ἐκστάσει, Acts xi. 5; ἐγένετο ἐπ' αὐτὸν ἔκστασις, Acts x. 10), and that his opponents availed themselves of this experience, in which he had passed, for a time, out of his own control, to whisper the malicious accusation that he had once not been quite right in his mind, and that this explained much. The Apostle, we should have to assume, admits the fact alleged, but protests against the inference drawn from it, and the use made of the inference. "I *was* beside myself," he says; "but it was an experience which had nothing to do with my ministry; it was between God and my solitary self; and to drag it into my relations with you is a mere impertinence." That the "ecstasis" in question was his vision of Jesus on the way to Damascus, and that his adversaries sought to discredit that, and the apostleship of Paul as grounded on that, is one of the extravagances of an irresponsible criticism. Of all experiences that ever befell him, his conversion is the very one which was *not* solely his own affair and God's, but the affair of the whole Church; and whereas he speaks of his ecstasies and visions with evident reluctance and embarrassment, as in chap. xii. 1 ff., or refuses to speak of them at all, as here (assuming this interpretation to be the true one), he makes his conversion and the appearance of the Lord the very foundation of his preaching, and treats of both with the utmost frankness. It must be something quite different from this—something analogous perhaps to me speaking with tongues, in which "the understanding was unfruitful," but for which Paul was distinguished (1 Cor. xiv. 14-18)—that is intended here. Such rapt conditions are certainly open to misinterpretation; and as their spiritual value is merely personal, Paul declines to discuss any allusion to them, as if it affected his relation to the Corinthians.

The strongest point in favour of this interpretation seems to me not the tense of ἐξέστημεν, but the use of Θεῷ: "it is unto God." If the meaning were the one first suggested, and the madness were the holy enthusiasm of the Evangelist, that would be distinctly a thing which did concern the Corinthians, and it would not be natural to withdraw it from their censure as God's affair. Nevertheless, one can conceive Paul saying that he was answerable for his extravagances, not to them, but to his Master; and that his sober-mindedness, at all events, had their interests in view. On a survey of the whole case, and especially with Mark iii. 21, and the New Testament use of the verb ἐξίσταμαι before us, I incline to think that the text of the Revised Version is to be preferred to the margin. The "being beside himself" with which Paul was charged will not, then, be an isolated incident in his career—an incident which Jewish teachers, remembering the ecstasies of Peter and John, could hardly object to—but the spiritual tension in which he habitually lived and wrought. The language, so far as I can judge, admits of this interpretation, and it brings the Apostle's experience into line, not only with that of his Master, but with that of many who have succeeded him. But how great and rare is the self-conquest of the man who can say that in his enthusiasm and his sobriety alike—when he is beside himself, and when his spirit is wholly subject to him—the one thing which never intrudes, or troubles his singleness of mind, is the thought of his own private ends.

In the verses which follow, Paul lets us into the secret of this unselfishness, this freedom from by-ends and ambition: "For the love of Christ constraineth us; because we thus judge, that One died for all, therefore all [of them] died." "Constraineth" is one of the most expressive words in the New Testament; the love of Christ has hold of the Apostle on both sides, as it were, and urges him on in a course which he cannot avoid. It has him in its grasp, and he has no choice, under its irresistible constraint, but to be what he is, and to do what he does, whether men think him in his mind or out of his mind. That the love of Christ means Christ's love to us, and not our love to Him, is shown by the fact that Paul goes on at once to describe in what it consists. "It constrains us," he says, "because we have come to this mind about it: One died for all; so then all died." Here, we may say, is the content of Christ's love, the essence of it, that which gives it its soul-subduing and constraining power: He loved us, *and gave Himself for us*; He died for all, *and in that death of His all died*.

It may seem a hazardous thing to give a definition of love, and especially to shut up within the boundaries of a human conception that love of Christ which passes knowledge. But the intelligence must get hold somehow even of things inconceivably great, and the New Testament writers, with all their diversity of spiritual gifts, are at one as to what is essential here.

They all find Christ's love concentrated and focussed in His death. They all find it there inasmuch as that death was a death *for us*. Perhaps St. Paul and St. John penetrated further, intellectually, than any of the others into the mystery of this "for"; but if we cannot give it a natural interpretation, and an interpretation in which an absolutely irresistible constraint is hidden for heart and will, we do not know what the Apostles meant when they spoke of Christ's love. There has been much discussion about the "for" in this place. It is ὑπέρ, not ἀντί, and many render it simply "on our behalf," or "for our advantage." That Christ did die for our advantage is not to be questioned. Neither is it to be questioned that this is a fair rendering of ὑπέρ. But what *does* raise question is whether this interpretation of the "for" supplies sufficient ground for the immediate inference of the Apostle "so then all died." Is it logical to say, "One died for the benefit of all: *hence* all died"? From that premiss is not the only legitimate conclusion "hence all remained alive"? Plainly, if *Paul's* conclusion is to be drawn, the "for" must reach deeper than this mere suggestion of our advantage: if we all *died*, in that Christ died *for* us, there must be a sense in which that death of His is *ours*; He must be identified with *us* in it: there, on the cross, while we stand and gaze at Him, He is not simply a person doing us a service; He is a person doing us a service *by filling our place and dying our death*. It is out of this deeper relation that all services, benefits, and advantages flow; and that deeper sense of "for," to which Christ in His death is at once the representative and the substitute of man, is essential to do justice to the Apostle's thought. Without the ideas involved in these words we cannot conceive, as he conceived it, the love of Christ. We cannot understand how that force, which exercised such absolute authority over his whole life, appealed to his intelligence. We do not mean what he meant even when we use his words; we gain currency, under cover of them, for ideas utterly inadequate to the spiritual depth of his.

If this were an exposition of St. Paul's theology, and not of the Second Epistle to the Corinthians, I should be bound to consider the connexion between that outward death of Christ in which the death of all is involved, and the appropriation of that death to themselves by individual men. But the Apostle does not directly raise this question here; he only adds in the fifteenth verse a statement of the purpose for which Christ died, and in doing so suggests that the connecting link is to be sought, in part at least, in the feeling of gratitude. "He died for all, that they which live should no longer live unto themselves, but unto Him who died for them and rose again." In dying our death Christ has done something for us so immense in love that we ought to be His, and only His, for ever. To make us His is the very object of His death. Before we know Him we are naturally selfish; we are an end to ourselves, in the bad sense; we are our own. Even the sacrifices which men make for their families, their country, or their order, are but qualifications of selfishness; it is not eradicated and exterminated till we see and feel what is meant by this—that *Christ died our death*. The life we have after we have apprehended this can never be our own; nay, we ourselves are not our own; we are bought with a price; life has been given a ransom for us, and our life is due to him "who died for us and rose again." I believe the Authorised Version is right in this rendering, and that it is a mistake to say, "who for our sakes died and rose again." The Resurrection has certainly significance in the work of Christ, but not in precisely the same way as His death; and Paul mentions it here, not to define its significance, but simply because he could not think of living except for One who was Himself alive.

One point deserves especial emphasis here—the universality of the expressions. Paul has been speaking of himself, and of the constraint which the love of Christ, as he apprehends it, exercises upon him. But he no sooner begins to define his thought of Christ's love than he passes over from the first person to the third. The love of Christ was not to be limited; what it is to the Apostle it is to the world: He died for all, and so all died. Whatever blessing Christ's death contained, it contains for all. Whatever doom it exhausts and removes, it exhausts and removes for all. Whatever power it breaks, it breaks for all. Whatever ideal it creates, whatever obligation it imposes, it creates and imposes for all. There is not a soul in the world which is excluded from an interest in that knowledge-surpassing love which made our death its own. There is not one which ought not to feel that omnipotent constraint which enchained and swayed the strong, proud spirit of Paul. There is not one which ought not to be pouring out its life for Him who died in its place, and rose to receive its service.

XV
THE NEW WORLD

> "Wherefore we henceforth know no man after the flesh: even though we have known Christ after the flesh, yet now we know *Him so* no more. Wherefore if any man *is* in Christ, *he* is a new creature [or, *there is* a new creation]: the old things are passed away; behold, they are become new."—2 Cor. v. 16, 17 (R.V.).

The inferences which are here drawn depend upon what has just been said of Christ's death for all and the death of all in that death of His. In that death, as inclusive of ours, the old life died, and with it died all its distinctions. All that men were, apart from Christ, all that constituted the "appearance" (πρόσωπον, ver. 12) of their life, all that marked them off from each other as such and such outwardly, ceased to have significance the moment Christ's death was understood as Paul here understands it. He dates his inference with ἀπὸ τοῦ νῦν ("henceforth"). This does not mean from the time at which he writes, but from the time at which he saw that One had died for all, and so all died. Here, as in other places, he divides his life into "now" and "then," the Christian and the pre-Christian stage (Rom. v. 9; Eph. ii. 11-13). The transition from one to the other was revolutionary, and one of its most startling results is that which he here describes. "Then," the distinctions between men, the "appearances" in which they boasted, had been important in his eyes; "now," they have ceased to be, *He* [47] never asks whether a man is Jew or Greek, rich or poor, bond or free, learned or unlearned; these are classifications "after the flesh," and have died in Christ's death *for all*. To recognise them any longer, to admit the legitimacy of claims based upon them—such claims as his opponents in Corinth seem to have been putting forth—would be to make Christ's death, in a sense, of no effect. It would be to deny that when He died for all, all died in Him; it would be to reanimate distinctions that should have been annihilated in His death.

To this rule of knowing no one after the flesh Paul can admit no exception. Not even Christ is excepted. "Even though we have known Christ after the flesh, yet now we know Him so no more." This is a difficult saying, and has been very variously interpreted. The English reader inevitably supposes that Paul *had* known Christ "after the flesh," but had outgrown that kind of knowledge; and that he is intimating these two facts. But it is quite possible to take the words[48] as purely hypothetical: "Supposing us to have known even Christ after the flesh—a case which in point of fact was never ours—yet now we know Him so no more." Grammar does not favour this last rendering, though it does not preclude it; and however the matter may be settled, the bare supposition, as much as the fact, requires us to give a definite meaning to the words about knowing Christ after the flesh, and ceasing so to know Him.

Some have inferred from them that when Paul became a Christian, and for some time after, his conception of Christ had resembled that of the persons whom he is here controverting: his Christ had been to all intents and purposes a Jewish Messiah, and he had only been able by degrees to overcome, though he had at last overcome, the narrowness and nationalism of his early years as a disciple. To know Christ after the flesh would be to know Him in the character of a deliverer of the Jews: His Jewish descent, His circumcision, His observance of the Temple worship, His limitation of His ministry to the Holy Land, would be matters of great significance; and Jewish descent might naturally be supposed to establish a prerogative in relation to the Messiah for Jews as opposed to Gentiles. Probably there were Christians whose original conception of the Saviour was of this kind, and it is a fair enough description to say that this amounts only to a knowing of Christ after the flesh; but Paul can hardly have been one of them. His Christian knowledge of Christ dates from his vision of the Risen Lord on the way to Damascus, and in that appearance there was no room for anything that could be called "flesh." It was an appearance of the Lord of Glory. It determined all Paul's thoughts thenceforth. Nothing is more remarkable in his Epistles than the strong sense that what he calls his Gospel is one, unchanged, and unchangeable. It is not Yes and No. Neither man nor angel may modify it by preaching another Jesus than he preaches. He is quite unconscious of any such transformation of his Christology as is indicated above; and in the absence of any trace elsewhere of a change so important, it is impossible to read it into the verse before us.

Another interpretation of the words would make "knowing Christ after the flesh" refer to a knowledge at first hand of the facts and outward conditions of Christ's life in this world: a knowledge which Paul had in his early Christian days valued highly, but for which he no longer cared. There were numbers of men alive then who had known Christ in this sense. They had seen and heard Him in Galilee and Jerusalem; they had much to tell about Him which would no doubt be very interesting to believers;

and more than likely some of them emphasised this distinction of theirs, and were disposed to be pretentious on the strength of it. Whether Paul had ever known Christ in this sense, it is impossible to say. But it is certain that to such knowledge he would have assigned no Christian importance whatever. And in doing so, he would have been following the example of Christ Himself. "Then shall ye begin to say, We have eaten and drunk in Thy presence, and Thou hast taught in our streets. And He shall say, I tell you, I know you not whence ye are." But it is impossible to suppose that this is a matter on which Paul as a Christian had ever needed to change his mind.

It is an interpretation in part akin to this which makes St. Paul here decry all knowledge of the historical Christ in comparison with the understanding of His death and resurrection. To know Christ after the flesh is in this case to know Him as He is represented in Matthew, Mark, and Luke; and Paul is supposed to say that, though narratives like these once had an interest and value for him, they really have it no longer: they are not essential to his Gospel, which is constituted by the death and resurrection alone. These great events and their consequences are all he is concerned with; to know Christ after the Evangelists is merely to know Him after the flesh; and flesh, even *His* flesh, ought to have no significance since His death.

It is a little difficult to take this quite seriously, though it has a serious side. St. Paul, no doubt, makes very few references to incidents in the life of our Lord, or even to words which He spoke.[49] But he is not singular in this. The Epistles of Peter and John are historically as barren as his. They do not add a word to the Gospel story; there is no new incident, no new trait in the picture of Jesus, no new oracle. Indeed, the only genuine addition to the record is that one made by Paul himself—"the word of the Lord Jesus, how He said, It is more blessed to give than to receive." The truth seems to be that it is not natural for an apostle, nor for any inspired man, to fall back on quotations, like a preacher gravelled for lack of matter, or conscious of wanting authority. Paul and his colleagues in apostleship had Christ living in them, and recognised the spirit by which they spoke as the spirit of their Master. So far as this was the case, it was certainly a matter of indifference to them whether they were acquainted with this or that incident in His life, with this or that syllable that He spoke on such and such an occasion. One casual occurrence, one scene in Christ's sufferings, one discourse which He delivered, would inevitably be known with more exact and literal precision to one person than to another; and there is no difficulty in believing that the casual advantage which any individual might thus possess was regarded by St. Paul as a thing of no Christian consequence. Similar differences exist still, and in principle are to be disregarded. But it is another thing to say that all knowledge of the historical Christ is irrelevant to Christianity, and yet another to father such an opinion on St. Paul. The attempt to do so is due in part, I believe, to a misinterpretation of κατὰ σάρκα. Paul has been read as if what he disclaimed and decried were knowledge of Christ ἐν σαρκί. But the two things are quite distinct. Christ lived *in the flesh*; but the life that He lived in the flesh He lived *after the spirit*, and when its spiritual import is regarded, it is safe to say that no one ever knew Christ as He was *in the flesh*—the Christ of Matthew, Mark, and Luke—better than Paul. No one had been initiated into Christ's character, as that character is revealed in the story of the Evangelists, more fully than he. No one ever knew the mind, the temper, the new moral ideal of Christianity, better than Paul, and there is no ultimate source for this knowledge but the historical Christ. Paul could not in his work as an evangelist preach salvation through the death and resurrection of an unknown person; the story which was the common property of the Church, and with which her catechists everywhere indoctrinated the new disciples, must have been as familiar to him, in substance, as it is to us; and his evident knowledge and appreciation of the character embodied in it forbids us to think of this acquaintance with Christ as what he means by knowing Him after the flesh. He might have had the Gospel narratives by heart, and counted them inestimably precious, and yet have spoken exactly as he speaks here.

Nevertheless, this interpretation, though mistaken, has a certain truth in it. There *is* a historical knowledge of Christ which is a mere irrelevance to Christianity, and it has sometimes a stress laid upon it by its possessors which tempts one to speak of it in St. Paul's scornful tone. Many so-called "Lives" of Christ abound in it. They aim at a historical realism which, to speak the plain truth, has simply no religious value. Knowledge of localities, customs, costumes, and so forth, is interesting enough; but if it should be ever so full and ever so exact, it is not the knowledge of Jesus Christ in any sense which makes a Gospel. It is quite possible, nay it is more than possible, that such knowledge may come between the soul and the Lord. It was so when Jesus lived. There were people who knew so well what He was like that they were blind to what He was. In St. Paul's phrase we may say that they knew Him "after the flesh," and it kept them from knowing Him truly. They asked, "Is not this the carpenter?" as if that were a piece of undeniable insight; and they were not conscious that only men blind to what He really was could ever have asked a question so absurd. It was *not* the carpenter who spoke with authority in the synagogues, and cast out devils, and brought in the kingdom; it was the Son of Man, the Son of God; and whether Paul meant it so or not, we may use his language in this passage to express the conviction, that one may really know Christ, to whom the whole outward aspect of His life, represented by "the carpenter of Nazareth," is indifferent; nay, that one cannot know Him in any real sense until these external things *are* indifferent. Or to put the same thing in other words, we may say that the knowledge of Christ which constitutes the Christian is not the knowledge of what He was, but of what he is; and if we know what He is, then all that is merely outward in the history may pass away.

But if none of these interpretations answers exactly to the Apostle's thought, where are we to seek the meaning of his words? All these, it will be observed, assume that Paul knew Christ "after the flesh," subsequent to his conversion; that he shared, as a Christian, views about Christ which he is now combating. As these interpretations, however, are untenable, we must assume that the time when he thus knew Christ was *before* his conversion. He could look back to days when his Messianic conceptions were carnal; when the Christ was to be identified, for him, by tokens in the domain of "appearance," or "flesh"; when He was to be a national, perhaps merely a political deliverer, and the Saviour of the Jews in a sense which gave them an advantage over the Gentiles. But these days were gone for ever. "Henceforth"—from the very instant that the truth flashed on him, One died *for all*, and so *all* died—they belonged to a past which could never be revived or recalled. One died for all: that means that Christ is Universal Redeemer. That same One rose again: that means He is Universal Lord. He has done the same infinite service for all, He makes the same infinite claim upon all; there are no prerogatives for any race, for any caste, for any individual men, in relation to Him. In presence of His cross, there is no difference: in His death, and in our death in Him, all carnal distinctions die; "henceforth we know no man after the flesh." Even kinship to Jesus "after the flesh" does not base any prerogative in the kingdom of God; even to have eaten and drunk in His presence, and listened to His living voice, confers no distinction there; He has not done more for His brethren and His companions than He has done for us all. And not only the carnal distinctions of men have vanished away; the carnal Jewish conception of Christ has vanished with them.

The seventeenth verse seems a new inference from the same ground as the fifteenth. Indeed, it connects so naturally with ver. 15 that one critic has suggested that ver. 16 is spurious, and another that it was a later insertion by the Apostle. Perhaps we may assume that St. Paul, who had no fear of such critics before his eyes, was capable of setting his sentences down just as they occurred to him, and did not mind an occasional awkwardness. When he writes "Wherefore if any man is in Christ, he is a new creature," he is indeed drawing an inference from ver. 15, but he is at the same time generalising and carrying on the thought of ver. 16. The idea of the new creature occurs in other places in his writings (*e.g.*, Eph. ii. 10; Gal. vi. 15), but both here and in Gal. vi. 15 I prefer the rendering in the margin of the Revised Version—"If any man is in Christ, there is a new creation: the things passed away (when he died in Christ);[50] behold, they have become new." We may say, if we please, that it is the new creature which makes the new creation; the change in the soul which revolutionises the world. Still, it is this universal change which the Apostle, apparently, wishes to describe; and in the sudden note of triumph with which he concludes—"Behold! all is become new"—we feel, as it were, one throb of that glad surprise with which he had looked out on the world after God had reconciled him to Himself by His Son. The past was dead to him, as dead as Christ on His cross; all its ideas, all its hopes, all its ambitions, were dead; *in Christ*, he was another man in another universe.

This is the first passage in 2 Corinthians in which this Pauline formula for a Christian—a man in Christ—is used.[51] It denotes the most intimate possible union, a union in which the believer's faith identifies him with Jesus in His death and resurrection, so that he can say, "I live no longer, but Christ liveth in me." It is the Apostle's profoundest word, not on the Gospel, but on the appropriation of the Gospel; not on Christ, but on the Christian religion.[52] It is mystical, as every true word must be which speaks of the relation of the soul to the Saviour; but it is intelligible to every one who knows what it is to trust and to love, and through trust and love to lose self in another whose life is greater and better than his own. And when we have seen, even for a moment, what it is to live in self or in the world, and what to live in Christ, we can easily believe that this union is equivalent to a re-creating and transfiguring of all things.

It is impossible to point to all the applications of this truth: "all things" is too wide a text. Every reader knows the things which bulked most largely in his life before he knew Christ, and it is easy for him to tell the difference due to being in the Lord. In a sense the new creation is in process as long as we live; it is ideally that faith in Christ means death in His death; ideally that with faith the old passes and the new is there; the actual putting away of the old, the actual production of the new, are the daily task of faith as it unites the soul to Christ. We are *in* Him the moment faith touches Him, but we have to grow up *into* Him in all things. Only as we do so does the world change all around us, till the promise is fulfilled of new heavens and a new earth.

But there is one application of these words, directly suggested by the context, which we ought not to overlook: I mean their application to men, and the old ways of estimating men. Those who are in Christ have died to the whole order of life in which men are judged "after the flesh." Perhaps the Christian Church has almost as much need as any other society to lay this to heart. We are still too ready to put stress upon distinctions which are quite in place in the world, but are without ground in Christ. Even in a Christian congregation there is a recognition of wealth, of learning, of social position, in some countries of race, which is not Christian. I do not say these distinctions are not real, but they are meaningless in relation to Christ, and ought not to be made. To make them narrows and impoverishes the soul. If we associate only with people of a certain station, and because of their station, all our thoughts and feelings are limited to a very small area of human life; but if distinctions of station, of intelligence, of manners, are lost in the common relation to Christ, then life is open to us in all its length and breadth; all things are ours, because we are His. To be guided by worldly distinctions is to know only a few people, and to know them by what is superficial in their nature; but to see that such distinctions died in Christ's death, and to look at men in relation to Him who is Redeemer and Lord of all, is to know all our brethren, and to know them not on the surface, but to the heart. People lament everywhere the want of a truly social and brotherly feeling in the Church, and try all sorts of well-meant devices to stimulate it, but nothing short of this goes to the root of the matter. The social, in this universal sense, is dependent upon the religious. Those who have died in Christ to the world in which these separative distinctions reign will have no difficulty in recognising each other as one in Him. Society is transfigured for each of us when this union is accomplished; the old things have passed, and all has become new.

XVI
RECONCILIATION

"But all things are of God, who reconciled us to Himself through Christ, and gave unto us the ministry of reconciliation; to wit, that God was in Christ reconciling the world unto Himself, not reckoning unto them their trespasses, and having committed unto us the word of reconciliation. We are ambassadors therefore on behalf of Christ, as though God were intreating by us: we beseech *you* on behalf of Christ, be ye reconciled to God. Him who knew no sin He made *to be* sin on our behalf; that we might become the righteousness of God in Him."—2 Cor. v. 18-21 (R.V.).

"Est hic insignis locus, si quis alius est in toto Paulo: proinde diligenter excutere singulas particulas convenit."—Calvin.

"If any man be in Christ," Paul has said, "there is a new creation; he is another man and lives in another world. But the new creation has the same Author as the original one: it is all of God, who reconciled us to Himself by Jesus Christ, and gave to us the ministry of reconciliation." It is plain from these last words that "us" does not mean Christians in general, but in the first instance Paul himself. He is a typical example of what it is to be in Christ; he understands what his own words mean—"the old things passed away; behold, they have become new"; he understands also how this stupendous change has been brought about. "It is due to God," he says, "who reconciled us to Himself through Christ."

The great interest of this passage is its bearing upon the Christian doctrine of reconciliation, and before we go further it is necessary to explain precisely what this word means. It presupposes a state of estrangement. Now, a state of estrangement may be of two kinds: the feeling of alienation and hostility may exist upon one side only, or it may exist upon both. What, then, is the character of that state of estrangement which subsists between God and man independently of the Gospel, and which the Gospel, as a ministry of reconciliation, is designed to overcome? Is it one-sided, or two-sided? Is there something to be put away in man only, or something to be put away in God as well, before reconciliation is effected?

These questions have been answered very confidently in different ways. Many, especially in modern times, assert with passionate eagerness that the estrangement is merely one-sided. Man is alienated from God by sin, fear, and unbelief, and God reconciles him to Himself when He prevails with him to lay aside these evil dispositions, and trust Him as his Father and his Friend. "All things are of God, who reconciled us to Himself through Christ," would mean in this case, "All things are of God, who has won our friendship through His Son." That this describes in part the effect of the Gospel, no one will deny. It is one of its blessed results that fear and distrust of God are taken away, and that we learn to trust and love Him. Nevertheless, this is not what the New Testament means by reconciliation, though it is one of its fruits.

To St. Paul the estrangement which the Christian reconciliation has to overcome is indubitably two-sided; there is something in God as well as something in man which has to be dealt with before there can be peace. Nay, the something on God's side is so incomparably more serious that in comparison with it the something on man's side simply passes out of view. It is God's earnest dealing with the obstacle on His own side to peace with man which prevails on man to believe in the seriousness of His love, and to lay aside distrust. It is God's earnest dealing with the obstacle on His own side which constitutes the reconciliation; the story of it is "the word of reconciliation"; when men receive it, they *receive* (Rom. v. 10) the reconciliation. "Reconciliation" in the New Testament sense is not something which *we accomplish* when we lay aside our enmity to God; it is something which *God accomplished* when in the death of Christ He put away everything that on His side meant estrangement, so that He might come and preach peace. To deny this is to take St. Paul's Gospel away root and branch. He always conceives the Gospel as the revelation of God's wisdom and love in view of a certain state of affairs as subsisting between God and man. Now, what is the really serious element in this situation? What is it that makes a Gospel necessary? What is it that the wisdom and love of God undertake to deal with, and do deal with, in that marvellous way which constitutes the Gospel? Is it man's distrust of God? is it man's dislike, fear, antipathy, spiritual alienation? Not if we accept the Apostle's teaching. The serious thing which makes the Gospel necessary, and the putting away of which constitutes the Gospel, is God's condemnation of the world and its sin; it is God's wrath, "revealed from heaven against all ungodliness and unrighteousness of men" (Rom. i. 16-18). The putting away of this is "reconciliation": the preaching of *this* reconciliation is the preaching of the Gospel.

Much impatience has been shown in the criticism of this conception. Clever men have exhibited their talent and courage by calling it "heathenish"; and others have undertaken to apologise for St. Paul by describing this objection as "modern." I cannot understand how any one should feel entitled either to flout the Apostle on this matter, or to take him under his patronage. If any one ever had the sense to distinguish between what is real and unreal in regard to God, between what is true and false spiritually, it was he; even with Ritschl on one side and Schmiedel on the other he is not dwarfed, and may be permitted to speak for himself. The wrath of God, the condemnation of God resting on the sinful world, are not, whatever speculative theologians may think, unreal things: neither do they belong only to ancient times. They are the most real things of which human nature has any knowledge till it receives the reconciliation. They are as real as a bad conscience; as real as misery, impotence, and despair. And it is the glory of the Gospel, as St. Paul understood it, that it deals with them as real. It does not tell men that they are illusions, and that only their own groundless fear and distrust have ever stood between them and God. It tells them that God has dealt seriously with these serious things for their removal, that awful as they are He has put them away by an awful demonstration of His love; it tells them that God has made peace at an infinite cost, and that the priceless peace is now freely offered to them.

When St. Paul says that God has given him the ministry of reconciliation, he means that he is a preacher of this peace. He ministers reconciliation to the world. His work has no doubt a hortatory side, as we shall see, but that side is secondary. It is not the main part of his vocation to tell men to make their peace with God, but to tell them that God has made peace with the world. At bottom, the Gospel is not good advice, but good news. All the good advice it gives is summed up in this—Receive the good news. But if the good news be taken away; if we cannot say, God has made peace, God has dealt seriously with His condemnation of sin, so that it no longer stands in the way of your return to Him; if we cannot say, Here *is* the reconciliation, receive it,—then for man's actual state we have no Gospel at all.

In the nineteenth verse St. Paul explains more fully the way in which he is looking at the subject:[53] "to wit, that God was in Christ reconciling the world to Himself, not reckoning unto them their trespasses, and having committed unto us the word of reconciliation." The English Authorised Version puts a comma at Christ: "God was in Christ, reconciling the world to Himself." It is safe to say that "God was in Christ" is a sentence which neither St. Paul nor any other New Testament writer could have conceived; the "was" and the "reconciling" must be taken together, and "in Christ" is practically equivalent to "through Christ" in the previous verse—God was by means of Christ reconciling the world to Himself. "Reconciling," of course, must be taken in the sense already explained. The sentence does not mean that God was trying to convert men, or to prevail with them to lay aside their enmity, but that He was disposing of everything that on His part made peace impossible. When Christ's work was done, the reconciliation of the world was accomplished. When men were called to receive it, they were called to a relation to God; not in which they would no more be against Him—though that is included—but in which they would no more have Him against them (Hofmann). There would be no condemnation thenceforth to those who were in Christ Jesus.

The connexion of the words "not reckoning unto them their trespasses, and having committed unto us the word of reconciliation," is rather difficult. The last clause certainly refers to something which took place after the work of reconciliation had been wrought; Paul was commissioned to tell the story of it. It seems most probable that the other is co-ordinate with this, so that both are in a sense the evidence for the main proposition. It is as if he had said: "God was by means of Christ establishing friendly relations between the world and Himself, as appears from this, that He does not reckon their trespasses unto them,[54] and has made us preachers of His grace." The very universality of the expression—reconciling a world to Himself—is consistent only with an objective reconciliation. It cannot mean that God was overcoming the world's enmity (though that is the ulterior object) it means that God was putting away His own condemnation and wrath. When this was done, He could send, and did send, men to declare that it was done; and among these men, none had a profounder appreciation of what God had wrought, and what he himself had to declare as God's glad tidings, than the Apostle Paul.

This is the point we reach in ver. 20: "We are ambassadors therefore on behalf of Christ, as though God were intreating you by us; we beseech you, on behalf of Christ, be ye reconciled to God." The Apostle has just told us that all is of God, but all is at the same time "in Christ," or "through Christ." Hence it is on Christ's behalf he comes forward; it is the furtherance of Christ's interests he has at heart. Nay, it is that same interest which is at the heart of the Father, who desires now to glorify the Son; so that when Paul appeals to men on Christ's behalf it is as though God Himself entreated them. Most expositors notice the amazing contrast between πρεσβεύομεν ("we are ambassadors") and δεόμεθα ("we beseech you"). The ambassador, as a rule, stands upon his dignity; he maintains the greatness of the person whom he represents. But Paul in this lowly passionate entreaty is not false to his Master; he is preaching the Gospel in the spirit of the Gospel; he shows that he has really learned of Christ; the very conception of the ambassador descending to entreaty is, as Calvin says, an incomparable commendation of the grace of Christ. One can imagine how Saul the Pharisee would have spoken on God's behalf; with what rigour, what austerity, what unbending, uncompromising assurance. But old things have passed away; behold, they have become new. This single verse illumines, as by a lightning flash, the new world into which the Gospel has translated Paul, the new man it has made of him. The fire that burned in Christ's heart has caught hold in his; his soul is tremulous with passion; he is conscious of the grandeur of his calling, yet there is nothing that he would not do to win men for his message. It would go to his heart like a sword if he had to take up the old lament, "Who hath believed our report?" In his dignity as Christ's ambassador and as the mouthpiece of God, in his humility, in his passionate earnestness, in the urgency and directness of his appeal, St. Paul is the supreme type and example of the Christian minister. In the passage before us he presents the appeal of the Gospel in its simplest form: wherever he stands before men on Christ's behalf his prayer is, "Be ye reconciled unto God." And once more we must insist on the apostolic import of these words. It is the misleading *nuance* of "reconcile" in English that makes so many take them as if they meant, "Lay aside your enmity to God; cease to regard Him with distrust, hatred, and fear"; in other words, "Show yourselves His friends." In St. Paul's lips they cannot possibly mean anything but, "Accept *His* offered friendship; enter into that peace which He has made for the world through the death of His Son; believe that He has at infinite cost put away all that on His part stood between you and peace; *receive* the reconciliation."

The Received Text and the Authorised Version attach the twenty-first verse to this exhortation by γὰρ ("for"): "For Him who knew no sin He made *to be* sin on our behalf." The "for" is spurious, and though it is not inept the sentence gains greatly in impressiveness by its omission. The Apostle does not point out the connexion for us: in simply declaring the manner in which God reconciled the world to Himself—the process by which, the cost at which, He made peace—he leaves us to feel how vast is the boon which is offered to us in the Gospel, how tremendous the responsibility of rejecting it. To refuse "the reconciliation" is to contemn the death in which the Sinless One was made sin on our behalf.

This wonderful sentence is the inspired commentary on the statement of ver. 15—"One died for all." It takes us into the very heart of the Apostolic Gospel. Just because it does so, it has always been felt to be of critical importance, alike by those who welcome and by those who reject it; it condenses and concentrates in itself the attraction of Christ and the offence of Christ. It is a counsel of despair to evade it. It is not the puzzle of the New Testament, but the ultimate solution of all puzzles; it is not an irrational quantity that has to be eliminated or explained away, but the key-stone of the whole system of apostolic thought. It is not a blank obscurity in revelation, a spot of impenetrable blackness; it is the focus in which the reconciling love of God burns with the purest and intensest flame; it is the fountain light of all day, the master light of all seeing, in the Christian revelation. Let us look at it more closely.

God, we must observe in the first place, is the subject. "All" is of him in the work of reconciliation, and this above all, that He made the Sinless One to be sin. I have read a book on the Atonement which quoted this sentence three times, or rather misquoted it, never once recognising that an action of God is involved. But without this, there is no coherence in the Apostle's thoughts at all. Without this, there would be no explanation of reconciliation as God's work. God reconciled the world to Himself—made peace into which the world might enter—in making Christ sin on its behalf. What precisely this means we shall inquire further on; but it is essential to remember, whatever it mean, that God is the doer of it.

Observe next the description of Christ—"Him that knew no sin." The Greek negative (μὴ), as Schmiedel remarks, implies that this is regarded as the verdict of some one else than the writer. It was Christ's own verdict upon Himself. He whose words search our very hearts, and bring to light unsuspected seeds of badness, never Himself betrays the faintest consciousness of guilt. He challenges His enemies directly: "Which of you convinceth Me of sin?" It is the verdict of all sincere human souls, as uttered by the soldier who watched His cross—"Truly this was a righteous man." It is the verdict even of the great enemy who assailed Him again and again, and found nothing in Him, and whose agents recognised Him as the Holy One of God. Above all, it is the verdict of God. He was the beloved Son, in whom the Father was well pleased. For three-and-thirty years, in daily contact with the world and its sins, Christ lived and yet knew no sin. To His will and conscience it was a foreign thing. What infinite worth that sinless life possessed in God's sight! When He looked down to earth it was the one absolutely precious thing. Filled full of righteousness, absolutely well-pleasing in His eyes, it was worth more to God than all the world beside.

Now, God reconciled the world to Himself—He made a peace which could be proclaimed and offered to the world—when, all sinless as Christ was, He made Him to be sin on our behalf. What does this mean? Not, exactly, that He made Him a sin-offering on our behalf. The expression for a sin-offering is distinct (περὶ ἁμαρτίας), and the parallelism with δικαιοσύνη in the next clause forbids that reference here. The sin-offering of the Old Testament can at most have pointed towards and dimly suggested so tremendous an utterance as this; and the profoundest word of the New

Testament cannot be adequately interpreted by anything in the Old. When St. Paul says, "Him that knew no sin God made sin," he must mean that in Christ on His cross, by divine appointment, the extremest opposites met and became one—incarnate righteousness and the sin of the world. The sin is laid by God on the Sinless One; its doom is laid on Him; His death is the execution of the divine sentence upon it. When He dies, He has put away sin; it no longer stands, as it once stood, between God and the world. On the contrary, God has made peace by this great transaction; He has wrought out reconciliation; and its ministers can go everywhere with this awful appeal: "Receive the reconciliation; Him who knew no sin God hath made sin on our behalf, and there is henceforth no condemnation to them that are in Christ."

No one who has felt the power of this appeal will be very anxious to defend the Apostolic Gospel from the charges which are sometimes made against it. When he is told that it is impossible for the doom of sin to fall on the Sinless One, and that even if it were conceivable it would be frightfully immoral, he is not disquieted. He recognises in the moral contradictions of this text the surest sign that the secret of the Atonement is revealed in it: he feels that God's work of reconciliation necessarily involves such an identification of sinlessness and sin. He knows that there is an appalling side to sin, and he is ready to believe that there is an appalling side to redemption also—a side the most distant sight of which makes the proudest heart quail, and stops every mouth before God. He knows that the salvation which he needs must be one in which God's mercy comes *through*, and not *over*, His judgment; and this is the redemption which is in Christ Jesus. But without becoming controversial on a subject on which more than on any other the temper of controversy is unseemly, reference may be made to the commonest form of objection to the apostolic doctrine, in the sincere hope that some one who has stumbled at that doctrine may see it more truly. The objection I refer to discredits propitiation in the alleged interest of the love of God. "We do not need," the objectors say, "to propitiate an angry God. This is a piece of heathenism, of which a Christian ought to be ashamed. It is a libel on the God and Father of our Lord Jesus Christ, whose name is love, and who waits to be gracious." What are we to say to such words, which are uttered as boldly as if there were no possible reply, or rather as if the Apostles had never written, or had been narrow-minded unreceptive souls, who had not only failed to understand their Master, but had taught with amazing perversity the very opposite of what He taught on the most essential of all points—the nature of God and His relation to sinful men? We must say this. It is quite true that we have not to propitiate an offended God: the very fact upon which the Gospel proceeds is that we *cannot* do any such thing. But it is not true that no propitiation is needed. As truly as guilt is a real thing, as truly as God's condemnation of sin is a real thing, a propitiation is needed. And it is here, I think, that those who make the objection referred to part company, not only with St. Paul, but with all the Apostles. God is love, they say, and therefore He does not require a propitiation. God is love, say the Apostles, and therefore He provides a propitiation. Which of these doctrines appeals best to the conscience? Which of them gives reality, and contents, and substance, to the love of God? Is it not the apostolic doctrine? Does not the other cut out and cast away that very thing which made the soul of God's love to Paul and John? "Herein is love, not that we loved God, but that *He loved us, and sent His Son to be the propitiation for our sins.*" "*God commendeth His love toward us, in that, while we were yet sinners, Christ died for us.... Him that knew no sin He made to be sin on our behalf.*" That is how they spoke in the beginning of the Gospel, and so let us speak. Nobody has any right to borrow the words "God is love" from an apostle, and then to put them in circulation after carefully emptying them of their apostolic import. Still less has any one a right to use them as an argument against the very thing in which the Apostles placed their meaning. But this is what they do who appeal to love against propitiation. To take the condemnation out of the Cross is to take the nerve out of the Gospel; it will cease to hold men's hearts with its original power when the reconciliation which is preached through it contains the mercy, but not the judgment of God. Its whole virtue, its consistency with God's character, its aptness to man's need, its real dimensions as a revelation of love, depend ultimately on this, that mercy comes to us in it through judgment.

In the last words of the passage the Apostle tells us the object of this great interposition of God: "He made Christ to be sin on our behalf, that we might become the righteousness of God in Him." Our condemnation is made His; it is accepted, exhausted, annihilated, on His cross; and when we receive the reconciliation—when we humble ourselves to be forgiven and restored at this infinite cost—there is no longer condemnation for us: we are justified by our faith, and have peace with God through our Lord Jesus Christ. This is what is meant by becoming the righteousness of God in Him. It is not, as the very next sentence suggests, all that is included in the Christian salvation, but it is all that the words themselves contain. "*In Him*" has all promise in it, as well as the present possession of reconciliation, with which the Christian life begins; but it is this present possession, and not the promise involved in it, which St. Paul describes as the righteousness of God. In Christ, that Christ who died for us, and in Him in virtue of that death which by exhausting condemnation put away sin, we are accepted in God's sight.

XVII
THE SIGNS OF AN APOSTLE

"And working together *with Him* we intreat also that ye receive not the grace of God in vain (for He saith,
At an acceptable time I hearkened unto thee,
And in a day of salvation did I succour thee:
behold, now is the acceptable time; behold, now is the day of salvation): giving no occasion of stumbling in anything, that our ministration be not blamed; but in everything commending ourselves, as ministers of God, in much patience, in afflictions, in necessities, in distresses, in stripes, in imprisonments, in tumults, in labours, in watchings, in fastings; in pureness, in knowledge, in long-suffering, in kindness, in the Holy Ghost, in love unfeigned, in the word of truth, in the power of God; by the armour of righteousness on the right hand and on the left, by glory and dishonour, by evil report and good report; as deceivers, and *yet* true; as unknown, and yet well known; as dying, and behold, we live; as chastened, and not killed; as sorrowful, yet alway rejoicing; as poor, yet making many rich; as having nothing, and *yet* possessing all things.

"Our mouth is open unto you, O Corinthians, our heart is enlarged. Ye are not straitened in us, but ye are straitened in your own affections. Now for a recompense in like kind (I speak as unto *my* children), be ye also enlarged."—2 Cor. vi. 1-13 (R.V.).

The ministry of the Gospel is a ministry of reconciliation; the preacher of the Gospel is primarily an evangelist. He has to proclaim that wonderful grace of God which made peace between heaven and earth through the blood of the Cross, and he has to urge men to receive it. Until this is done, there is nothing else that he can do. But when sinful men have welcomed the glad tidings, when they have consented to accept the peace bought for them with so great a price, when they have endured to be forgiven and restored to God's favour, not for what they are, nor for what they are going to be, but solely for what Christ did for them on the cross, then a new situation is created, and the minister of the Gospel has a new task. It is to that situation St. Paul addresses himself here. Recognising the Corinthians as people reconciled to God by the death of His Son, he entreats them not to receive the grace of God in vain. He does so, according to our Bibles, as a fellow-worker with God. This is probably right, though some would take the word as in chap. i. 24, and make it mean "as fellow-workers with you." But it is more natural, when we look to what precedes, to think that St. Paul is here identifying himself with God's interest in the world, and that he speaks out of the proud consciousness of doing so. "All is of God," in the great work of redemption; but God does not disdain the sympathetic co-operation of men whose hearts He has touched.

But what is meant by receiving the grace of God in vain, or to no purpose? That might be done in an infinite variety of ways, and in reading the words for edification we naturally grasp at any clue suggested by our circumstances. An expositor is bound to seek his clue rather in the circumstances of the Corinthians; and if we have regard to the general tenor of this Epistle, and especially to such a passage as chap. xi. 4, we shall find the true interpretation without difficulty. Paul has explained his Gospel—his proclamation of Jesus as Universal Redeemer in virtue of His dying the sinner's death, and as Universal Lord in virtue of His resurrection from the dead—so explicitly, because he fears lest through the influence of some false teacher the minds of the Corinthians should be corrupted from the simplicity that is toward Christ. It would be receiving the grace of God in vain, if, after receiving those truths concerning Christ which he had taught them, they were to give up his Gospel for another in which these truths had no place. This is what he dreads and deprecates, both in Corinth and Galatia: the precipitate removal from the grace of Christ to another Gospel which is no Gospel at all, but a subversion of the truth. This is what he means by receiving the grace of God in vain.

There are some minds to which this will not be impressive, some to which it will only be provoking. It will seem irrelevant and pithless to those who take for granted the finality of the distinction between religion and theology, or between the theory, as it is called, and the fact of the Atonement. But for St. Paul, as for all sufficiently earnest and vigorous minds, there is a point at which these distinctions disappear. A certain theory is seen to be essential to the fact, a certain theology to be the constitutive force in the religion. The death of Christ was what it was to him only because it was capable of a certain interpretation: his theory of it, if we choose to put it so, gave it its power over him. The love of Christ constrained him "because he thus judged"—*i.e.*, because he construed it to his intelligence in a way which showed it to be irresistible. If these interpretations and constructions are rejected, it must not be in the name of "fact" as opposed to "theory," but in the name of other interpretations more adequate and constraining. A fact of which there is absolutely *no* theory is a fact which is without relation to anything in the universe—a mere irrelevance in man's mind—a blank incredibility—a rock in the sky. Paul's "theory" about Christ's death for sin was not to him an excrescence on the Gospel, or a superfluous appendage to it: it was itself the Gospel; it was the thing in which the very soul of God's redeeming love was brought to light; it was the condition under which the love of Christ became to him a constraining power; to receive it and then reject it was to receive the grace of God in vain.

This does not preclude us from the edifying application of these words which a modern reader almost instinctively makes. Peace with God is the first and deepest need of the sinful soul, but it is not the sum-total of salvation. It would, indeed, be received in vain, if the soul did not on the basis of it proceed to build up the new life in new purity and power. The failure to do this is, unhappily, only too common. There is no mechanical guarantee for the fruits of the Spirit; no assurance, such as would make this appeal unnecessary, that every man who has received the word of reconciliation will also walk in newness of life. But if an evangelical profession, and an immoral life, are the ugliest combination of which human nature is capable, the force of this appeal ought to be felt by the weakest and the worst. "The Son of God loved me, and gave Himself for me": can any of us hide that word in his heart, and live on as if it meant nothing at all?

Paul emphasises his appeal to the Corinthians by a striking quotation from an ancient prophet (Isa. xlix. 8): "At an acceptable time did I hearken unto thee, And in a day of salvation did I succour thee"; and he points it by the joyful exclamation: "Behold, now is the acceptable time; behold, now is the day of salvation." The passage in Isaiah refers to the servant of Jehovah, and some scholars would insist that even in the quotation a primary application must be made to Christ. The ambassadors of the Gospel represent *His* interest (chap. v. 20); this verse is, as it were, the answer to *His* prayer: "Father, the hour is come: glorify Thy Son." In answering the Son, the Father introduces the era of grace for all who are, or shall be, Christ's: behold, now is the time in which God shows us favour; now is the day on which He saves us. This is rather scholastic than apostolic, and it is far more probable that St. Paul borrows the prophet's words, as he often does, because they suit him, without thinking of their original application. What is striking in the passage, and characteristic both of the writer and of the New Testament, is the union of urgency and triumph in the tone. "Now" does certainly mean "now or never"; but more prominently still it means "in a time so favoured as this: in a time so graced with opportunity." The best illustration of it is the saying of Jesus to the Apostles: "Blessed are your eyes, for they see; and your ears, for they hear. For verily I say unto you, That many prophets and righteous men have desired to see those things which ye see, and have not seen them; and to hear those things which ye hear, and have not heard them." *Now*, that we live under the reign of grace; *now*, when God's redeeming love, omnipotent to save, shines on us from the Cross; *now*, that the last days have come, and the Judge is at the door, let us with all seriousness, and all joy, work out our own salvation, lest we make the grace of God of no effect.

St. Paul is as careful himself as he would have the Corinthians to be. He does not wish them to receive the Gospel in vain, and he takes pains that it shall not be frustrated through any fault of his: "working together with God we intreat you ... giving no occasion of stumbling in anything, that our ministration be not blamed." It is almost implied in a sentence like this that there are people who will be glad of an excuse not to listen to the Gospel, or not to take it seriously, and that they will look for such an excuse in the conduct of its ministers. Anything in the minister to which objection can be raised will be used as a shield against the Gospel. It does not matter that in nine cases out of ten this plea for declining the grace of God is impudent hypocrisy; it is one which the non-Christian should never have. If it is not the chief end of the evangelist to give no occasion of stumbling, it is one of his chief rules. This is a matter on which Jesus lays great stress. The severest words He ever spoke were spoken against those whose conduct made faith hard and unbelief easy. Of course they were spoken to all, but they have special application to those who are so directly identified with the Gospel as its ministers. It is to them men naturally look for the proof of what grace does. If its reception has been in vain in them; if they have not learned the spirit of their message; if their pride, or indolence, or avarice, or ill-nature, provoke the anger or contempt of those to whom they preach,—then their ministration is blamed, and the shadow of that censure falls upon their message. The grace of God which has to be proclaimed through human lips, and to attest itself by its power over human lives, might seem to be put in this way to too great hazard in the world; but it has God behind it, or rather it is itself God at work in His ministers as their humility and fidelity allow Him; and in spite of the occasions of stumbling for which there is no excuse, God is always able to make grace prevail. Through the faults of its ministers, nay, sometimes even with those faults as a foil, men see how good and how strong that grace is.

It is not easy to comment on the glowing passage (vv. 4-10) in which St. Paul expands this sober habit of giving no occasion of stumbling in anything into a description of his apostolic ministry. Logically, its value is obvious enough. He means the Corinthians to feel that if they turn away from the Gospel which he has preached to them they are passing censure lightly on a life of unparalleled devotion and power. He commends himself to them, as God's servants ought always to do,[55] by the life which he leads in the exercise of his ministry; and to reject his Gospel is to condemn his life as worthless or misspent. Will they venture to do that when they are reminded of what it is, and when they feel that it is all this for them? No right-minded man will, without provocation, speak about himself, but Paul is doubly protected. He is challenged, by the threatened desertion from the Gospel of some, at least, of the Corinthians; and it is not so much of himself he speaks, as of the ministers of Christ; not so much on his own behalf, as on behalf of the Gospel. The fountains of the great deep are broken up within him as he thinks of what is at issue; he is in all straits, as he begins, and can speak only in unconnected words, one at a time; but before he stops he has won his liberty, and pours out his soul without restraint.

It is needless to comment on each of the eight-and-twenty separate phrases in which St. Paul characterises his life as a minister of the Gospel. But there are what might be called breathing-places, if not logical pauses, in the outburst of feeling, and these, as it happens, coincide with the introduction of new aspects of his work. (1) At first he depicts exclusively, and in single words, its passive side. Christ had shown him at his conversion how great things he must suffer for His name's sake (Acts ix. 16), and here is his own confirmation of the Lord's word: he has ministered "in much patience—in afflictions, in necessities, in distresses; in stripes, in imprisonments, in tumults"—where the enmity of men was conspicuous; "in labours, in watchings, in fastings"—freely exacted by his own devotion. These nine words are all, in a manner, subordinated to "much patience"; his brave endurance was abundantly shown in every variety of pain and distress. (2) At ver. 6 he makes a new start, and now it is not the passive and physical aspect of his work that is in view, but the active and spiritual. All that weight of suffering did not extinguish in him the virtues of the new life, or the special gifts of the Christian minister. He wrought, he reminds them, "in purity, in knowledge, in long-suffering, in kindness, in the Holy Spirit, in love unfeigned, in the word of truth, in the power of God." The precise import of some of these expressions may be doubtful, but this is of less consequence than the general tenor of the whole, which is unmistakable. Probably some of the terms, strictly taken, would cross each other. Thus the Holy Spirit and the power of God, if we compare such passages as 1 Cor. ii. 4, 1 Thess. i. 5, are very nearly akin. The same remark would apply to "knowledge," and to "the word of truth," if the latter refers, as I cannot but think it does,[56] to the Gospel. "Purity" is naturally taken in the widest sense, and "undissembled love" is peculiarly appropriate when we think of the feelings with which some of the Corinthians regarded Paul. But the main thing to notice is how the "much endurance," which, to a superficial observer, is the most conspicuous characteristic of the Apostle's ministry, is balanced by a great manifestation of spiritual force from within. Of all men in the world he was the weakest to look at, the most battered, burdened, and depressed, yet no one else had in him such a fountain as he of the most powerful and gracious life. And then (3) after another pause, marked this time by a slight change in the construction (from ἐν to διὰ), he goes on to enlarge upon the whole conditions under which his ministry is fulfilled, and especially on the extraordinary contrasts which are reconciled in it. We commend ourselves in our work he says, "by the armour of righteousness on the right hand and the left, by glory and dishonour, by evil report and good report: as deceivers, and yet true; as unknown, and yet coming to be well known; as dying, and behold, we live; as chastened, and not killed; as sorrowing, yet ever rejoicing; as poor, yet making many rich; as having nothing, and yet possessing all things." Here again it is not the details that are important, but the whole, and yet the details require notice. The armour of righteousness is that which righteousness supplies, or it may even be that which righteousness is: Paul's character equips him right and left; it is both spear and shield, and makes him competent either for attack or defence. Without righteousness, in this sense of integrity, he could not commend himself in his work as a minister of God.[57] But not only does his real character commend him; his reputation does the same service, however various that reputation may be. Through honour and dishonour, through evil report and good report—through the truth that is told about him, and through the lies—through the esteem of his friends, the malignity of his enemies, the contempt of strangers—the same man comes out, in the same character, devoted always in the same spirit to the same calling. It is indeed his very devotion which produces these opposite estimates, and hence, inconsistent as they are, they agree in recommending him as a servant of God. Some said "He is beside himself," and others would have plucked out their eyes for his sake, yet both these extremely opposite attitudes were produced by the very same thing—the passionate earnestness with which he served Christ in the Gospel. There are good scholars who think that the clauses beginning "as deceivers, and true," are the Apostle's own commentary on "through evil report and good report"; in other words, that in these clauses he is giving samples of the way in which he was spoken of, to his honour or dishonour, and glorying that honour and dishonour alike only guaranteed more thoroughly his claim to be a minister of God. This might suit the first two pairs of contrasts ("as deceivers, and true; as unknown, and gaining recognition"), but it does not suit the next ("as dying, and behold we live"), in which, as in those that follow, the Apostle is not repeating what was said by others, but speaking for himself, and stating truth equally on both sides of the account. After the first pair, there is no "dishonour," or "evil report," in any of the states which he contrasts with each other: though opposites, they have each their truth, and the power and beauty of the passage, and of the life which it describes, lie simply in this, that both *are* true, and that through all such contrasts St. Paul can prove himself the same loyal minister of the reconciliation.

Each pair of opposites might furnish by itself a subject for discourse, but what we are rather concerned with is the impression produced by the whole. In their variety they give us a vivid idea of the range of St. Paul's experiences; in the regularity with which he puts the higher last, and in the climax with which he concludes, they show the victorious spirit with which he confronted all that various life. An ordinary Christian—an ordinary minister of the Gospel—may well feel, as he reads, that his own life is by comparison empty and commonplace. There is not that terrible pressure on him from without; there is not that irrepressible fountain of grace within; there is not that triumphant spirit which can subdue all the world contains—honour and dishonour, evil report and good report—and make it pay tribute to the Gospel, and to himself as a Gospel minister. Yet the world has still all possible experiences ready for those who give themselves to the service of God with the wholeheartedness of Paul: it will show them its best and its worst; its reverence, affection, and praise; its hatred, its indifference, its scorn. And it is in the facing of all such experiences by God's ministers that the ministry receives its highest attestation: they are enabled to turn all to profit; in ignominy and in honour alike they are made more than conquerors through Him who loved them. St. Paul's plea rises involuntarily into a pæan; he begins, as we saw, with the embarrassed tone of a man who wishes to persuade others that he has taken sincere pains not to frustrate his work by faults he could have avoided—"giving no occasion of stumbling in anything, that the ministry be not blamed"; but he is carried higher and higher, as the tide of feeling rises within him, till it sets him beyond the reach of blame or praise—at Christ's right hand, where all things are his. Here is a signal fulfilment of that word of the Lord: "I am come that they might have life, and might have it more abundantly." Who could have it more abundantly, more triumphantly strong through all its vicissitudes, than the man who dictated these lines?

The passage closes with an appeal in which Paul descends from this supreme height to the most direct and affectionate address. He names his readers by name: "Our mouth is open unto you, O Corinthians;[58] our heart is enlarged." He means that he has treated them with the utmost frankness and cordiality. With strangers we use reserve; we do not let ourselves go, nor indulge in any effusion of heart. But he has not made strangers of them; he has relieved his overcharged heart before them, and he has established a new claim on their confidence in doing so. "Ye are not straitened in us," he writes; that is, "The awkwardness and constraint of which you are conscious in your relations with me are not due to anything on my side; my heart has been made wide, and you have plenty of room in it. But you are straitened in your own affections. It is *your* hearts that are narrow: cramped and confined with unworthy suspicions, and with the feeling that you have done me a wrong which you are not quite prepared to rectify. Overcome these ungenerous thoughts at once. Give me a recompense in kind for my treatment of you. I have opened my heart wide, to you and for you; open your hearts as freely, to me and for me. I am your father in Christ, and I have a right to this from my children."

When we take this passage as a whole, in its original bearings, one thing is plain: that want of love and confidence between the minister of the Gospel and those to whom he ministers has great power to frustrate the grace of God. There may have been a real revival under the minister's preaching—a real reception of the grace which he proclaims—but all will be in vain if mutual confidence fails. If he gives occasion of stumbling in something, and the ministry is blamed; or if malice and falsehood sow the seeds of dissension between him and his brethren, the grand condition of an effective ministry is gone. "Beloved, let us love one another," if we do not wish the virtue of the Cross to be of no effect in us.

XVIII
NEW TESTAMENT PURITANISM

"Be not unequally yoked with unbelievers: for what fellowship have righteousness and iniquity? or what communion hath light with darkness? And what concord hath Christ with Belial? or what portion hath a believer with an unbeliever? And what agreement hath a temple of God with idols? for we are a temple of the living God; even as God said, I will dwell in them, and walk in them; and I will be their God, and they shall be My people. Wherefore

Come ye out from among them, and be ye separate, saith the Lord,
And touch no unclean thing;
And I will receive you,
And will be to you a Father,
And ye shall be to Me sons and daughters,

saith the Lord Almighty. Having therefore these promises, beloved, let us cleanse ourselves from all defilement of flesh and spirit, perfecting holiness in the fear of God."—2 Cor. vi. 14-vii. 1 (R.V.).

This is one of the most peculiar passages in the New Testament. Even a careless reader must feel that there is something abrupt and unexpected in it; it jolts the mind as a stone on the road does a carriage wheel. Paul has been begging the Corinthians to treat him with the same love and confidence which he has always shown to them, and he urges this claim upon them up to ver. 13. Then comes this passage about the relation of Christians to the world. Then again, at chap. vii. 2—"Open your hearts to us; we wronged no man, we corrupted no man, we took advantage of no man"—he returns to the old subject without the least mark of transition. If everything were omitted from chap. vi. 14 to chap. vii. 1 inclusive, the continuity both of thought and feeling would be much more striking. This consideration alone has induced many scholars to believe that these verses do not occupy their original place. The ingenious suggestion has been made that they are a fragment of the letter to which the Apostle refers in the First Epistle (chap. v.

9): the sentiment, and to some extent even the words, favour this conjecture. But as there is no external authority for any conjecture whatever, and no variation in the text, such suggestions can never become conclusive. It is always possible that, on reading over his letter, the Apostle himself may have inserted a paragraph breaking to some extent the closeness of the original connexion. If there is nothing in the contents of the section inconsistent with his mind, the breach of continuity is not enough to discredit it.

Some, however, have gone further than this. They have pointed to the strange formulæ of quotation—"as God said," "saith the Lord," "saith the Lord Almighty"—as unlike Paul. Even the main idea of the passage—"touch not any unclean thing"—is asserted to be at variance with his principles. A narrow Jewish Christian might, it is said, have expressed this shrinking from what is unclean, in the sense of being associated with idolatry, but not the great Apostle of liberty. At all events he would have taken care, in giving such an advice under special circumstances, to safeguard the principle of freedom. And, finally, an argument is drawn from language. The only point at which it is even plausible is that which touches upon the use of the terms "flesh" and "spirit" in chap. vii. 1. Schmiedel, who has an admirable excursus on the whole question, decides that this, and this only, is certainly un-Pauline. It is certainly unusual in Paul, but I do not think we can say more. The "rigour and vigour" with which Paul's use of these terms is investigated seems to me largely misplaced. They did undoubtedly tend to become technical in his mind, but words so universally and so vaguely used could never become simply technical. If any contemporary of Paul could have written, "Let us cleanse ourselves from all defilement of flesh and spirit," then Paul himself could have written it. Language offers the same latitudes and liberties to everybody, and one could not imagine a subject which tempted less to technicality than the one urged in these verses. Whatever the explanation of their apparently irrelevant insertion here, I can see nothing in them alien to Paul. Puritanism is certainly more akin to the Old Testament than to the New, and that may explain the instinctiveness with which the writer seems to turn to the law and the prophets, and the abundance of his quotations; but though "all things are lawful" to the Christian, Puritanism has a place in the New Testament too. There is no conception of "holiness" into which the idea of "separation" does not enter; and though the balance of elements may vary in the New Testament as compared with the Old, none can be wanting. From this point of view we can best examine the meaning and application of the passage. If a connexion is craved, the best, I think, is that furnished by a combination of Calvin and Meyer. *Quasi recuperata auctoritate*, says Calvin, *liberius jam eos objurgat*: this supplies a link of feeling between vv. 13 and 14. A link of thought is supplied if we consider with Meyer that inattention to the rule of life here laid down was a notable cause of receiving the grace of God in vain (ver. 1).[59] Let us notice (1) the moral demand of the passage; (2) the assumption on which it rests; (3) the Divine promise which inspires its observance.

(1) The moral demand is first put in the negative form: "Be not unequally yoked with unbelievers." The peculiar word ἑτεροζυγοῦντες ("unequally yoked") has a cognate form in Lev. xix. 19, in the law which forbids the breeding of hybrid animals. God has established a good physical order in the world, and it is not to be confounded and disfigured by the mixing of species. It is that law (or perhaps another form of it in Deut. xxii. 10, forbidding an Israelite to plough with an ox and an ass under the same yoke) that is applied in an ethical sense in this passage. There is a wholesome moral order in the world also, and it is not to be confused by the association of its different kinds. The common application of this text to the marriage of Christians and non-Christians is legitimate, but too narrow. The text prohibits every kind of union in which the separate character and interest of the Christian lose anything of their distinctiveness and integrity. This is brought out more strongly in the free quotation from Isa. lii. 11 in ver. 17: "Come out from among them, and be separate, saith the Lord, and touch not anything unclean." These words were originally addressed to the priests who, on the redemption of Israel from Babylon, were to carry the sacred temple vessels back to Jerusalem. But we must remember that, though they are Old Testament words, they are quoted by a New Testament writer, who inevitably puts his own meaning into them. "The unclean thing" which no Christian is to touch is not to be taken in a precise Levitical sense; it covers, and I have no doubt was intended by the writer to cover, all that it suggests to any simple Christian mind now. We are to have no compromising connexion with anything in the world which is alien to God. Let us be as loving and conciliatory as we please, but as long as the world is what it is, the Christian life can only maintain itself in it in an attitude of protest. There always will be things and people to whom the Christian has to say No!

But the moral demand of the passage is put in a more positive form in the last verse: "Let us cleanse ourselves from all defilement of flesh and spirit, perfecting holiness in the fear of God." That is the ideal of the Christian life. There is something to be overcome and put away; there is something to be wrought out and completed; there is a spiritual element or atmosphere—the fear of God—in which alone these tasks can be accomplished. The fear of God is an Old Testament name for true religion, and even under the New Testament it holds its place. The Seraphim still veil their faces while they cry "Holy, holy, holy is the Lord of Hosts," and still we must feel that great awe descend upon our hearts if we would be partakers of His holiness. It is this which withers up sin to the root, and enables us to cleanse ourselves from all defilement of flesh and spirit. St. Paul includes himself in his exhortation here: it is one duty, one ideal, which is set before all. The prompt decisive side of it is represented in καθαρίσωμεν ("let us cleanse": observe the aorist); its patient laborious side in ἐπιτελοῦντες ἁγιωσύνην ("carrying holiness to completion)." Almost everybody in a Christian Church makes a beginning with this task: we cleanse ourselves from obvious and superficial defilements; but how few carry the work on into the spirit, how few carry it on ceaselessly towards perfection. As year after year rolls by, as the various experiences of his come to us with their lessons and their discipline from God, as we see the lives of others, here sinking ever deeper and deeper into the corruptions of the world, there rising daily nearer and nearer to the perfect holiness which is their goal, does not this demand assert its power over us? Is it not a great thing, a worthy thing, that we should set ourselves to purge away from our whole nature, outward and inward, whatever cannot abide the holy eye of God; and that we should regard Christian holiness, not as a subject for casual thoughts once a week, but as the task to be taken up anew, with unwearying diligence, every day we live? Let us be in earnest with this, for surely God is in earnest.

(2) Observe now the assumption on which the demand not to be unequally yoked with unbelievers is based. It is that there are *two* ethical or spiritual interests in the world, and that these are fundamentally inconsistent with each other. This implies that in choosing the one, the other has to be rejected. But it implies more: it implies that at bottom there are only two kinds of people in the world—those who identify themselves with the one of these interests, and those who identify themselves with the other.

Now, as long as this is kept in an abstract form people do not quarrel with it. They have no objection to admit that good and evil are the only spiritual forces in the world, and that they are mutually exclusive. But many will not admit that there are only two kinds of persons in the world, answering to these two forces. They would rather say there is only *one* kind of persons, in whom these forces are with infinite varieties and modifications combined. This seems more tolerant, more humane, more capable of explaining the amazing mixtures and inconsistencies we see in human lives. But it is not more true. It is a more penetrating insight which judges that every man—despite his range of neutrality—would in the last resort choose his side; would, in short, in a crisis of the proper kind, prove finally that he was not good *and* bad, but good *or* bad. We cannot pretend to judge others, but sometimes men judge themselves, and always God can judge. And there is an instinct in those who are perfecting holiness in the fear of God which tells them, without in the least making them Pharisaical, not only what things, but what persons—not only what ideas and practices, but what individual characters—are not to be made friends of. It is no pride, or scorn, or censoriousness, which speaks thus, but the voice of all Christian experience. It is recognised at once where the young are concerned: people are careful of the friends their children make, and a schoolmaster will dismiss inexorably, not only a bad habit, but a bad boy, from the school. It ought to be recognised just as easily in maturity as in childhood: there are men and women, as well as boys and girls, who distinctly represent evil, and whose society is to be declined. To protest against them, to repel them, to resent their life and conduct as morally offensive, is a Christian duty; it is the first step towards evangelising them.

It is worth noticing in the passage before us how the Apostle, starting from abstract ideas, descends, as he becomes more urgent, into personal relations. What fellowship have righteousness and lawlessness? None. What communion has light with darkness? None. What concord has Christ with Belial? Here the persons come in who are the heads, or representatives, of the opposing moral interests, and it is only now that we feel the completeness of the antagonism. The interest of holiness is gathered up in Christ; the interest of evil in the great adversary; and they have nothing in common. And so with the believer and the unbeliever. Of course there is ground on which they can meet: the same sun shines on them, the same soil supports them, they breathe the same air. But in all that is indicated by those two names—believer and unbeliever—they stand quite apart; and the distinction thus indicated reaches deeper than any bond of union. It is not denied that the unbeliever may have much that is admirable about him; but for the believer the one supremely important thing in the world is that which the unbeliever denies, and therefore the more he is in earnest the less can he afford the unbeliever's friendship. We need all the help we can get to fight the good fight of faith, and to perfect holiness in the fear of God; and a friend whose silence numbs faith, or whose words trouble it, is a friend no earnest Christian dare keep. Words like these would not seem so hard if the common faith of Christians were felt to be a real bond of union among them, and if the recoil from the unbelieving world were seen to be the action of the whole Christian society, the instinct of self-preservation in the new Christian life. But, at whatever risk of seeming harsh, it must be repeated that there has never been a state of affairs in the world in which the commandment had no meaning, "Come out from among them, and be ye separate"; nor an obedience to this commandment which did not involve separation from persons as well as from principles.

(3) But what bulks most largely in the passage is the series of divine promises which are to inspire and sustain obedience. The separations which an earnest Christian life requires are not without their compensation; to leave the world is to be welcomed by God. It is probable that the pernicious association which the writer had immediately in view was association with the heathen in their worship, or at least in their sacrificial feasts. At all events it is the inconsistency of this with the worship of the true God that forms the climax of his expostulation—What agreement hath a temple of God with idols? and it is to this, again, that the encouraging promises are attached. "*We*," says the Apostle, "are a temple of the living God." This carries with it all that he has claimed: for a temple means a house in which God dwells, and God can only dwell in a holy place. Pagans and Jews alike recognised the sanctity of their temples: nothing was guarded more jealously; nothing, if violated, was more promptly and terribly avenged. Paul had seen the day when he gave his vote to shed the blood of a man who had spoken disrespectfully of the Temple at Jerusalem, and the day was coming when he himself was to run the risk of his life on the mere suspicion that he had taken a pagan into the holy place. He expects Christians to be as much in earnest as Jews to keep the sanctity of God's house inviolate; and now, he says, that house are we: it is ourselves we have to keep unspotted from the world.

We are God's temple in accordance with the central promise of the old covenant: as God said, "I will dwell in them and walk in them, and I will be their God, and they shall be My people." The original of this is Lev. xxvi. 11, 12. The Apostle, as has been observed already, takes the Old Testament words in a New Testament sense: as they stand here in Second Corinthians they mean something much more intimate and profound than in their old place in Leviticus. But even there, he tells us, they are a promise to us. What God speaks, He speaks to His people, and speaks once for all. And if the divine presence in the camp of Israel—a presence represented by the Ark and its tent—was to consecrate that nation to Jehovah, and inspire them with zeal to keep the camp clean, that nothing might offend the eyes of His glory, how much more ought those whom God has visited in His Son, those in whom He dwells through His Spirit, to cleanse themselves from every defilement, and make their souls fit for His habitation? After repeating the charge to come out and be separate, the writer heaps up new promises, in which the letter and the spirit of various Old Testament passages are freely combined.[60] The principal one seems to be 2 Sam. vii., which contains the promises originally made to Solomon. At ver. 14 of that chapter we have the idea of the paternal and filial relation, and at ver. 8 the speaker is described in the LXX., as here, as the Lord Almighty. But passages like Jer. xxxi. 1, 9, also doubtless floated through the writer's mind, and it is the substance, not the form, which is the main thing. The very freedom with which they are reproduced shows us how thoroughly the writer is at home, and how confident he is that he is making the right and natural application of these ancient promises.

Separate yourselves, for you are God's temple: separate yourselves, and you will be sons and daughters of the Lord Almighty, and He will be your Father. *Hæc una ratio instar mille esse debet.* The friendship of the world, as James reminds us, is enmity with God; it is the consoling side of the same truth that separation from the world means friendship with God. It does not mean solitude, but a more blessed society; not renunciation of love, but admission to the only love which satisfies the soul, because that for which the soul was made. The Puritanism of the New Testament is no harsh, repellent thing, which eradicates the affections, and makes life bleak and barren; it is the condition under which the heart is opened to the love of God, and filled with all comfort and joy in obedience. With Him on our side—with the promise of His indwelling Spirit to sanctify us, of His fatherly kindness to enrich and protect us—shall we not obey the exhortation to come out and be separate, to cleanse ourselves from all that defiles, to perfect holiness in His fear?

XIX
REPENTANCE UNTO LIFE

"Open your hearts to us: we wronged no man, we corrupted no man, we took advantage of no man. I say it not to condemn *you*: for I have said before, that ye are in our hearts to die together and live together. Great is my boldness of speech toward you, great is my glorying on your behalf: I am filled with comfort, I overflow with joy in an our affliction.

"For even when we were come into Macedonia, our flesh had no relief, but *we were* afflicted on every side; without *were* fightings, within *were* fears. Nevertheless He that comforteth the lowly, *even* God, comforted us by the coming of Titus; and not by his coming only, but also by the comfort wherewith he was comforted in you, while he told us your longing, your mourning, your zeal for me; so that I rejoiced yet more. For though I made you sorry with my epistle, I do not regret it, though I did regret; for I see that that epistle made you sorry, though but for a season. Now I rejoice, not that ye were made sorry, but that ye were made sorry unto repentance: for ye were made sorry after a godly sort, that ye might suffer loss by us in nothing. For godly sorrow worketh repentance unto salvation, *a repentance* which bringeth no regret: but the sorrow of the world worketh death. For behold, this selfsame thing, that ye were made sorry after a godly sort, what earnest care it wrought in you, yea, what clearing of yourselves, yea, what indignation, yea, what fear, yea, what longing, yea, what zeal, yea, what avenging! In everything ye approved yourselves to be pure in the matter. So although I wrote unto you, *I wrote* not for his cause that did the wrong, nor for his cause that suffered the wrong, but that your earnest care for us might be made manifest unto you in the sight of God. Therefore we have been comforted: and in our comfort we joyed the more exceedingly for the joy of Titus, because his spirit hath been refreshed by you all. For if in anything I have gloried to him on your behalf, I was not put to shame; but as we spake all things to you in truth, so our glorying also, which I made before Titus, was found to be truth. And his inward affection is more abundantly toward you, whilst he remembereth the obedience of you all, how with fear and trembling ye received him. I rejoice that in everything I am of good courage concerning you."—2 Cor. vii. 2-16 (R.V.).

In this fine passage St. Paul completes, as far as it lay upon his side to do so, his reconciliation with the Corinthians. It concludes the first great division of his Second Epistle, and henceforth we hear no more of the sinner censured so severely in the First (chap. v.),[61] or of the troubles which arose in the Church over the disciplinary treatment of his sin. The end of a quarrel between friends is like the passing away of a storm; the elements are meant to be at peace with each other, and nature never looks so lovely as in the clear shining after rain. The effusion of feeling in this passage, so affectionate and unreserved; the sense that the storm-clouds have no more than left the sky, yet that fair weather has begun, make it conspicuously beautiful even in the writings of St. Paul.

He begins by resuming the appeal interrupted at chap. vi. 13. He has charged the Corinthians with being straitened in their own affections: distrust and calumny have narrowed their souls, nay, shut them against him altogether. "Receive us," he exclaims here—*i.e.*, open your hearts to us. "You have no cause to be reserved: we wronged no man, ruined no man, took advantage of no man." Such charges had doubtless been made against him. The point of the last is clear from chap. xii. 16-18: he had been accused of making money out of his apostolic work among them. The other words are less precise, especially the one rendered "corrupted" (ἐφθείραμεν), which should perhaps be rather explained, as in 1 Cor. iii. 17, "destroyed." Paul has not wronged or ruined any one in Corinth. Of course, his Gospel made serious demands upon people: it insisted on readiness to make sacrifices, and on actual sacrifice besides; it proceeded with extreme severity against sinners like the incestuous man; it entailed obligations, as we shall presently hear, to help the poor even of distant lands; and then, as still, such claims might easily be resented as ruinous or unjust. St. Paul simply denies the charge. He does not retort it; it is not his object to condemn those whom he loves so utterly. He has told them already that they are in his heart to die together and to live together (vi. 11); and when this is so, there is no place for recrimination or bandying of reproaches. He is full of confidence in them;[62] he can freely make his boast of them. He has had affliction enough, but over it all he has been filled with consolation; even as he writes, his joy overflows (observe the present: ὑπερπερισσεύομαι).

That word—"ye are in our hearts to die together and to live together"—is the key to all that follows. It has suffered much at the hands of grammarians, for whom it has undeniable perplexities; but vehement emotion may be permitted to be in some degree inarticulate, and we can always feel, even if we cannot demonstrate, what it means. "Your image in my heart accompanies me in death and life,"[63] is as nearly as possible what the Apostle says; and if the order of the words is unusual—for "life" would naturally stand first—that may be due to the fact, so largely represented in chap. iv., that his life was a series of deadly perils, and of ever-renewed deliverances from them, a daily dying and a daily resurrection, through all the vicissitudes of which the Corinthians never lost their place in his heart. More artificial interpretations only obscure the intensity of that love which united the Apostle to his converts. It is levelled here, unconsciously no doubt, but all the more impressively, with the love which God in Christ Jesus our Lord bears to His redeemed. "I am persuaded," St. Paul writes to the Romans, "that neither death nor life can separate us from that." "You may be assured," he writes here to the Corinthians, "that neither death nor life can separate you from my love." The reference of death and life is of course different, but the strength of conviction and of emotion is the same in both cases. St. Paul's heart is pledged irrevocably and irreversibly to the Church. In the deep feeling that he is theirs, he has an assurance that they also are his. The love with which he loves them is bound to prevail; nay, it has prevailed, and he can hardly find words to express his joy. *En qualiter affectos esse omnes Pastores conveniat* (Calvin).

The next three verses carry us back to chap. ii. 12 ff., and resume the story which was interrupted there at ver. 14. The sudden thanksgiving of that passage—so eager and impetuous that it left the writer no time to tell what he was thankful for—is explained here. Titus, whom he had expected to see in Troas, arrived at length, probably at Philippi, and brought with him the most cheering news. Paul was sadly in need of it. His flesh had no rest: the use of the perfect (ἔσχηκεν) almost conveys the feeling that he began to write whenever he got the news, so that up to this moment the strain had continued. The fights without were probably assaults upon himself, or the Churches, of the nature of persecution; the fears within, his anxieties about the state of morals, or of Gospel truth, in the Christian communities. Outworn and depressed, burdened both in body and mind (cf. the expressions in ii. 13 and vii. 5), he was suddenly lifted on high by the arrival and the news of Titus. Here again, as in ii. 14, he ascribes all to God. It was He whose very nature it is to comfort the lowly who so graciously comforted him. Titus apparently had gone himself with a sad and apprehensive heart to Corinth; he had been away longer than he had anticipated, and in the interval St.

Paul's anxiety had risen to anguish; but in Corinth his reception had been unexpectedly favourable, and when he returned he was able to console his master with a consolation which had already gladdened his own heart. Paul was not only comforted, his sorrow was turned into joy, as he listened to Titus telling of the longing of the Corinthians to see him, of their mourning over the pain they had given him by their tolerance for such irregularities as that of the incestuous man or the unknown insulter of the Apostle, and of their eagerness to satisfy him and maintain his authority. The word "your" (ὑμῶν) in ver. 7 has a certain emphasis which suggests a contrast. Before Titus went to Corinth, it was Paul who had been anxious to see *them*, who had mourned over their immoral laxity, who had been passionately interested in vindicating the character of the Church he had founded; now it is *they* who are full of longing to see *him*, of grief, and of moral earnestness; and it is this which explains his joy. The conflict between the powers of good in one great and passionate soul, and the powers of evil in a lax and fickle community, has ended in favour of the good; Paul's vehemence has prevailed against Corinthian indifference, and made it vehement also in all good affections, and he rejoices now in the joy of his Lord.

Then comes the most delicate part of this reconciliation (vv. 8-12). It is a good rule in making up disputes to let bygones be bygones, as far as possible; there may be a little spark hidden here and there under what seem dead ashes, and there is no gain in raking up the ashes, and giving the spark a chance to blaze again. But this is a good rule only because we are bad men, and because reconciliation is seldom allowed to have its perfect work. We feel, and say, after we have quarrelled with a person and been reconciled, that it can never be the same again. But this ought not to be so; and if we were perfect in love, or ardent in love at all, it would not be so. If we were in one another's hearts, to die together and to live together, we should retrace the past together in the very act of being reconciled; and all its misunderstandings and bitterness and badness, instead of lying hidden in us as matter of recrimination for some other day when we are tempted, would add to the sincerity, the tenderness, and the spirituality of our love. The Apostle sets us an example here, of the rarest and most difficult virtue, when he goes back upon the story of his relations with the Corinthians, and makes the bitter stock yield sweet and wholesome fruit.[64]

The whole result is in his mind when he writes, "Although I made you sorry with the letter, I do not regret it." The letter is, on the simplest hypothesis, the First Epistle; and though no one would willingly speak to his friends as Paul in some parts of that Epistle speaks to the Corinthians, he cannot pretend that he wishes it unwritten. "Although I did regret it," he goes on, "now I rejoice." He regretted it, we must understand, before

Titus came back from Corinth. In that melancholy interval, all he saw was that the letter made them sorry; it was bound to do so, even if it should only be temporarily; but his heart smote him for making them sorry at all. It vexed him to vex them. No doubt this is the plain truth he is telling them, and it is hard to see why it should have been regarded as inconsistent with his apostolic inspiration. He did not cease to have a living soul because he was inspired; and if in his despondency it crossed his mind to say, "That letter will only grieve them," he must have said in the same instant, "I wish I had never written it." But both impulses were momentary only; he has heard now the whole effect of his letter, and rejoices that he wrote it. Not, of course, that they were made sorry—no one could rejoice for that—but that they were made sorry to repentance. "For ye were made sorry according to God, that in nothing ye might suffer loss on our part. For sorrow according to God worketh repentance unto salvation, a repentance which bringeth no regret. But the sorrow of the world worketh death."

Most people define repentance as a kind of sorrow, but this is not exactly St. Paul's view here. There is a kind of sorrow, he intimates, which issues in repentance, but repentance itself is not so much an emotional as a spiritual change. The sorrow which ends in it is a blessed experience; the sorrow which does not end in it is the most tragical waste of which human nature is capable. The Corinthians, we are told, were made sorry, or grieved, according to God. Their sorrow had respect to Him: when the Apostle's letter pricked their hearts, they became conscious of that which they had forgotten—God's relation to them, and His judgment on their conduct. It is this element which makes any sorrow "godly," and without this, sorrow does not look towards repentance at all. All sins sooner or later bring the sense of loss with them; but the sense of loss is not repentance. It is not repentance when we discover that our sin has found us out, and has put the things we most coveted beyond our reach. It is not repentance when the man who has sown his wild oats is compelled in bitterness of soul to reap what he has sown. It is not a sorrow according to God when our sin is summed up for us in the pain it inflicts upon ourselves—in our own loss, our own defeat, our own humiliation, our own exposure, our own unavailing regret. These are not healing, but embittering. The sorrow according to God is that in which the sinner is conscious of his sin in relation to the Holy One, and feels that its inmost soul of pain and guilt is this, that he has fallen away from the grace and friendship of God. He has wounded a love to which he is dearer than he is to himself: to know this is really to grieve, and that not with a self-consuming, but with a healing, hopeful sorrow. It was such a sorrow to which Paul's letter gave rise at Corinth: it is such a sorrow which issues in repentance, that complete change of spiritual attitude which ends in salvation, and need never be regretted. Anything else—the sorrow, *e.g.*, which is bounded by the selfish interests of the sinner, and is not due to his sinful act, but only to its painful consequences—is the sorrow of the world. It is such as men feel in that realm of life in which no account is taken of God; it is such as weakens and breaks the spirit, or embitters and hardens it, turning it now to defiance and now to despair, but never to God, and penitent hope in Him. It is in this way that it works death. If death is to be defined at all, it must be by contrast with salvation: the grief which has not God as its rule can only exhaust the soul, wither up its faculties, blight its hopes, extinguish and deaden all.

St. Paul can point to the experience of the Corinthians themselves as furnishing a demonstration of these truths. "Consider your own godly sorrow," he seems to say, "and what blessed fruits it bore. What earnest care it wrought in you! how eager became your interest in a situation to which you had once been sinfully indifferent!" But "earnest care" is not all. On the contrary (ἀλλὰ), Paul expands it into a whole series of acts or dispositions, all of which are inspired by that sorrow according to God. When they thought of the infamy which sin had brought upon the Church, they were eager to clear themselves of complicity in it (ἀπολογίαν), and angry with themselves that they had ever allowed such a thing to be (ἀγανάκτησιν); when they thought of the Apostle, they feared lest he should come to them with a rod (φόβον), and yet their hearts went out in longing desires to see him (ἐπιπόθησιν); when they thought of the man whose sin was at the bottom of all this trouble, they were full of moral earnestness, which made lax dealing with him impossible (ζῆλον), and compelled them to punish his offence (ἐκδίκησιν). In every way they made it evident that, in spite of early appearances, they were really pure in the matter. They were not, after all, making themselves partakers, by condoning it, of the bad man's offence.

A popular criticism disparages repentance, and especially the sorrow which leads to repentance, as a mere waste of moral force. We have nothing to throw away, the severely practical moralist tells us, in sighs and tears and feelings: let us be up and doing, to rectify the wrongs for which we are responsible; that is the only repentance which is worth the name. This passage, and the experience which it depicts, are the answer to such precipitate criticism. The descent into our own hearts, the painful self-scrutiny and self-condemnation, the sorrowing according to God, are not waste of moral force. Rather are they the only possible way to accumulate moral force; they apply to the soul the pressure under which it manifests those potent virtues which St. Paul here ascribes to the Corinthians. All sorrow, indeed, as he is careful to tell us, is not repentance; but he who has no sorrow for his sin has not the force in him to produce earnest care, fear, longing, zeal, avenging. The fruit, of course, is that for which the tree is cultivated; but who would magnify the fruit by disparaging the sap? That is what they do who decry "godly sorrow" to exalt practical amendment.

With this reference to the effect of his letter upon them, the Apostle virtually completes his reconciliation to the Corinthians. He chooses to consider the effect of his letter as the purpose for which it was written, and this enables him to dismiss what had been a very painful subject with a turn as felicitous as it is affectionate. "So then, though I did write to you, it was not for his sake who did the wrong [the sinner of 1 Cor. v.], nor for his who had it done to him [his father][65]; but that you yourselves might become conscious of your earnest care of our interests in the sight of God." Awkward as some of the situations had been, all that remained, so far as the Apostle and the Corinthians were concerned, was this: they knew better than before how deeply they were attached to him, and how much they would do for his sake. He chooses, as I have said, to regard this last result of his writing as the purpose for which he wrote; and when he ends the twelfth verse with the words, "For this cause, we have been comforted,"[66] it is as if he said, "I have got what I wanted now, and am content."

But content is far too weak a word. Paul had heard all this good news from Titus, and the comfort which it gave him was exalted into abounding joy when he saw how the visit to Corinth had gladdened and refreshed the spirit of his friend. Evidently Titus had accepted Paul's commission with misgivings: possibly Timothy, who had been earlier enlisted for the same service (1 Cor. xvi. 10), had found his courage fail him, and withdrawn. At all events, Paul had spoken encouragingly to Titus of the Corinthians before he started; as he puts it in ver. 14, he had boasted somewhat to him on their account; and he is delighted that their reception of Titus has shown that his confidence was justified. He cannot refrain here from a passing allusion to the charges of prevarication discussed in the first chapter; he not only tells the truth *about* them (as Titus has seen), but he has always told the truth *to* them. These verses present the character of Paul in an admirable light: not only his sympathy with Titus, but his attitude to the Corinthians, is beautifully Christian. What in most cases of estrangement makes reconciliation hard is that the estranged have allowed themselves to speak of each other to outsiders in a way that cannot be forgotten or got over. But even when the tension between Paul and the Corinthians was at its height, he boasted of them to Titus. His love to them was so real that nothing could blind him to their good qualities. He could say severe things to them, but he would never disparage or malign them to other people; and if we wish friendships to last, and to stand the strains to which all human ties are occasionally subject, we must never forget this rule. "Boast somewhat," even of the man who has wronged you, if you possibly can. If you have ever loved him, you certainly can, and it makes reconciliation easy.

The last results of the painful friction between Paul and the Corinthians were peculiarly happy. The Apostle's confidence in them was completely restored, and they had completely won the heart of Titus. "His affections are more abundantly toward you, as he remembers the obedience of you all, how with fear and trembling ye received him." "Fear and trembling" is an expression which St. Paul uses elsewhere, and which is liable to be misunderstood. It does not suggest panic, but an anxious scrupulous desire not to be wanting to one's duty, or to do less than one ought to do. "Work out your salvation with fear and trembling, for it is God that worketh in you," does not mean "Do it in a constant state of agitation or alarm," but "Work on with this resource behind you, in the same spirit with which a young man of character would work, who was starting in business on capital advanced by a friend." He would proceed, or ought to proceed, with fear and trembling, not of the sort which paralyse intelligence and energy, but of the sort which peremptorily preclude slackness or failure in duty. This is the meaning here also. The Corinthians were not frightened for Paul's deputy, but they welcomed him with an anxious conscientious desire to do the very utmost that duty and love could require. This, says Calvin, is the true way to receive ministers of Christ: and it is this only which will gladden a true minister's heart. Sometimes, with the most innocent intention, the whole situation is changed, and the minister, though received with the utmost courtesy and kindness, is not received with fear and trembling at all. Partly through his own fault, and partly through the fault of others, he ceases to be the representative of anything that inspires reverence, or excites to conscientious earnestness of conduct. If, under these circumstances, he continues to be kindly treated, he is apt to end in being, not the pastor, but the pet lamb of his flock. In apostolic times there was no danger of this, but modern ministers and modern congregations have sometimes thrown away all the possibilities of good in their mutual relations by disregarding it. The affection which they ought to have to each other is Christian, not merely natural; controlled by spiritual ideas and purposes, and not a matter of ordinary good feeling; and where this is forgotten, all is lost.

XX
THE GRACE OF LIBERALITY

"Moreover, brethren, we make known to you the grace of God which hath been given in the Churches of Macedonia; how that in much proof of affliction the abundance of their joy and their deep poverty abounded unto the riches of their liberality. For according to their power, I bear witness, yea and beyond their power, *they gave* of their own accord, beseeching us with much intreaty in regard of this grace and the fellowship in the ministering to the saints: and *this*, not as we had hoped, but first they gave their own selves to the Lord, and to us by the will of God. Insomuch that we exhorted Titus, that as he had made a beginning before, so he would also complete in you this grace also. But as ye abound in everything, *in* faith, and utterance, and knowledge, and *in* all earnestness, and *in* your love to us, *see* that ye abound in this grace also. I speak not by the way of commandment, but as proving through the earnestness of others the sincerity also of your love. For ye know the grace of our Lord Jesus Christ, that, though He was rich, yet for your sakes He became poor, that ye through His poverty might become rich. And herein I give *my* judgment: for this is expedient for you, who were the first to make a beginning a year ago, not only to do, but also to will. But now complete the doing also; that as *there was* the readiness to will, so *there may be* the completion also out of your ability. For if the readiness is there, *it is* acceptable according as *a man* hath, not according as *he* hath not. For *I say* not *this*, that others may be eased, *and* ye distressed: but by equality; your abundance *being a supply* at this present time for their want, that their abundance also may become *a supply* for your want; that there may be equality: as it is written, He that *gathered* much had nothing over; and he that *gathered* little had no lack."—2 Cor. viii. 1-15 (R.V.).

With the eighth chapter begins the second of the three great divisions of this Epistle. It is concerned exclusively with the collection which the Apostle was raising in all the Gentile Christian communities for the poor of the Mother Church at Jerusalem. This collection had great importance in his eyes, for various reasons: it was the fulfilment of his undertaking, to the original Apostles, to remember the poor (Gal. ii. 10); and it was a testimony to the saints in Palestine of the love of the Gentile brethren in Christ. The fact that Paul interested himself so much in this collection, destined as it was for Jerusalem, proves that he distinguished broadly between the primitive Church and its authorities on the one hand, and the Jewish emissaries whom he treats so unsparingly in chaps. x. and xi. on the other.

Money is usually a delicate topic to handle in the Church, and we may count ourselves happy in having two chapters from the pen of St. Paul in which he treats at large of a collection. We see the mind of Christ applied in them to a subject which is always with us, and sometimes embarrassing; and if there are traces here and there that embarrassment was felt even by the Apostle, they only show more clearly the wonderful wealth of thought and feeling which he could bring to bear on an ungrateful theme. Consider only the variety of lights in which he puts it, and all of them ideal. "Money," as such, has no character, and so he never mentions it. But he calls the thing which he wants a grace (χάρις), a service (διακονία), a communion in service (κοινωνία), a munificence (ἁδρότης), a blessing (εὐλογία), a manifestation of love. The whole resources of Christian imagination are spent in transfiguring, and lifting into a spiritual atmosphere, a subject on which even Christian men are apt to be materialistic. We do not need to be hypocritical when we speak about money in the Church; but both the charity and the business of the Church must be transacted as Christian, and not as secular, affairs.

Paul introduces the new topic with his usual felicity. He has got through some rough water in the first seven chapters, but ends with expressions of joy and satisfaction. When he goes on in the eighth chapter, it is in the same cheerful key. It is as though he said to the Corinthians: "You have made me very happy, and now I must tell you what a happy experience I have had in Macedonia. The grace of God has been poured out on the Churches, and they have given with incredible liberality to the collection for the Jewish poor. It so moved me that I begged Titus, who had already made some arrangements in connexion with this matter among you, to return and complete the work."

Speaking broadly, the Apostle invites the Corinthians to look at the subject through three media: (1) the example of the Macedonians; (2) the example of the Lord; and (3) the laws by which God estimates liberality.

(1) The liberality of the Macedonians is described as "the grace of God given in the Churches." This is the aspect of it which conditions every other; it is not the native growth of the soul, but a divine gift for which God is to be thanked. Praise Him when hearts are opened, and generosity shown; for it is His work. In Macedonia this grace was set off by the circumstances of the people. Their Christian character was put to the severe proof of a great affliction (see 1 Thess. ii. 14 f.); they were themselves in deep poverty; but their joy abounded nevertheless (1 Thess. i. 6), and joy and poverty together poured out a rich stream of liberality.[67] This may sound paradoxical, but paradox is normal here. Strange to say, it is not those to whom the Gospel comes easily, and on whom it imposes little, who are most generous in its cause. On the contrary, it is those who have suffered for it, those who have lost by it, who are as a rule most open-handed. Comfort makes men selfish, even though they are Christian; but if they are Christian, affliction, even to the spoiling of their goods, teaches them generosity. The first generation of Methodists in England—the men who in 1843 fought the good fight of the faith in Scotland—illustrate this law; in much proof of affliction, it might be said of them also, the abundance of their joy, and their deep poverty, abounded unto the riches of their liberality. Paul was almost embarrassed with the liberality of the Macedonians. When he looked at their poverty, he did not hope for much (ver. 5). He would not have felt justified in urging people who were themselves in such distress to do much for the relief of others. But they did not need urging: it was they who urged him. The Apostle's sentence breaks down as he tries to convey an adequate impression of their eagerness (ver. 4), and he has to leave off and begin again (ver. 5). To their power, he bears witness, yes and beyond their power, they gave of their own accord. They importuned him to bestow on them also the favour of sharing in this service to the saints. And when their request was granted, it was no paltry contribution that they made; they gave *themselves* to the Lord, to begin with, and to the Apostle, as His agent in the transaction, by the will of God. The last words resume, in effect, those with which St. Paul introduced this topic: it was God's doing, the working of His will on their wills, that the Macedonians behaved as they did. I cannot think the English version is right in the rendering: "And this, not as we had hoped, but first they gave their own selves to the Lord." This inevitably suggests that afterwards they gave something else—viz., their subscriptions. But this is a false contrast, and gives the word "first" (πρῶτον) a false emphasis, which it has not in the original. What St. Paul says is virtually this: "We expected little from people so poor, but by God's will they literally put *themselves* at the service of the Lord, in the first instance, and of us as His administrators. They said to us, to our amazement and joy, 'We are Christ's, and yours after Him, to command in this matter.'" This is one of the finest

and most inspiring experiences that a Christian minister can have, and, God be thanked, it is none of the rarest. Many a man besides Paul has been startled and ashamed by the liberality of those from whom he would not have ventured to beg. Many a man has been importuned to take what he could not have dared to ask. It is a mistake to refuse such generosity, to decline it as too much; it gladdens God, and revives the heart of man. It is a mistake to deprive the poorest of the opportunity of offering this sacrifice of praise; it is the poorest in whom it has most munificence, and to whom it brings the deepest joy. Rather ought we to open our hearts to the impression of it, as to the working of God's grace, and rouse our own selfishness to do something not less worthy of Christ's love.

This was the application which St. Paul made of the generosity of the Macedonians. Under the impression of it he exhorted Titus, who on a previous occasion[68] had made some preliminary arrangements about the matter in Corinth, to return thither and complete the work. He had other things also to complete, but "this grace" was to be specially included (καὶ τὴν χάριν ταύτην). Perhaps one may see a gentle irony in the tone of ver. 7. "Enough of argument," the Apostle says:[69] "let Christians distinguished as you are in every respect—in faith and eloquence and knowledge and all sorts of zeal, and in the love that comes from you and abides in us—see that they are distinguished in this grace also." It is a real character that is suggested here by way of contrast, but not exactly a lovely one: the man who abounds in spiritual interests, who is fervent, prayerful, affectionate, able to speak in the Church, but unable to part with money.

(2) This brings the Apostle to his second point, the example of the Lord. "I do not speak by way of commandment," he says, "in urging you to be liberal; I am only taking occasion, through the earnestness of others, to put the sincerity of your love to the proof. If you truly love the brethren you will not grudge to help them in their distress. The Macedonians, of course, are no law for you; and though it was from them I started, I do not need to urge their example; 'for ye know the grace of our Lord Jesus Christ, that, though He was rich, yet for your sakes He became poor, that ye through His poverty might become rich.'" This is the one pattern that stands for ever before the eyes of Christian men, the fountain of an inspiration as strong and pure to-day as when Paul wrote these words.

Read simply, and by one who has the Christian creed in his mind, the words do not appear ambiguous. Christ was rich, they tell us; He became poor for our sakes, and by His poverty we become rich. If a commentary is needed, it is surely to be sought in the parallel passage Phil. ii. 5 ff. The rich Christ is the pre-existent One, in the form of God, in the glory which He had with the Father before the world was; He became poor when He became man. The poor men are those whose lot Christ came to share, and in consequence of that self-impoverishment of His they become heirs of a kingdom. It is not necessary, indeed it is utterly misleading, to ask curiously *how* Christ became poor, or what kind of experience it was for Him when He exchanged heaven for earth, and the form of God for the form of a servant. As Mr. Gore has well said, it is not the metaphysics of the Incarnation that St. Paul is concerned with, either here or in Philippians, but its ethics. We may never have a scientific key to it, but we have a moral key. If we do not comprehend its method, at least we comprehend its motive, and it is in its motive that the inspiration of it lies. We know *the grace* of our Lord Jesus Christ; and it comes home to our hearts when the Apostle says, "Let that *mind*—that moral temper—be in you which was also in Him." Ordinary charity is but the crumbs from the rich man's table; but if we catch Christ's spirit, it will carry us far beyond that. He was rich, and gave up all for our sakes; it is no less than poverty on His part which enriches us.

The older theologians, especially of the Lutheran Church, read this great text differently, and their opinion is not yet quite extinct. They referred ἐπτώχευσεν, not to Christ's entrance on the incarnate state, but to His existence in it;[70] they puzzled themselves to conceive of Him as rich and poor at the same time; and they quite took the point from St. Paul's exhortation by making ἐπτώχευσεν πλούσιος ὤν describe a combination, instead of an interchange, of states. It is a counsel of despair when a recent commentator (Heinrici), sympathising with this view, but yielding to the comparison of Phil. ii. 5 ff., tries to unite the two interpretations, and to make ἐπτώχευσεν cover both the coming to earth from heaven and the life in poverty on earth. No word can mean two different things at the same time: and in this daring attempt we may fairly see a final surrender of the orthodox Lutheran interpretation.

Some strange criticisms have been passed on this appeal to the Incarnation as a motive to liberality. It shows, Schmiedel says, Paul's contempt for the knowledge of Christ after the flesh, when the Incarnation is all he can adduce as a pattern for such a simply human thing as a charitable gift. The same contempt, then, we must presume, is shown in Philippians, when the same great pattern is held up to inspire Christians with lowly thoughts of themselves, and with consideration for others. It is shown, perhaps, again at the close of that magnificent chapter—the fifteenth in First Corinthians— where all the glory to be revealed when Christ transfigures His people is made a reason for the sober virtues of stedfastness and patience. The truth is rather that Paul knew from experience that the supreme motives are needed on the most ordinary occasions. He never appeals to incidents, not because he does not know them, or because he despises them, but because it is far more potent and effectual to appeal to Christ. His mind gravitates to the Incarnation, or the Cross, or the Heavenly Throne, because the power and virtue of the Redeemer are concentrated there. The spirit that wrought redemption, and that changes men into the image of the Lord—the spirit without which *no* Christian disposition, not even the most "simply human," can be produced—is felt there, if one may say so, in gathered intensity; and it is not the want of a concrete vision of Jesus such as Peter and John had, nor a scholastic insensibility to such living and love-compelling details as our first three Gospels furnish, that makes Paul have recourse thither; it is the instinct of the evangelist and pastor who knows that the hope of souls is to live in the presence of the very highest things. Of course Paul believed in the pre-existence and in the Incarnation. The writer quoted above does not, and naturally the appeal of the text is artificial and unimpressive to him. But may we not ask, in view of the simplicity, the unaffectedness, and the urgency with which St. Paul uses this appeal both here and in Philippians, whether *his* faith in the pre-existence can have had no more than the precarious speculative foundation which is given to it by so many who reconstruct his theology? "Christ, the perfect reconciler, must be the perfect revealer of God; God's purpose—that for which He made all things—must be seen in Him; but that for which God made all things must have existed (in the mind of God) before all things; therefore Christ is (ideally) from everlasting." This is the substance of many explanations of how St. Paul came by his Christology; but if this had been all, *could* St. Paul by any possibility have appealed thus naïvely to the Incarnation *as a fact*, and a fact which was one of the mainsprings of Christian morality?

(3) The Apostle pauses for a moment to urge his plea in the interest of the Corinthians themselves. He is not commanding, but giving his judgment: "this," he says, "is profitable for you, who began[71] a year ago, not only to do, but also to will.[72] But now complete the doing also." Every one knows this situation, and its evils. A good work which has been set on foot with interest and spontaneity enough, but which has begun to drag, and is in danger of coming to nothing, is very demoralising. It enfeebles the conscience, and spoils the temper. It develops irresolution and incapacity, and it stands perpetually in the way of anything else that has to be done. Many a bright idea stumbles over it, and can get no further. It is not only worldly wisdom, but divine wisdom, which says: "Whatsoever thy hand findeth to do, do it with thy might." If it is the giving of money, the building of a church, the insuring of a life, complete the doing. To be always thinking about it, and always in an ineffective way busy about it, is not profitable for you.

It is in this connexion that the Apostle lays down the laws of Christian liberality. In these verses (11 to 15) there are three. (*a*) First, there must be readiness, or, as the Authorised Version puts it, a willing mind. What is given must be given freely; it must be a gracious offering, not a tax. This is fundamental. The law of the Old Testament is re-enacted in the New: "Of every man *whose heart maketh him willing* shall ye take the Lord's offering." What we spend in piety and charity is not tribute paid to a tyrant, but the response of gratitude to our Redeemer: and if it has not this character He does not want it. If there be *first* a willing mind, the rest is easy; if not, there is no need to go on. (*b*) The second law is, "according as a man has." *Readiness* is the acceptable thing, not this or that proof of it. If we cannot give much, then a ready mind makes even a little acceptable. Only let us remember this, that readiness always gives all that is in its power. The readiness of the poor widow in the Temple could only give two mites, but two mites were all her living; the readiness of the Macedonians was in the depths of poverty, but they gave *themselves* to the Lord. The widow's mites are an illustrious example of sacrifice, and this word of the Apostle contains a moving appeal for generosity; yet the two together have been profaned times innumerable to cloak the meanest selfishness. (*c*) The third law is reciprocity. Paul does not write that the Jews may be relieved and the Corinthians burdened, but on the principle of equality: at this crisis the superfluity of the Corinthians is to make up what is wanting to the Jews, and at some other the situation will be exactly reversed. Brotherhood cannot be one-sided; it must be mutual, and in the interchange of services equality is the result. This, as the quotation hints, answers to God's design in regard to worldly goods, as that design is indicated in the story of the manna: He that gathered much had no more than his neighbours, and he that gathered little had no less. To be selfish is not an infallible way of getting more than your share; you may cheat your neighbour by that policy, but you will not get the better of God. In all probability men are far more nearly on an equality, in respect of what their worldly possessions yield, than the rich in their pride, or the poor in their envious discontent, would readily believe; but where inequality is patent and painful—a glaring violation of the divine intention here suggested—there is a call for charity to redress the balance. Those who give to the poor are co-operating with God, and the more a community is Christianised, the more will that state be realised in which each has what he needs.

XXI
THE FRUITS OF LIBERALITY

"But thanks be to God, which putteth the same earnest care for you into the heart of Titus. For indeed he accepted our exhortation; but being himself very earnest, he went forth unto you of his own accord. And we have sent together with him the brother whose praise in the Gospel *is spread* through all the Churches; and not only so, but who was also appointed by the Churches to travel with us in *the matter of* this grace, which is ministered by us to the glory of the Lord, and *to show* our readiness: avoiding this, that any man should blame us in *the matter of* this bounty which is ministered by us: for we take thought for things honourable, not only in the sight of the Lord but also in the sight of men. And we have sent with them our brother, whom we have many times proved earnest in many things, but now much more earnest by reason of the great confidence which *he hath* in you. Whether *any inquire* about Titus, *he is* my partner, and *my* fellow-worker to you-ward; or our brethren, *they are* the messengers of the Churches, *they are* the glory of Christ. Show ye therefore unto them in the face of the Churches the proof of your love, and of our glorying on your behalf.

"For as touching the ministering to the saints, it is superfluous for me to write to you: for I know your readiness, of which I glory on your behalf to them of Macedonia, that Achaia hath been prepared for a year past; and your zeal hath stirred up very many of them. But I have sent the brethren, that our glorying on your behalf may not be made void in this respect; that, even as I said, ye may be prepared: lest by any means, if there come with me any of Macedonia, and find you unprepared, we (that we say not, ye) should be put to shame in this confidence. I thought it necessary therefore to intreat the brethren, that they would go before unto you, and make up beforehand your afore-promised bounty, that the same might be ready, as a matter of bounty, and not of extortion.

"But this *I say*, He that soweth sparingly shall reap also sparingly; and he that soweth bountifully shall reap also bountifully. *Let* each man *do* according as he hath purposed in his heart; not grudgingly, or of necessity: for God loveth a cheerful giver. And God is able to make all grace abound unto you; that ye, having always all sufficiency in everything, may abound unto every good work: as it is written,

He hath scattered abroad, he hath given to the poor; His righteousness abideth for ever.

And He that supplieth seed to the sower and bread for food, shall supply and multiply your seed for sowing, and increase the fruits of your righteousness: ye being enriched in everything unto all liberality, which worketh through us thanksgiving to God. For the ministration of this service not only filleth up the measure of the wants of the saints, but aboundeth also through many thanksgivings unto God; seeing that through the proving *of you* by this ministration they glorify God for the obedience of your confession unto the Gospel of Christ, and for the liberality of your contribution unto them and unto all; while they themselves also, with supplication on your behalf, long after you by reason of the exceeding grace of God in you. Thanks be to God for His unspeakable gift." —2 Cor. viii. 16-ix. 15 (R.V.).

This long passage has a good many difficulties of detail, for the grammarian and the textual critic. Where it seems necessary, these will be referred to in the notes; but as the large meaning of the writer is hardly affected by them, they need not interrupt the course of exposition. It falls into three parts, which are clearly marked as such in the Revised Version: (1) Chap. viii. 16-24, commending to the Corinthians the three brethren who were to precede Paul and prepare the collection; (2) Chap. ix. 1-5, appealing to the motives of emulation and shame to reinforce love in the matter; and (3) Chap. ix. 6-15, urging liberality, and enlarging on the blessed fruits it yields. The first of these divisions begins, and the last ends, with an exclamatory ascription of thanks to God.

(1) Chap. viii. 16-24. Of the three men who acted as commissioners in this delicate undertaking, only one, Titus, is known to us by name. He had just returned from Corinth; he knew all the critical points in the situation; and no doubt the Apostle was glad to have such a man at the head of the

little party. He was thankful to God that on the occasion of that previous visit the Corinthians had completely won the heart of Titus, and that his loyal fellow-worker needed no compulsion to return. He was leaving[73] Paul of his own accord, full of earnest care for his Achaian friends. Along with him went a second—the brother whose praise in the Gospel was through all the Churches. It is useless to ask who the brother was. A very early opinion, alluded to by Origen, and represented apparently in the traditional subscription to this Epistle, identified him with Luke. Probably the ground for this identification was the idea that his "praise in the Gospel" referred to Luke's work as an evangelist. But this cannot be: first, because Luke's Gospel cannot have been written so early; and, secondly, because "the Gospel" at this date does not mean a written thing at all. This man's praise in the Gospel must mean the credit he had acquired by his services to the Christian faith; it might be by some bold confession, or by activity as an evangelist, or by notable hospitality to missionaries, or by such helpful ministries as the one he was now engaged in. The real point of interest for us in the expression is the glimpse it gives us of the unity of the Church, and the unimpeded circulation of one life through all its members. Its early divisions, theological and racial, have been sufficiently emphasised; it is well worth while to observe the unity of the spirit. It was this, eventually, which gave the Church its power in the decline of the Empire. It was the only institution which extended over the area of civilisation with a common spirit, common sympathies, and a common standard of praise. It was a compliment to the Corinthians to include in this embassy one whose good name was honoured wherever men met in the name of Jesus. This brother was at the same time a deputy in a special sense. He had been elected by the Churches who were contributing to the collection, that he might accompany the Apostle when it was taken to Jerusalem. This, in itself, is natural enough, and it would not call for comment but for the remark to which the Apostle proceeds—"avoiding this, that any man should blame us in the matter of this bounty which is ministered by us to the glory of the Lord, and *to show our*[74] *readiness:* for we take thought for things honourable, not only in the sight of the Lord, but also in the sight of men."

There was evidently an unpleasant side to this transaction. Paul's interest in the collection, his enemies had plainly said (chap. xii. 17, 18), was not quite disinterested. He was capable of putting his own hand into the bag. What ought a Christian man to do in such a case? We shall see in a later chapter how keenly Paul felt this unworthy imputation, and with what generous passion he resented it; but here he betrays no indignation; he joins with the Churches who are making the collection in so ordering matters as to preclude suspicion. Wherever the money is concerned, his responsibility is to be shared with another. It is a pity that Christ should not be glorified, and the Apostle's zeal to help the poor saints made known, without the accompaniment of these base suspicions and precautionary measures; but in all things human, evil will mingle with good, and the humble course is best, which does not only what God knows to be honourable, but what men must see to be so too. In handling money especially, it is best to err on the safe side. If most men are too readily suspected by others, it only answers to the fact that most men are too ready to trust themselves. We have an infinite faith in our own honesty; and when auditors are appointed to examine their books, the inexperienced are apt to think it needless, and even impertinent. If they were wise, they would welcome it as a protection against suspicion and even against themselves. Many a man has ruined himself—not to speak of those who trusted him—by too blind a belief in his own integrity. The third brother who accompanied Titus seems to have been more closely associated with Paul than the second. He had proved him often, in many things, and found him uniformly earnest; and at this juncture the confidence he had in the Corinthians made him more earnest than ever. Paul extols the three in the highest terms before he sends them off; if anybody in Corinth wishes to know what they are, he is proud to tell. Titus is his partner in the apostolic calling, and has shared his work among them; the other brethren are deputies (apostles) of Churches, a glory of Christ. What an idealist Paul was! What an appreciation of Christian character he had when he described these nameless believers as reflections of the splendour of Christ! To common eyes they might be commonplace men; but when Paul looked at them he saw the dawning of that brightness in which the Lord appeared to him by the way. Contact with the grimy side of human nature did not blind him to this radiance; rather did this glory of Christ in men's souls strengthen him to believe all things, to hope all things, to endure all things. In showing before these honoured messengers the proof of their love, and of his boasting on their behalf, the Corinthians will show it,[75] he says, before the face of the Churches. It will be officially reported throughout Christendom.

(2) Chap. ix. 1-5. This section strikes one at first as greatly wanting in connexion with what precedes. It looks like a new beginning, an independent writing on the same or a similar subject. This has led some scholars to argue that either chap. viii. or chap. ix. belongs to a different occasion, and that only resemblance in subject has led to one of them being erroneously inserted here beside the other. This, in the absence of any external indication, is an extremely violent supposition; and closer examination goes to dissipate that first impression. The statements, *e.g.*, in vv. 3-5 would be quite unintelligible if we had not chap. viii. 16-24 to explain them; and instead of saying there

is no connexion between ix. 1 and what precedes, we should rather say that the connexion is somewhat involved and circuitous—as will happen when one is handling a topic of unusual difficulty. It is to be explained thus. The Apostle feels that he has said a good deal now about the collection, and that there is a danger in being too urgent. He uses what he has just said about the reception of the brethren as a stepping-stone to another view of the subject, more flattering to the Corinthians, to begin with, and less importunate. "Maintain your character before them," he says in effect; "for as for the ministering to the saints, it is superfluous for me to be writing to you as I do."[76] Instead of finding it necessary to urge their duty upon them, he has been able to hold up their readiness as an example to the Macedonians. "Achaia has been prepared for a year past," he said to his fond disciples in Thessalonica and Philippi; and the zeal of the Achaians, or rivalry of them, roused the majority of the Macedonians. This is one way of looking at what happened; another, and surely Paul would have been the first to say a more profound, is that of chap. viii. 1—the grace of God was given in the Churches of Macedonia. But the grace of God takes occasions, and uses means; and here its opportunity and its instrument for working in Macedonia was the ready generosity of the Corinthians. It has wrought, indeed, so effectively that the tables are turned, and now it is the liberality of Macedonia which is to provoke Corinth. Paul is sending on these brethren beforehand, lest, if any of the Macedonians should accompany him when he starts for Corinth himself, they should find matters not so flourishing as he had led them to believe. "That would put me to shame," he says to the Corinthians, "not to speak of you. I have been very confident in speaking of you as I have done in Macedonia: do keep up my credit and your own. Let this blessing, which you are going to bestow on the poor, be ready *as* a blessing—*i.e.*, as something which one gives willingly, and as liberally as he can; and not as a matter of avarice,[77] in which one gives reluctantly, keeping as much as he can."

The legitimacy of such motives as are appealed to in this paragraph will always be more or less questioned among Christian men, but as long as human nature is what it is they will always be appealed to. Ζηλότυπον γὰρ τὸ τῶν ἀνθρώπων γένος (Chrys.). A great man of action like St. Paul will of course find his temptations along this line. He is so eager to get men to act, and the inertness of human nature is so great, that it is hard to decline anything which will set it in motion. It is not the highest motive, certainly, when the forwardness of one stimulates another; but in a good cause, it is better than none. A good cause, too, has a wonderful power of its own when men begin to attend to it; it asserts itself, and takes possession of souls on its own account. Rivalry becomes generous then, even if it remains; it is a race in love that is being run, and all who run obtain the prize. Competitions for prizes which only one can gain have a great deal in them that is selfish and bad; but rivalry in the service of others—rivalry in unselfishness—will not easily degenerate in this direction. Paul does not need to be excused because he stimulates the Macedonians by the promptitude of the Corinthians— though he had his misgivings about this last—and the Corinthians by the liberality of the Macedonians. The real motive in both cases was "the grace of our Lord Jesus Christ, who, though He was rich, yet for our sakes became poor." It is this which underlies everything in the Christian heart, and nothing can do harm which works as its auxiliary.

(3) Chap. ix. 6-15. In the third and last section the Apostle resumes his direct and urgent tone. "I do not need to write to you," he seems to say, "but one thing I cannot but set down: He that soweth sparingly shall reap also sparingly; and he that soweth bountifully[78] shall reap also bountifully." That is the law of God, and the nature of things, whether men regard or disregard it. Charity is in a real sense an investment, not a casting away of money; it is not fruitless, but bears fruit in the measure in which it is sown. Of course it cannot be enforced—that would be to deny its very nature. Each is to give what he has purposed in his heart, where he is free and true: he is not to give out of grief, mourning over what he gives and regretting he could not keep it; neither is he to give out of necessity, because his position, or the usages of his society, or the comments of his neighbours, put a practical compulsion upon him. God loves a cheerful giver. Money is nothing to Him but as an index to the soul; unless the soul gives it, and gives itself with it, He takes no account. But He does take account of true charity, and because He does, the charitable may be of good cheer: He will not allow them to be without the means of manifesting a spirit so grateful to Him. If we really wish to be generous, He will not withhold from us the power of being so. This is what the Apostle says in ver. 8: "God is able to make all grace abound toward you, that ye, having always all sufficiency in everything, may abound unto every good work." There is, indeed, another way of rendering αὐτάρκεια (sufficiency). Some take it subjectively, not objectively, and make it mean, not sufficiency, but contentment. But though a contented spirit disposes people wonderfully to be generous, and the discontented, who have never enough for themselves, can never, of course, spare anything for anybody else, this meaning is decidedly to be rejected. The sufficiency, as ver. 10 also shows, is outward: we shall always, if we are charitable, have by God's grace the means of being more so. He is able to bless us abundantly, that we may be able for every good work. Observe the purpose of God's blessing. This is the import of the quotation from the 112th Psalm, in which we have the portrait of the good man: "He hath dispersed"—what uncalculating

liberality there is in the very word—"he hath given to the poor: his righteousness abideth for ever." The approximation, in the Jewish morals of later times, of the ideas of righteousness and almsgiving, has led some to limit δικαιοσύνη in this passage (as in Matt. vi. 1) to the latter sense. This is extremely improbable—I think impossible. In the Psalm, both in ver. 3 and ver. 10 (LXX.), the expression "his righteousness abideth for ever" reflects God's verdict on the character as a whole. The character there described, and here referred to by the relevant trait of generosity, is one which need fear no chances of the future. He who supplies seed to the sower and bread for food will supply and multiply the seed sown by the generous Corinthians (that they may ever be in a position to be generous), and will cause also the fruits of their righteousness to grow. Their righteousness, as it figures in this last phrase, is of course represented, for the time being, by their generosity; and the poetic expression "fruits of righteousness," which is borrowed from Hosea, designates the results which that generosity produces. It is not only an investment which guarantees to them the generous care of God for their own welfare; it is a seed which bears another and more spiritual harvest. With some expansion of heart on this the Apostle concludes.

(*a*) It yields a rich harvest of thanksgiving to God. This is expressed in ver. 12, and is the principal point. It is something to fill up further the measure of a brother's needs by a timely gift, but how much more it is to change the tune of his spirit, and whereas we found him cheerless or weak in faith, to leave him gratefully praising God. True thankfulness to the Heavenly Father is an atmosphere in which all virtues flourish: and those whose charity bears fruit in this grateful spirit are benefactors of mankind to an extent which no money can estimate. It is probably forcing the Apostle's language to insist that λειτουργία, as a name for the collection, has any priestly or sacrificial reference;[79] but unfeigned charity is in its very nature a sacrifice of praise to God—the answer of our love to His; and it has its best effect when it evokes the thanksgivings to God of those who receive it. Wherever love is, He must be first and last.

(*b*) The charity of the Corinthians bore another spiritual fruit: in consequence of it the saints at Jerusalem were won to recognise more unreservedly the Christian standing of the Gentile brethren. This is what we read in ver. 13. Taking occasion from the proof of what you are, which this ministration of yours has given them, they glorify God "for the obedience of your confession unto the Gospel of Christ, and for the liberality of your contribution unto them and unto all." The verbal combinations possible here give free scope to the ingenuity and the caprice of grammarians; but the kind of thing meant remains plain. Once the Christians of Jerusalem had had their doubts about the Corinthians, and the other pagans who were said to have received the Gospel; they had heard marvellous reports about them certainly, but it remained to be seen on what these reports rested. They would not commit themselves hastily to any compromising relation to such outsiders. Now all their doubts have been swept away; the Gentiles have actually come to the relief of their poverty, and there is no mistaking what that means. The language of love is intelligible everywhere, and there is only One who teaches it in such relations as are involved here—Jesus Christ. Yes, once they had their doubts of you; but now they will praise God that you have obediently confessed the Gospel, and frankly owned a fellowship with them and with all. The last words mean, in effect, that the Corinthians had liberally shared what they had with them and with all; but the terms are so chosen as to obliterate, as far as possible, all but the highest associations. This, then, is another fruit of charity: it widens the thoughts— it often improves the theology—of those who receive it. All goodness, men feel instinctively, is of God; and they cannot condemn as godless, or even as beyond the covenant, those through whom goodness comes to them.

(*c*) Finally, among the fruits of charity is to be reckoned the direct response of brotherly love, expressed especially in intercessory prayer, and in a longing to see those on whom God's grace rests so abundantly. An unknown and distant benefactor is sometimes better than one near at hand. He is regarded simply in his character as a benefactor; we know nothing of him that can possibly discount his kindness; our mind is compelled to rest upon his virtues and remember them gratefully before God. One of the meanest experiences of human nature that we can have—and it is not an imaginary one—is to see people paying the debt of gratitude, or at least mitigating the sense of obligation, by thinking over the deficiencies in their benefactor's character. "He is better off than we are; it is nothing to him; and if he *is* kind to the poor, he has need to be. It will take a lot of charity to cover all he would like to hide." This revolting spirit is the extreme opposite of the intercessory prayer and brotherly yearning which St. Paul sees in his mind's eye among the saints at Jerusalem. Perhaps he saw almost more than was really to be seen. The union of hearts he aimed at was never more than imperfectly attained. But to have aimed at it was a great and generous action, and to have brought so many Gentile Churches to co-operate to this end was a magnificent service to the kingdom of God.

These "fruits" are not as yet actually borne, but to the Apostle's loving anticipation they are as good as real. They are the fruits of "the righteousness" of the Corinthians, the harvest that God has caused to grow out of their liberality. From the very beginning there have been two opinions as to what St. Paul means by the exclamation with which he closes—"Thanks be unto God for His unspeakable gift." On the one hand, it is read as if it were a part of what precedes, the unspeakable gift of God being the numberless blessings that charity yields, by God's goodness, both to those who give and to those who receive it. Paul in this case would be thinking, when he wrote, of the joy with which the Gentiles gave, and of the gratitude, the willing recognition, and the brotherly prayers and longing, with which the Jews received, help in the hour of need. These would be the unspeakable gift. On the other hand, the sentence is read as if it stood apart, not the continuation of what immediately precedes, but the overflow of the Apostle's heart in view of the whole situation. It becomes possible, then, to regard "God's unspeakable gift" as the gift of redemption in His Son—the great, original, unsearchable gift, in which everything else is included, and especially all such manifestations of brotherly love as have just been in view. Sound feeling, I think, unequivocally supports the last interpretation. The very word "unspeakable" is one of a class that Paul reserves for this particular object; the wisdom and love of God as displayed in man's salvation are unspeakable, unsearchable, passing knowledge; but nothing else is. It is to this his mind goes back, instinctively, as he contemplates what has flowed from it in the particular case before us; but it is the great divine gift, and not its fruits in men's lives, however rich and various, that it passes the power of words to characterise. It is for it, and not for its results in Jew or Gentile, that the Apostle so devoutly thanks God.

XXII
WAR

"Now I Paul myself intreat you by the meekness and gentleness of Christ, I who in your presence am lowly among you, but being absent am of good courage toward you: yea, I beseech you, that I may not when present show courage with the confidence wherewith I count to be bold against some, which count of us as if we walked according to the flesh. For though we walk in the flesh, we do not war according to the flesh (for the weapons of our warfare are not of the flesh, but mighty before God to the casting down of strong holds); casting down imaginations, and every high thing that is exalted against the knowledge of God, and bringing every thought into captivity to the obedience of Christ; and being in readiness to avenge all disobedience, when your obedience shall be fulfilled."—2 Cor. x. 1-6 (R.V.).

The last four chapters of the Second Epistle to the Corinthians stand as manifestly apart as the two about the collection. A great deal too much has been made of this undeniable fact. If a man has a long letter to write, in which he wishes to speak of a variety of subjects, we may expect variations of tone, and more or less looseness of connexion. If he has something on his mind which it is difficult to speak about, but which cannot be suppressed, we may expect him to keep it to the end, and to introduce it, perhaps, with awkward emphasis. The scholars who have argued, on the ground of the extreme difference of tone, and want of connexion, that chaps. x.-xiii. of this Epistle were originally a separate letter, either earlier (Weisse) or later (Semler) than the first seven chapters, seem to have overlooked these obvious considerations.[80] If Paul stopped dictating for the day at the end of chap. ix.—if he even stopped a few moments in doubt how to proceed to the critical subject he had still to handle—the want of connexion is sufficiently explained; the tone in which he writes, when we consider the subject, needs no justification. The mission of Titus had resulted very satisfactorily, so far as one special incident was concerned—the treatment of a guilty person by the Church; the tension of feeling over that case had passed by. But in the general situation of affairs at Corinth there was much to make the

Apostle anxious and angry. There were Judaists at work, impugning his authority and corrupting his Gospel; there was at least a minority of the Church under their influence; there were large numbers living, apparently, in the grossest sins (chap. xii. 20 f.); there was something, we cannot but think, approaching spiritual anarchy. The one resource the Apostle has with which to encounter this situation—his one standing ground alike against the Church and those who were corrupting it—is his apostolic authority; and to the vindication of this he first addresses himself. This, I believe, explains the peculiar emphasis with which he begins: "Now I myself, I Paul intreat you." Αὐτὸς ἐγὼ Παῦλος is not only the grammatical subject of the sentence, but if one may say so, the subject under consideration; it is the very person whose authority is in dispute who puts himself forward deliberately in this authoritative way. The δέ ("now") is merely transitional; the writer moves on, without indicating any connexion, to another matter.

In the long sentence which makes up the first and second verses, everything comes out at once—the Apostle's indignation, in that extreme personal emphasis; his restraint of it, in the appeal to the meekness and gentleness of Christ; his resentment at the misconstruction of his conduct by enemies, who called him a coward at hand, and a brave man only at a safe distance; and his resolve, if the painful necessity is not spared him, to come with a rod and not spare. It is as if all this had been dammed up in his heart for long, and to say a single word was to say everything. The appeal to the meekness and gentleness of Christ is peculiarly affecting in such a connexion; it is intended to move the Corinthians, but what we feel is how it has moved Paul. It may be needful, on occasion, to assert oneself, or at least one's authority; but it is difficult to do it without sin. It is an exhilarating sensation to human nature to be in the right, and when we enjoy it we are apt to enlist our temper in the divine service, forgetting that the wrath of man does not work the righteousness of God. Paul felt this danger, and in the very sentence in which he puts himself and his dignity forward with uncompromising firmness, he recalls to his own and his readers' hearts the characteristic temper of the Lord. How far He was, under the most hateful provocation, from violence and passion! How far from that sinful self-assertion, which cannot consider the case and claims of others! It is when we are in the right that we must watch our temper, and, instead of letting anger carry us away, make our appeal for the right by the meekness and gentleness of Jesus. This, when right is won, makes it twice blessed. The words, "who in your presence am lowly among you, but being absent am of good courage toward you," are one of the sneers current in Corinth at Paul's expense. When he was there, his enemies said, face to face with them, he was humble enough;[81] it was only when he left them he became so brave. This mean slander must have stung the proud soul of the Apostle—the mere quotation of it shows this; but the meekness and gentleness of Christ have entered into him, and instead of resenting it he continues in a still milder tone. He descends from urging or entreating (παρακαλῶ) to beseeching (δέομαι). The thought of Christ has told already on his heart and on his pen. He begs them so to order their conduct that he may be spared the pain of demonstrating the falsehood of that charge. He counts on taking daring action against some at Corinth who count of him as though he walked after the flesh; but they can make this face-to-face hardihood needless, and in the name, not of his own cowardice, but of his Lord's meekness and considerateness, he appeals to them to do so. Δυσφημούμενοι παρακαλοῦμεν.

The charge of walking after the flesh is one that needs interpretation. In a general way it means that Paul was a worldly, and not a spiritual, man; and that the key to his character and conduct—even in his relations with Churches—was to be sought in his private and personal interests. What this would mean in any particular case would depend upon the circumstances. It might mean that he was actuated by avarice, and, in spite of pretences to be disinterested, was ruled at bottom by the idea of what would pay; or it might mean—and in this place probably does mean—that he had an undue regard for the opinion of others, and acted with feeble inconsistency in his efforts to please them. A man of whom either of these things could be truly said would be without spiritual authority, and it was to discredit the Apostle in the Church that the vague and damaging charge was made.

He certainly shows no want of courage in meeting it. That he walks *in* the flesh, he cannot deny. He is a human being, wearing the weak nature, and all its maladies are incident to him. As far as that nature goes, it is as possible that he, as that any man, should be ruled by its love of ease or popularity; or, on the other hand, should be overcome by timidity, and shrink from difficult duties. But he denies that this is his case. He spends his life *in* this nature, with all its capacity for unworthy conduct; but in his Christian warfare he is not ruled by it—he has conquered it, and it has no power over him at all. "I was with you," he wrote in the First Epistle, "with weakness and fear and much trembling"; but "my speech and my preaching were ... with demonstration of the Spirit and of power." This is practically what he says here, and what must be said by every *man* who undertakes to do anything for *God*. No one can be half so well aware as he, if he is sincere at all, of the immense contrast between the nature in which he lives and the service to which he is called. None of his enemies can know so well as he the utter earthenness of the vessel in which the heavenly treasure is deposited.

But the very meaning of a divine call is that a man is made master of this weakness, and through whatever pain and self-repression can disregard it for his work's sake. With some men timidity *is* the great trial: for them, it is the flesh. They are afraid to declare the whole counsel of God; or they are afraid of some class, or of some particular person: they are brave with a pen perhaps, or in a pulpit, or surrounded by sympathising spectators; but it is not in them to be brave alone, and to find in the Spirit a courage and authority which overbear the weakness of the flesh. From all such timidity, as an influence affecting his apostolic work, Paul can pronounce himself free. Like Jeremiah (Jer. i. 6-8) and Ezekiel (Ezek. ii. 6-8), he is naturally capable, but spiritually incapable of it. He is full of might by the Spirit of the Lord: and when he takes the field in the Lord's service, the flesh is as though it were not. Since the expression ἐν σαρκὶ περιπατοῦντες refers to the whole of the Apostle's life, it seems natural to take στρατευόμεθα as referring to the whole of his ministry, and not solely to his present campaign against the Corinthians. It is of his apostolic labours in general—of course including that which lay immediately before him—that he says: "The weapons of our warfare are not of the flesh, but mighty before God[82] to the casting down of strong holds."

Nobody but an evangelist could have written this sentence. Paul knew from experience that men fortify themselves against God: they try to find impregnable positions in which they may defy Him, and live their own life. Human nature, when God is announced to speak, instinctively puts itself on its guard; and you cannot pass that guard, as Paul was well aware, with weapons furnished by the flesh. The weapons need to be divinely strong; mighty in God's sight, for God's service, with God's own might. There is an answer in this to many of the questions that are being asked at present about methods of evangelising; where the divinely powerful weapons are found, such questions give no trouble. No man who has ever had a direct and unmistakable blessing on his work as an evangelist has ever enlisted "the flesh" in God's service. No such man has ever seen, or said, that learning, eloquence, or art in the preacher; or bribes of any sort to the hearer; or approaches to the "strong holds," constructed of amusements, lectures, concerts, and so forth, were of the very slightest value. He who knows anything about the matter knows that it is a life-and-death interest which is at stake when the soul comes face to face with the claims and the mercy of God; and that the preacher who has not the hardihood to represent it as such will not be listened to, and should not be. Paul was armed with this tremendous sense of what the Gospel was—the immensity of grace in it, the awfulness of judgment; and it was this which gave him his power, and lifted him above the arts, the wisdom, and the timidity of the flesh. A man will hold his own against anything but this. He will parley with any weapon flesh can fashion or wield; this is the only one to which he surrenders.

Perhaps in the fifth verse, which is an expansion of "the casting down of strong holds," a special reference to the Corinthians begins to be felt: at all events they might easily apply it to themselves. "Casting down imaginations," the Apostle says, "and every high thing that is exalted against the knowledge of God." "Imaginations" is probably a fair enough rendering of λογισμούς, though the margin has "reasonings," and the same word in Rom. ii. 15 is rendered "thoughts." To what it applies is not very obvious. Men do certainly fortify themselves against the Gospel in their thoughts. The proud wisdom of the Greek was familiar to the Apostle, and even the obvious fact that it had not brought the world salvation was not sufficient to lower its pride. The expression has sometimes been censured as justifying the *sacrificium intellectus*, or as taking away freedom of thought in religion. To think of Paul censuring the free exercise of intelligence in religion is too absurd; but there is no doubt that, with his firm hold of the great facts on which the Christian faith depends, he would have dealt very summarily with theories, ancient or modern, which serve no purpose but to fortify men against the pressure of these facts. He would not have taken excessive pains to put himself in the speculator's place, and see the world as he sees it, with the most stupendous realities left out; he would not have flattered with any affected admiration that most self-complacent of mortals—the wise of this world. He would have struck straight at the heart and conscience with the spiritual weapons of the Gospel; he would have spoken of sin and judgment, of reconciliation and life in Christ, till these great realities had asserted their greatness in the mind, and in doing so had shattered the proud intellectual structures which had been reared in ignorance or contempt of them. "Thoughts" and "imaginations" must yield to things, and make room for them: it was on this principle Paul wrought. And to "thoughts" or "imaginations" he adds "every high thing [ὕψωμα] that exalts itself against the knowledge of God." The emphasis is on "every"; the Apostle generalises the opposition which he has to encounter. It may not be so much in the "thoughts" of men, as in their tempers, that they fortify themselves. Pride, which by the instinct of self-preservation sees at once to the heart of the Gospel, and closes itself against it; which hates equally the thought of absolute indebtedness to God and the thought of standing on the same level with others in God's sight,—this pride raises in every part of our nature its protest against the great surrender. It is implied in the whole structure of this passage that "the knowledge of God" against which every high thing in man rises defiantly is a humbling knowledge. In other words, it is not speculative merely, but has an ethical significance, which the human heart is conscious of even at a distance, and makes ready to acknowledge or to resist. No high thing lifts itself up in us against a mere theorem—a doctrine of God which is as a doctrine in algebra; it is the practical import of knowing God which excites the rebellion of the soul. No doubt, for the Apostle, the knowledge of God was synonymous with the Gospel: it was the knowledge of His glory in the face of Jesus Christ; it was concentrated in the Cross and the Throne of His Son, in the Atonement and the Sovereignty of Christ. The Apostle had to beat down all the barriers by which men closed their minds against this supreme revelation; he had to win for these stupendous facts a place in the consciousness of humanity answering to their grandeur. *Their* greatness made *him* great: he was lifted up on them; and though he walked in the flesh, in weakness and fear and much trembling, he could confront undaunted the pride and the wisdom of the world, and compel them to acknowledge his Lord.

This meaning is brought out more precisely in the words with which he continues—"bringing every thought into captivity to the obedience of Christ." If we suppose a special reference here to the Corinthians, it will be natural to take νόημα ("thought") in a practical sense—as, *e.g.*, in chap. ii. 11, where it is rendered "devices." The Corinthians had notions of their own, apparently, about how a Church should be regulated—wild, undisciplined, disorderly notions; and in the absence of the Apostle they were experimenting with them freely. It is part of his work to catch these runaway thoughts, and make them obedient to Christ again. It seems, however, much more natural to allow the wider reference of αἰχμαλωτίζοντες to the whole of Paul's apostolic work; and then νόημα also will be taken in a less restricted sense. Men's minds, and all that goes on in their minds (νοήματα covers both: see chaps, ii. 11, iii. 14, iv. 4), are by nature lawless: they are without the sense of responsibility to guard and consecrate the sense of freedom. When the Gospel makes them captive, this lawless liberty comes to an end. The mind, in all its operations, comes under law to Christ: in its every thought it is obedient to Him. The supremacy which Christ claims and exercises is over the whole nature: the Christian man feels that nothing—not even a thought—lies beyond the range in which obedience is due to Him. This practical conviction will not paralyse thinking in the very least, but it will extinguish many useless and bad thoughts, and give their due value to all.

The Apostle descends unmistakably from the general to the particular in ver. 6: "Being in readiness to avenge all disobedience, when your obedience is fulfilled." Apparently what he contemplates in Corinth is a disobedience which in part at least will refuse to surrender to Christ. There is a spirit abroad there, in the Judaists especially, and in those whom they have influenced, which will not bend, and must be broken. How Paul means to take vengeance on it, he does not say. He is confident himself that the divinely powerful weapons which he wields will enable him to master it, and that is enough. Whatever the shape the disobedience may assume,—hostility to the Gospel of Paul, as subversive of the law; hostility to his apostolic claims, as unequal to those of the Twelve; hostility to the practical authority he asserted in Churches of his founding, and to the moral ideals he established there,—whatever the face which opposition may present, he declares himself ready to humble it. One limitation only he imposes on himself—he will do this, "when the obedience of the Corinthians is fulfilled." He expressly distinguishes the Church as a whole from those who represent or constitute the disobedient party. There have been misunderstandings between the Church and himself; but as chaps. i. to vii. show, these have been so far overcome: the body of the Church has reconciled itself to its founder; it has returned, so to speak, to its allegiance to Paul, and has busied itself in carrying out his will. When this process, at present only in course, is completed, his way will be clear. He will be able to act with severity and decision against those who have troubled the Church, without running any risk of hurting the Church itself. This leads again to the reflection that, with all his high consciousness of spiritual power, with all his sense of personal wrong, the most remarkable characteristic of Paul is love. He waits to the last moment before he resorts to severer measures; and he begs those who may suffer from them, begs them by the meekness and gentleness of Christ, to spare him such pain.

XXIII
COMPARISONS

"Ye look at the things that are before your face. If any man trusteth in himself that he is Christ's, let him consider this again with himself, that, even as he is Christ's, so also are we. For though I should glory somewhat abundantly concerning our authority (which the Lord gave for building you up, and not for casting you down), I shall not be put to shame: that I may not seem as if I would terrify you by my letters. For, His letters, they say, are weighty and strong; but his bodily presence is weak, and his speech of no account. Let such a one reckon this, that, what we are in word by letters when we are absent, such *are we* also in deed when we are present. For we are not bold to number or compare ourselves with certain of them that commend themselves: but they themselves, measuring themselves by themselves, and comparing themselves with themselves, are without understanding. But we will not glory beyond *our* measure, but according to the measure of the province which God apportioned to us as a measure, to reach even unto you. For we stretch not ourselves overmuch, as though we reached not unto you: for we came even as far as unto you in the Gospel of Christ: not glorying beyond *our* measure, *that is*, in other men's labours; but having hope that, as your faith groweth, we shall be magnified in you according to our province unto *further* abundance, so as to preach the Gospel even unto the parts beyond you, *and* not to glory in another's province in regard of things ready to our hand. But he that glorieth, let him glory in the Lord. For not he that commendeth himself is approved, but whom the Lord commendeth."—2 Cor. x. 7-18 (R.V.).

This passage abounds with grammatical and textual difficulties, but the general import and the purpose of it are plain. The self-assertion of αὐτὸς ἐγὼ Παῦλος (ver. 1) receives its first interpretation and expansion here: we see what it is that Paul claims, and we begin to see the nature of the opposition against which his claim has to be made good. Leaving questions of grammatical construction aside, vv. 7 and 8 define the situation; and it is convenient to take them as if they stood alone.

There was a person in Corinth—more than one indeed, but one in particular, as the τις in ver. 7 and the singular φησὶν[83] in ver. 10 suggest—who claimed to be Christ's, or of Christ, in a sense which disparaged and was meant to disparage Paul. If we use the plural, to include them all, we must not suppose that they are identical with the party in the Church who are censured in the First Epistle for saying, "I am of Christ," just as others said, "I am of Paul," "I am of Apollos," "I am of Cephas." That party may have been dependent upon them, but the individuals here referred to are taxed with an exclusiveness and arrogance, and in the close of the chapter with a wanton trespassing on Paul's province, which show that they were not native to the Church, but intruders into it. They were confident that they were Christ's in a sense which discredited Paul's apostleship, and entitled them, so to speak, to legitimate a Church which his labours had called into being. Everything compels us to recognise in them Jewish Christians, who had been connected with Christ in a way in which Paul had not; who had known Him in the flesh, or had brought recommendatory letters from the Mother Church at Jerusalem; and who, on the strength of these accidents, gave themselves airs of superiority in Pauline Churches, and corrupted the simplicity of the Pauline Gospel.

The first words in ver. 7—τὰ κατὰ πρόσωπον βλέπετε—are no doubt directed to this situation, but they have been very variously rendered. Our Authorised Version has, "Do ye look on things after the outward appearance?" That is, "Are you really imposed upon by the pretensions of these men, by their national and carnal distinctions, as if these had anything to do with the Gospel?" This is a good Pauline idea, but it is doubtful whether τὰ κατὰ πρόσωπον can yield it. The natural sense of these words is, "What is before your face." The Revised Version accordingly renders, "Ye look at the things that are before your face": meaning, apparently, "You allow yourselves to be carried away by whatever is nearest to you—at present, by these interloping Jews, and the claims they flaunt before your eyes." It seems to me more natural, with many good scholars, to take βλέπετε, in spite of its unemphatic position, as imperative: "Look at the things which are before your faces! The most obvious and palpable facts discredit these Judaists and accredit me. A claim to be Christ's is not to be made out *à priori* by any carnal prerogatives, or any human recommendations; it is only made out by this—that Christ Himself attests it by giving him who makes it success as an evangelist. Look at what confronts you! There is not a single Christian thing you see which is not Christ's own testimony that I am His;

unless you are senseless and blind, my position and authority as an apostle can never be impugned among you." The argument is thus the same as that which he uses in chap. iii. 1-3, and in the First Epistle, chap. ix. 2.

At first Paul asserts only a bare equivalence to his Jewish opponent: "Let him consider this with himself, that, *even as* he is Christ's, *so also* are we." The historical, outward connexion with Christ, whatever it may have been, amounted in this relation to exactly nothing at all. Not what Christ was, but what He is, is the life and reality of the Christian religion. Not an accidental acquaintance with Him as He lived in Galilee or Jerusalem, but a spiritual fellowship with Him as He reigns in the heavenly places, makes a Christian. Not a letter written by human hands—though they should be the hands of Peter or James or John—legitimates a man in the apostolic career; but only the sovereign voice which says, "He is a chosen vessel unto Me, to bear My Name." Neither as Christian nor as apostle can one establish a monopoly by making his appeal to "the flesh." The application of this Christian truth has constantly to be made anew, for human nature loves a monopoly; it does not seem really to have a thing, unless its possession of it is exclusive. We are all too ready to unchurch, or unchristianise, others; to say, "*We* are Christ's," with an emphasis which means that others are not. Churches with a strong organisation are especially tempted to this unchristian narrowness and pride. Their members think almost instinctively of other Christians as outsiders and inferiors; they would like to take them in, to reordain their ministers, to reform their constitution, to give validity to their sacraments—in one word, to legitimate them as Christians and as Christian societies. All this is mere unintelligence and arrogance. Legitimacy is a convenient and respectable political fiction; but to make the constitution of any Christian body, which has developed under the pressure of historical exigences, the law for the legitimation of Christian life, ministry, and worship everywhere, is to deny the essential character of the Christian religion. It is to play toward men whom Christ has legitimated by His Spirit, and by His blessing on their work, precisely the part which the Judaisers played toward Paul; and to compromise with it is to betray Christ, and to renounce the freedom of the Spirit.

But the Apostle does not stop short with claiming a bare equality with his rivals. "For though[84] I should boast somewhat more abundantly concerning our authority ... I shall not be put to shame"—*i.e.*, "The facts I have invited you to look at will bear me out." The key to this passage is to be found in 1 Cor. xv. 15, where he boasts that, though the least of the apostles, and not worthy to be called an apostle, he had, through the grace of God given to him, laboured more abundantly than all the rest. If it came to comparison, then, of the attestation which Christ gave to their several labours, and so to their authority, by success in evangelising, it would not be Paul who would have to hide his head. But he does not choose to boast any more of his authority at this point. He has no desire to clothe himself in terrors; on the contrary, he wishes to avoid[85] the very appearance of scaring them out of their wits by his letters (for ἐκφοβεῖν compare Mark ix. 6; Heb. xii. 21). His authority has been given him, not for the pulling down, but for the building up, of the Church; it is not lordly (chap. i. 24), but ministerial; and he would wish, not only to show it in kindly service, but also in a kindly aspect. "Not for casting down," in ver. 8, is no contradiction of "mighty for casting down" in ver. 4: the object in the two cases is quite different. Many *things* in man must be cast down—many high thoughts, much pride, much wilfulness, much presumption and sufficiency—but the casting down of these is the building up of souls.

At this point comes what is logically a parenthesis, and we hear in it the criticisms passed at Corinth on Paul, and his own reply to them. "His letters," they say (or, he says), "are weighty and strong; but his bodily presence weak, and his speech of no account." The last part of this criticism has been much misunderstood; it is really of moral import, but has been read in a physical sense. It does not say anything at all about the Apostle's physique, or about his eloquence or want of eloquence; it tells us that (according to these critics), when he was actually present at Corinth, he was somehow or other ineffective; and when he spoke there, people simply disregarded him. An uncertain tradition no doubt represents Paul as an infirm and meagre person, and it is easy to believe that to Greeks he must sometimes have seemed embarrassed and incoherent in speech to the last degree (what, for instance, could have seemed more formless to a Greek than vv. 12-18 of this chapter?): nevertheless, it is nothing like this which is in view here. The criticism is not of his physique, nor of his style, but of his personality—what is described is not his appearance nor his eloquence, but the effect which the man produced when he went to Corinth and spoke. It was nothing. As a man, bodily present, he could get nothing done: he talked, and nobody listened. It is implied that this criticism is false; and Paul bids any one who makes it consider that what he is in word by letters when he is absent, that he will also be in deed when he is present. The double *rôle* of potent pamphleteer and ineffective pastor is not for him.

The kind of criticism which was here passed on St. Paul is one to which every preacher is obnoxious. An epistle is, so to speak, the man's words without the man; and such is human weakness, that they are often stronger than the man speaking in bodily presence, that is, than the man and his words together. The character of the speaker, as it were, discounts all he says; and when he is there, and delivers his message in person, the message itself suffers an immense depreciation. This ought not so to be, and with a man who cultivates sincerity will not so be. He will be, himself, as good as his words; his effectiveness will be the same whether he writes or speaks. Nothing ultimately counts in the work of a Christian minister but what he can say and do and get done when in direct contact, with living men. In many cases the modern sermon really answers to the epistle as it is referred to in this sarcastic comment; in the pulpit, people say, the minister is impressive and memorable; but in the ordinary intercourse of life, and even in the pastoral relation, where he has to meet people on an equal footing, his power quite disappears. He is an ineffective person, and his words have no weight. Where this is true, there is something very far wrong; and though it was not true in the case of Paul, there are cases in which it is. To bring the pastoral up to the level of the pulpit work—the care of individual souls and characters to the intensity and earnestness of study and preaching—would be the saving of many a minister and many a congregation.[86]

But to return to the text. The Apostle is disinclined to pursue this line further: in defending himself against these obscure detractors, he can hardly avoid the appearance of self-commendation, which of all things he abhors. An acute observer has remarked that when war lasts long the opposing combatants borrow each other's weapons and tactics: and it was this uninviting weapon that the policy of his opponents laid to the Apostle's hand. With ironical recognition of their hardihood, he declines it: "We are not bold—have not the courage—to number ourselves among, or compare ourselves with, certain of them that commend themselves"— *i.e.*, the Judaists who had introduced themselves to the Church. "Far be it from me," says the Apostle grimly, "to claim a place among, or near, such a distinguished company." But he is too much in earnest to prolong the ironical strain, and in the verses which follow, from 12 to 16, he states in good set terms the differences between himself and them. (1) They measure themselves by themselves, and compare themselves among themselves, and in so doing are without understanding.[87] They constitute a religious coterie, a sort of clique or ring in the Church, ignoring all but themselves, making themselves the only standard of what is Christian, and betraying, by that very proceeding, their want of sense. There is a fine liberality about this sharp saying, and it is as necessary now as in the first century. Men coalesce, within the limits of the Christian community, from affinities of various kinds—sympathy for a type or an aspect of doctrine, or liking for a form of polity; and as it is easy, so is it common, for those who have united like to like, to set up their own associations and preferences as the only law and model for all. They take the air of superior persons, and the penalty of the superior person is to be unintelligent. They are without understanding.

The standard of the coterie—be it "evangelical," "high church," "broad church," or what you please—is not the standard of God; and to measure all things by it is not only sinful but stupid. In contrast to this Judaistic clique, who saw no Christianity except under their own colours, Paul's standard is to be found in the actual working of God through the Gospel. He would have said with Ignatius, only with a deeper insight into every word, "Where Jesus Christ is, there is the Catholic Church." (2) Another point of difference is this: Paul works independently as an evangelist; it has always been his rule to break new ground. God has assigned him a province to labour in, large enough to gratify the highest ambition; he is not going beyond it, nor exaggerating his authority, when he asserts his apostolic dignity in Corinth; the Corinthians know as well as he that he came all the way to them, and was the first to come, ministering the Gospel of Christ. Nay, it is only the weakness of their faith that keeps him from going farther: and he has hope that as their faith grows it will set him free to carry the Gospel beyond them to Italy and Spain; this would be the crown of his greatness as an evangelist, and it depends *on them* (ἐν ὑμῖν μεγαλυνθῆναι) whether he is to win it; in any case, the winning of it would be in harmony with his vocation, the carrying of it out in glorious fulness (κατὰ τὸν κανόνα εἰς περισσείαν); for, like John Wesley, he could say the whole world was his parish. If he boasts at all, it is not immeasurably; it is on the basis of the gift and calling of God, within the limits of what God has wrought by him and by no other; he never intrudes into another's province and boasts of what he finds done to his hand. But this was what the Jews did. They did not propagate the Gospel with apostolic enthusiasm among the heathen; they waited till Paul had done the hard preliminary work, and formed Christian congregations everywhere, and then they slunk into them—in Galatia, in Macedonia, in Achaia—talking as if these Churches were *their* work, disparaging their real father in Christ, and claiming to complete and legitimate—which meant, in effect, to subvert—-his work. No wonder Paul was scornful, and did not venture to put himself in a line with such heroes.

Two feelings are compounded all through this passage: an intense sympathy with the purpose of God that the Gospel should be preached to every creature—Paul's very soul melts into that; and an intense scorn for the spirit that sneaks and poaches on another's ground, and is more anxious that some men should be good sectarians than that all men should be good disciples. This evil spirit Paul loathes, just as Christ loathed it; the temper of these verses is that in which the Master cried, "Woe unto you, scribes and Pharisees, hypocrites! for ye compass sea and land to make one proselyte; and when he is become so, ye make him twofold more a son of hell than yourselves." Of course the evil spirit must always be disguised, both from others and from itself: the proselytiser assumes the garb of the evangelist; but the proselytiser turned evangelist is the purest example in the world of Satan disguised as an angel of light. The show is divine, but the reality is diabolical. It does not matter what the special sectarianism is: the proselytising of a hierarchical Church, and the proselytising of the Plymouth Brethren, are alike dishonourable and alike condemned. And the safeguard of the soul against this base spirit is an interest like Paul's in the Christianising of those who do not know Christ at all. Why should Churches compete? why should their agencies overlap? why should they steal from each other's folds? why should they be anxious to seal all believers with their private seal, when the whole world lies in wickedness? That field is large enough for all the efforts of all evangelists, and till it has been sown with the good seed from end to end there can be nothing but reprobation for those who trespass on the province of others, and boast that they have made their own what they certainly did not make Christ's.

At the close, to borrow Bengel's expression, Paul sounds a retreat. He has liberated his mind about his adversaries—always a more or less dangerous process; and after the excitement and self-assertion are over, he composes it again in the presence of God. He checks himself, we feel, with that Old Testament word, "Now he that glorieth, let him glory in the Lord. I *have* always broken new ground; I *have* come as far as you, and wish to go farther, evangelising; I never *have* boasted of another man's labours as if they were mine, or claimed the credit of what he had done; but all this is mine only as God's gift. It is His grace bestowed on me, and not in vain. I would not boast except in Him; for not he who commends himself is approved, but only he whom the Lord commends." No character which is only self-certificated can stand the test: no claim to apostolic dignity and authority can be maintained which the Lord does not attest by granting apostolic success.

> Note on vv. 12 and 13.—In some MSS. (D*, F, G, 109, It., and some Latins) the last two words of ver. 12 and the first two of ver. 13 (οὐ συνιᾶσιν· ἡμεῖς δέ) are omitted. Most editors of the text (Tischdf. vii., Tregelles, Westcott and Hort) seem to think the omission accidental; among exegetes, the fact that it yields an easy and natural, though of course a quite different, sense, has caused some hesitation. Thus Bengel, and recently Schmiedel, reject the words. The latter renders the whole passage: "We do not venture to put ourselves on a level, or to compare ourselves, with certain of those who commend themselves; but in measuring ourselves by ourselves, and comparing ourselves with ourselves, we shall not boast

beyond measure, but according to the measure of the rule," etc. This is no doubt intelligible and appropriate enough, and certainly one's first impression is that ἀλλ' αὐτοί in ver. 12 ought to refer to Paul; but as the meaning yielded by the passage with the four words included is equally appropriate, and their insertion immeasurably harder to understand than their omission, it seems preferable to let them stand, in the sense explained above. They are found (with the variation of συνίσασιν for συνιᾶσιν in א*) in א**, B, minusc. Theodoret: in E, K, L, P, the form is συνιοῦσιν. Apparently it is only by an accident that their omission leaves good sense.

XXIV
GODLY JEALOUSY

"Would that ye could bear with me in a little foolishness: nay indeed bear with me. For I am jealous over you with a godly jealousy: for I espoused you to one husband, that I might present you *as* a pure virgin to Christ. But I fear, lest by any means, as the serpent beguiled Eve in his craftiness, your minds should be corrupted from the simplicity and the purity that is toward Christ. For if he that cometh preacheth another Jesus, whom we did not preach, or *if* ye receive a different spirit, which ye did not receive, or a different gospel, which ye did not accept, ye do well to bear with *him*. For I reckon that I am not a whit behind the very chiefest apostles. But though *I be* rude in speech, yet *am I* not in knowledge; nay, in everything we have made *it* manifest among all men to you-ward."—2 Cor. xi. 1-6 (R.V.).

All through the tenth chapter there is a conflict in the Apostle's mind. He is repeatedly, as it were, on the verge of doing something, from which he as often draws back. He does not like to boast—he does not like to speak of himself at all—but the tactics of his enemies, and the faithlessness of the Corinthians, are making it inevitable. In chap. xi. he takes the plunge. He adopts the policy of his adversaries, and proceeds to enlarge on his services to the Church; but with magnificent irony, he first assumes the mask of a fool. It is not the genuine Paul who figures here; it is Paul playing a part to which he has been compelled against his will, acting in a character which is as remote as possible from his own. It is the character native and proper to the other side; and when Paul, with due deprecation, assumes it for the nonce, he not only preserves his modesty and his self-respect, but lets his opponents see what he thinks of them. He plays the fool for the occasion, and of set purpose; they do it always, and without knowing it, like men to the manner born.

But it is the Corinthians who are directly addressed. "Would that ye could bear with me in a little foolishness: nay indeed bear with me." In the last clause, ἀνέχεσθε may be either imperative (as the Revised Version gives it in the text), or indicative (as in the margin: "but indeed ye do bear with me"). The use of ἀλλὰ rather favours the last; and it would be quite in keeping with the extremely ironical tone of the passage to render it so. Even in the First Epistle, Paul had reflected on the self-conceit of the Corinthians: "We are fools for Christ's sake, but ye are wise in Christ." That self-conceit led them to think lightly of him, but not just to cast him off; they still tolerated him as a feeble sort of person: "Ye do indeed bear with me." But whichever alternative be preferred, the irony passes swiftly into the dead earnest of the second verse: "For I am jealous over you with a godly jealousy: for I espoused you to one husband, that I might present you *as* a pure virgin to Christ."

This is the ground on which Paul claims their forbearance, even when he indulges in a little "folly." If he is guilty of what seems to them extravagance, it is the extravagance of jealousy—*i.e.*, of love tormented by fear. Nor is it any selfish jealousy, of which he ought to be ashamed. He is not anxious about his private or personal interests in the Church. He is not humiliated and provoked because his former pupils have come to their spiritual majority, and asserted their independence of their master. These are common dangers and common sins; and every minister needs to be on his guard against them. Paul's jealousy over the Corinthians was "a jealousy of God"; God had put it into his heart, and what it had in view was God's interest in them. It distressed him to think, not that his personal influence at Corinth was on the wane, but that the work which God had done in their souls was in danger of being frustrated, the inheritance He had acquired in them of being lost. Nothing but God's interest had been in the Apostle's mind from the beginning. "I betrothed you," he says, "to *one* husband"—the emphasis lies on *one*—"that I might present you as a pure virgin to Christ."[88]

It is the Church collectively which is represented by the pure virgin, and it ought to be observed that this is the constant use in Scripture, alike in the Old Testament and the New. It is Israel as a whole which is married to the Lord; it is the Christian Church as a whole (or a Church collectively, as here) which is the Bride, the Lamb's wife. To individualise the figure, and speak of Christ as the Bridegroom of the soul, is not Scriptural, and almost always misleads. It introduces the language and the associations of natural affection into a region where they are entirely out of place; we have no terms of endearment here, and should have none, but high thoughts of the simplicity, the purity, and the glory of the Church. Glory is especially suggested by the idea of "*presenting*" the Church to Christ. The presentation takes place when Christ comes again to be glorified in His saints; that great day shines unceasingly in the Apostle's heart, and all he does is done in its light. The infinite issues of fidelity and infidelity to the Lord, as that day makes them manifest, are ever present to his spirit; and it is this which gives such divine intensity to his feelings wherever the conduct of Christians is concerned. He sees everything, not as dull eyes see it now, but as Christ in His glory will show it then. And it takes nothing less than this to keep the soul absolutely pure and loyal to the Lord.

The Apostle explains in the third verse the nature of his alarm. "I fear," he says, "lest by any means, as the serpent beguiled Eve in his craftiness, your minds should be corrupted from the simplicity [and the purity][89] which is toward Christ." The whole figure is very expressive. "Simplicity" means singleness of mind; the heart of the "pure virgin" is undivided; she ought not to have, and will not have, a thought for any but the "one man" to whom she is betrothed. "Purity" again is, as it were, one species of "simplicity"; it is "simplicity" as shown in the keeping of the whole nature unspotted for the Lord. What Paul dreads is the spiritual seduction of the Church, the winning away of her heart from absolute loyalty to Christ. The serpent beguiled Eve by his craftiness; he took advantage of her unsuspecting innocence to wile her away from her simple belief in God and obedience to Him. When she took into her mind the suspicions he raised, her "simplicity" was gone, and her "purity" followed. The serpent's agents—the servants of Satan, as Paul calls them in ver. 15—are at work in Corinth; and he fears that their craftiness may seduce the Church from its first simple loyalty to Christ. It is natural for us to take ἁπλότης and ἁγνότης in a purely ethical sense, but it is by no means certain that this is all that is meant; indeed, if καὶ τῆς ἁγνότητος be a gloss, as seems not improbable, ἁπλότης may well have a different application. "The simplicity which is toward Christ," from which he fears lest by any means "their *minds*" or "*thoughts*" be corrupted, will rather be their whole-hearted acceptance of Christ as Paul conceived of Him and preached Him, their unreserved, unquestioning surrender to that form of doctrine (τύπον διδαχῆς, Rom. vi. 17) to which they had been delivered. This, of course, in Paul's mind, involved the other—there is no separation of doctrine and practice for him; but it makes a theological rather than an ethical interest the predominant one; and this interpretation, it seems to me, coheres best with what follows, and with the whole preoccupation of the Apostle in this passage. The people whose influence he feared were not unbelievers, nor were they immoral; they professed to be Christians, and indeed better Christians than Paul; but their whole conception of the Gospel was at variance with his; if they made way at Corinth, his work would be undone. The Gospel which he preached would no longer have that unsuspicious acceptance; the Christ whom he proclaimed would no longer have that unwavering loyalty; instead of simplicity and purity, the heart of the "pure virgin" would be possessed by misgivings, hesitations, perhaps by out-right infidelity; his hope of presenting her to Christ on the great day would be gone.

This is what we are led to by ver. 4, one of the most vexed passages in the New Testament. The text of the last word is uncertain: some read the imperfect ἀνείχεσθε; others, including our Revisers, the present ἀνέχεσθε. The last is the better attested, and suits best the connexion of thought. The interpretations may be divided into two classes. First, there are those which assume that the suppositions made in this verse are not true. This is evidently the intention in our Authorised Version. It renders, "For if he that cometh preacheth another Jesus, whom we have not preached, or if ye receive another spirit, which ye have not received, or another gospel, which ye have not accepted, *ye might well bear with him*." But—we must interpolate—nothing of this sort has really taken place; for Paul counts himself not a whit inferior to the very chiefest Apostles. No one—not even Peter or James or John—could have imparted anything to the Corinthians which Paul had failed to impart; and hence their spiritual seduction, no matter how or by whom accomplished, was perfectly unreasonable and gratuitous. This interpretation, with variations in detail which need not be pursued, is represented by many of the best expositors, from Chrysostom to Meyer. "If," says Chrysostom in his paraphrase, "if we had omitted anything that should have been said, and they had made up the omission, we do not forbid you to attend to them. But if everything has been perfectly done on our part, and no blank left, how did they [the Apostle's adversaries] get hold of you?" This is the broad result of many discussions; and it is usual—though not invariable—for those who read the passage thus to take τῶν ὑπερλίαν ἀποστόλων in a complimentary, not a contemptuous, sense, and to refer it, as Chrysostom expressly does, to the three pillars of the primitive Church.

The objections to this interpretation are obvious enough. There is first the grammatical objection, that a hypothetical sentence, with the present indicative in the protasis (εἰ ... κηρύσσει, εἰ ... λαμβάνετε), and the present indicative in the apodosis (ἀνέχεσθε), can by no plausibility of argument be made to mean, "If the interloper *were* preaching another Jesus ... you *would* be right to bear with him." Even if the imperfect is the true reading, which is improbable, this translation is unjustified.[90] But there is a logical as well as a grammatical objection. The use of γάρ ("for") surely implies that in the sentence which it introduces we are to find the reason for what precedes. Paul is afraid, he has told us, lest the Church should be seduced from the one husband to whom he has betrothed her. But he can never mean to explain a *real* fear by making a number of *imaginary* suppositions; and so we must find in the hypothetical clauses here the *real* grounds of his alarm. People had come to Corinth—ὁ ἐρχόμενος is no doubt collective, and characterises the troublers of the Church as intruders, not native to it, but separable from it—doing all the things here supposed. Paul has espoused the Church to *One* Husband; they preach *another* Jesus. Not, of course, a distinct Person, but certainly a distinct conception of the same Person. Paul's Christ was the Son of God, the Lord of Glory, He who by His death on the cross became Universal Redeemer, and by His ascension Universal Lord—the end of the law, the giver of the Spirit; it would be another Jesus if the intruders preached only the Son of David, or the Carpenter of Nazareth, or the King of Israel. According to the conception of Christ, too, would be "the spirit" which accompanied this preaching, the characteristic temper and power of the religion it proclaimed. The spirit ministered by Paul in his apostolic work was one of power, and love, and, above all things, liberty; it emancipated the soul from weakness, from scruples, from moral inability, from slavery to sin and law; but the spirit generated by the Judaising ministry, the characteristic temper of the religion it proclaimed, was servile and cowardly. It was a spirit of bondage tending always to fear (Rom. viii. 15). Their whole gospel—to give their preaching a name it did not deserve (Gal. i. 6-9)—was something entirely unlike Paul's both in its ideas and in its spiritual fruits. Unlike—yes, and immeasurably inferior, and yet in spite of this the Corinthians put up with it well enough. This is the plain fact (ἀνέχεσθε) which the Apostle plainly states. *He* had to plead for their toleration, but they had no difficulty in tolerating men who by a spurious gospel, an unspiritual conception of Christ, and an unworthy incapacity for understanding freedom, were undermining his work, and seducing their souls. No wonder he was jealous, and angry, and scornful, when he saw the true Christian religion, which has all time and all nations for its inheritance, in danger of being degraded into a narrow Jewish sectarianism; the kingdom of the Spirit lost in a society in which race gave a prerogative, and carnal ordinances were revived; and, worse still, Christ the Son of God, the Universal Reconciler, known only "after the flesh," and appropriated to a race, instead of being exalted as Lord of all, in whom there is no room for Greek or Jew, barbarian or Scythian, bond or free. The Corinthians bore with this nobly (καλῶς); but he who had begotten them in the true Gospel had to beg them to bear with him.

There is only one difficulty in this interpretation, and that is not a serious one: it is the connexion of ver. 5 with what precedes. Those who connect it immediately with ver. 4 are obliged to supply something: for example, "But you *ought* not to bear with them, for I consider that I am in nothing behind the very chiefest apostles." I have no doubt at all that οἱ ὑπερλίαν ἀπόστολοι—the superlative apostles—are *not* Peter, James, and John, but the teachers aimed at in ver. 4, the ψευδαπόστολοι of ver. 13; it is with them, and not with the Twelve or the eminent Three, that Paul is comparing himself.[91] But even so, I agree with Weizsäcker that the connexion for the γὰρ in ver. 5 must be sought further back—as far back, indeed, as ver. 1. "You bear well enough with them, and so you may well bear with me, as I beg you to do; for I consider," etc. This is effective enough, and brings us back again to the main subject. If there is a point in which Paul is willing to his inferiority to these superlative apostles, it is the non-essential one of utterance. He grants that he is rude in speech—not rhetorically gifted or trained—a plain, blunt man who speaks right on. But he is not rude in knowledge: in every respect he has made *that* manifest, among all men, toward them. The last clause is hardly intelligible, and the text is insecure. [92] The reading φανερώσαντες is that of all the critical editors; the object may either be indefinite (his competence in point of knowledge), or, more precisely, τὴν γνῶσιν itself, supplied from the previous clause. In no point whatever, under no circumstances, has Paul ever failed to exhibit to the Corinthians the whole truth of God in the Gospel. This it is which makes him scornful even when he thinks of the men whom the Corinthians are preferring to himself.

When we look from the details of this passage to its scope, some reflections are suggested, which have their application still.

(1) Our conception of the Person of Christ determines our conception of the whole Christian religion. What we have to proclaim to men as gospel—what we have to offer to them as the characteristic temper and virtue of the life which the Gospel originates—depends on the answer we give to Jesus' own question, "Whom say ye that I am?" A Christ who is simply human cannot be to men what a Christ is who is truly divine. The Gospel identified with Him cannot be the same; the spirit of the society which gathers round Him cannot be the same. It is futile to ask whether such a gospel and such a spirit can fairly be called Christian; they are in point of fact quite other things from the Gospel and the Spirit which are historically associated with the name. It is plain from this passage that the Apostle attached the utmost importance to his conceptions of the Person and Work of the Lord: ought not this to give pause to those who evacuate his theology of many of its distinctive ideas—especially that of the Pre-existence of Christ—on the plea that they are merely theologoumena of an individual Christian, and that to discard them leaves the Gospel unaffected? Certainly this was not what he thought. Another Jesus meant another spirit, another gospel—to use modern words, another religion and another religious consciousness; and *any* other, the Apostle was perfectly sure, came short of the grandeur of the

truth. The spirit of the passage is the same with that in Gal. i. 6 ff., where he erects the Gospel he has preached as the standard of absolute religious truth. "Though we, or an angel from heaven, should preach unto you any gospel other than that which we preached unto you, let him be anathema. As we have said before, so say I now again, If any man preacheth unto you any gospel other than that which ye received, let him be anathema."

(2) "The simplicity that is toward Christ"—the simple acceptance of the truth about Him, and undivided loyalty of heart to Him—may be corrupted by influences originating within, as well as without, the Church. The infidelity which is subtlest, and most to be dreaded, is not the gross materialism or atheism which will not so much as hear the name of God or Christ; but that which uses all sacred names, speaking readily of Jesus, the Spirit, and the Gospel, but meaning something else, and something less, than these words meant in apostolic lips. This it was which alarmed the jealous love of Paul; this it is, in its insidious influence, which constitutes one of the most real perils of Christianity at the present time. The Jew in the first century, who reduced the Person and Work of Christ to the scale of his national prejudices, and the theologian in the nineteenth, who discounts apostolic ideas when they do not suit the presuppositions of his philosophy, are open to the same suspicion, if they do not fall under the same condemnation. True thoughts about Christ—in spite of all the smart sayings about theological subtleties which have nothing to do with piety—are essential to the very existence of the Christian religion.

(3) There is no comparison between the Gospel of God in Jesus Christ His Son and any other religion. The science of comparative religion is interesting as a science; but a Christian may be excused for finding the religious use of it tiresome. There is nothing true in any of the religions which is not already in his possession. He never finds a moral idea, a law of the spiritual life, a word of God, in any of them, to which he cannot immediately offer a parallel, far more simple and penetrating, from the revelation of Christ. He has no interest in disparaging the light by which millions of his fellow-creatures have walked, generation after generation, in the mysterious providence of God; but he sees no reason for pretending that that light—which Scripture calls darkness and the shadow of death—can bear comparison with the radiance in which he lives. "If," he might say, misapplying the fourth verse—"if they brought us another saviour, another spirit, another gospel, we might be religiously interested in them; but, as it is, we have everything already, and they, in comparison, have nothing." The same remark applies to "theosophy," "spiritualism," and other "gospels." It will be time to take them seriously when they utter one wise or true word on God or the soul which is not an echo of something in the old familiar Scriptures.

XXV
FOOLISH BOASTING

"Or did I commit a sin in abasing myself that ye might be exalted, because I preached to you the Gospel of God for nought? I robbed other Churches, taking wages *of them* that I might minister unto you; and when I was present with you and was in want, I was not a burden on any man; for the brethren, when they came from Macedonia, supplied the measure of my want; and in everything I kept myself from being burdensome unto you, and *so* will I keep *myself*. As the truth of Christ is in me, no man shall stop me of this glorying in the regions of Achaia. Wherefore? because I love you not? God knoweth. But what I do, that I will do, that I may cut off occasion from them which desire an occasion; that wherein they glory, they may be found even as we. For such men are false apostles, deceitful workers, fashioning themselves into apostles of Christ. And no marvel; for even Satan fashioneth himself into an angel of light. It is no great thing therefore if his ministers also fashion themselves as ministers of righteousness; whose end shall be according to their works.

"I say again, Let no man think me foolish; but if *ye do*, yet as foolish receive me, that I also may glory a little. That which I speak, I speak not after the Lord, but as in foolishness, in this confidence of glorying. Seeing that many glory after the flesh, I will glory also. For ye bear with the foolish gladly, being wise *yourselves*. For ye bear with a man, if he bringeth you into bondage, if he devoureth you, if he taketh you *captive*, if he exalteth himself, if he smiteth you on the face. I speak by way of disparagement, as though we had been weak. Yet whereinsoever any is bold (I speak in foolishness), I am bold also. Are they Hebrews? so am I. Are they Israelites? so am I. Are they the seed of Abraham? so am I. Are they ministers of Christ? (I speak as one beside himself) I more; in labours more abundantly, in prisons more abundantly, in stripes above measure, in deaths oft. Of the Jews five times received I forty *stripes* save one. Thrice was I beaten with rods, once was I stoned, thrice I suffered shipwreck, a night and a day have I been in the deep; *in* journeyings often, *in* perils of rivers, *in* perils of robbers, *in* perils from *my* countrymen, *in* perils from the Gentiles, *in* perils in the city, *in* perils in the wilderness, *in* perils in the sea, *in* perils among false brethren; *in* labour and travail, in watchings often, in hunger and thirst, in fastings often, in cold and nakedness. Beside those things that are without, there is that which presseth upon me daily, anxiety for all the Churches. Who is weak, and I am not weak? who is made to stumble, and I burn not?"—2 Cor. xi. 7-29 (R.V.).

The connexion of ver. 7 with what precedes is not at once clear. The Apostle has expressed his conviction that he is in nothing inferior to "the superlative apostles" so greatly honoured by the Corinthians. Why, then, is he so differently treated? A rudeness in speech he is willing to concede, but that can hardly be the explanation, considering his fulness of knowledge. Then another idea strikes him, and he puts it, interrogatively, as an alternative. Can it be that he did wrong—humbling himself that they might be exalted—in preaching to them the Gospel of God for nought, *i.e.* in declining to accept support from them while he evangelised in Corinth? Do they appreciate the interlopers more highly than Paul, because they exact a price for their gospel, while he preached his for nothing? This, of course, is bitterly ironical; but it is not gratuitous. The background of fact which prompted the Apostle's question was no doubt this—that his adversaries had misinterpreted his conduct. A true apostle, they said, has a right to be maintained by the Church; the Lord Himself has ordained that they who preach the Gospel should live by the Gospel; but he claims no maintenance, and by that very fact betrays a bad conscience. He dare not make the claim which every true apostle makes without the least misgiving.

It would be hard to imagine anything more malignant in its wickedness than this. Paul's refusal to claim support from those to whom he preached is one of the most purely and characteristically Christian of all his actions. He felt himself, by the grace of Christ, a debtor to all men; he owed them the Gospel; it was as if he were defrauding them if he did not tell them of the love of God in His Son. He felt himself in immense sympathy with the spirit of the Gospel; it was the free gift of God to the world, and as far as it depended on him its absolute freeness would not be obscured by the merest suspicion of a price to be paid. He knew that in foregoing his maintenance he was resigning a right secured to him by Christ (1 Cor. ix. 14), humbling himself, as he puts it here, that others might be spiritually exalted; but he had the joy of preaching the Gospel in the spirit of the Gospel—of entering, in Christ's service, into the self-sacrificing joy of his Lord; and he valued this above all earthly reward. To accuse such a man, on such grounds, of having a bad conscience, and of being afraid to live by his work, because he knew it was not what it pretended to be, was to sound the depths of baseness. It gave Paul in some measure the Master's experience, when the Pharisees said, "He casteth out devils by Beelzebub, the prince of the devils." It is really the prince of the devils, the accuser of the brethren, who speaks in all such malignant insinuations; it is the most diabolical thing any one can do—the nearest approach to sinning against the Holy Ghost—when he sets himself to find out bad motives for good actions.

As we shall see further on, Paul's enemies made more specific charges: they hinted that he made his own out of the Corinthians indirectly, and that he could indemnify himself, for this abstinence, from the collection (chaps. xii. 16-18, chap. viii. and ix.). Perhaps this is why he describes his actual conduct at Corinth in such vigorous language (vv. 7-11), before saying anything at all of his motives. "I preached to you the Gospel of God," he says, "for nothing." He calls it "the Gospel of God" with intentional fulness and solemnity; the genuine Gospel, he means—not another, which is no gospel at all, but a subversion of the truth. He robbed other Churches, and took wages from them, in order to minister to the Corinthians. There is a mingling of ideas in the strong words here used. The English reader thinks of Paul's doing less than justice to other Churches that he might do more than justice to the Corinthians; but though this is true, it is not all. Both "robbed" (ἐσύλησα) and "wages" (ὀψώνιον), as Bengel has pointed out, are military words, and it is difficult to resist the impression that Paul used them as such; he did not come to Corinth to be dependent on any one, but in the course of a triumphant progress, in which he devoted the spoils of his earlier victories for Christ to a new campaign in Achaia.[93] Nay, even when he was with them and was "in want" (what a ray of light that one word ὑστερηθείς lets into his circumstances!), he did not throw himself like a benumbing weight on any one; what his own labours failed to supply, the brethren (perhaps Silas and Timothy) made good when they came from Macedonia. This has been his practice, and will continue to be so. He swears by the truth of Christ that is in him, that no man shall ever stop his mouth, so far as boasting of this independence is concerned, in the regions of Achaia. Why? His tender heart dismisses the one painful supposition which could possibly arise. "Because I love you not? God knoweth." Love is wounded when its proffered gifts are rejected with scorn, and when *their* rejection means that *it* is rejected; but that was not the situation here. Paul can appeal to Him who knows the heart in proof of the sincerity with which he loves the Corinthians.

His fixed purpose to be indebted to no one in Achaia has another object in view. What that is he explains in the twelfth verse. Strange to say, this verse, like ver. 4, has received two precisely opposite interpretations. (1) Some start with the idea that Paul's adversaries at Corinth were persons who took no support from the Church, and boasted of their disinterestedness in this respect. The "occasion" which they desired was an occasion of any sort for disparaging and discrediting Paul; and they felt they would have such an occasion if Paul accepted support from the Church, and so put himself in a position of inferiority to them. But Paul persists in his self-denying policy, with the object of depriving them of the opportunity they seek, and at the same time of proving them—in this very point of disinterestedness—to be in exactly the same position as himself. But surely, throughout both Epistles, a contrast is implied, in this very point, between Paul and his opponents: the tacit assumption is always that his line of conduct is singular, and is not to be made a rule. And in the face of ver. 20 it is too much to assume that it was the rule of his Judaising opponents in Corinth. (2) Others start with the idea, which seems to me indubitably right, that these opponents did accept support from the Church. But even on this assumption opinions diverge. (*a*) Some argue that Paul pursued his policy of abstinence partly to deprive them of any opportunity of disparaging him, and partly to compel them to adopt it themselves ("that they may be found even as we").[94] I can hardly imagine this being taken seriously. Why should Paul have wanted to lift these preachers of a false gospel to a level with himself in point of generosity? To coerce them into a reluctant self-denial could be no possible object to him either of wish or hope. Hence there seems only (*b*) the other alternative open, which makes the last clause—"that wherein they boast, they may be found even as we"—depend, not upon "what I do, that I will do," but upon "them that desire occasion."[95] What the adversaries desired was, not occasion to disparage Paul in general, but occasion of being on an equality with him in the matter in which they gloried—viz., their apostolic claims. They felt the advantage which Paul's disinterestedness gave him with the Corinthians; they had not themselves the generosity needed to imitate it; it was not enough to assail it with covert slanders (chap. xii. 16-18), or to say that he was afraid to claim an apostle's due; it would have been all they wanted had he resigned it. Then they could have said that in that in which they boasted—apostolic dignity—they were precisely on a level with him. But not to mention the spiritual motives for his conduct, which have been already explained, and were independent of all relation to his opponents, Paul was too capable a strategist to surrender such a position to the enemy. It would never be by action of his that he and they found themselves on the same ground.

At the very mention of such an equality his heart rises within him. "Found even as we! Why, such men are false apostles, deceitful workers, fashioning themselves into apostles of Christ." Here, at last, the irony is cast aside, and Paul calls a spade a spade. The conception of apostleship in the New Testament is not that dogmatic traditional one, which limits the name to the Twelve, or to the Twelve and the Apostle of the Gentiles; as we see from passages like chap. viii. 23, Acts xiv. 4, 14, it had a much larger application. What Paul means when he calls his opponents false apostles is not that persons *in their position* could have no right to the name; but that persons *with their character*, their aims, and their methods, would only deceive others when they used it. It ought to cover something quite different from what it actually did cover in them. He explains himself further when he calls them "deceitful workers." That they were active he does not deny; but the true end of their activity was not declared. As far as the word itself goes, the "deceit" which they used may have been intended to cloak either their personal or their proselytising views. After what we have read in chap. x. 12-18, the latter seems preferable. The Judaising preachers had shown their hand in Galatia, demanding openly that Paul's converts should be circumcised, and keep the law of Moses as a whole; but their experience there had made them cautious, and when they came to Corinth they proceeded more diplomatically. They tried to sap the Pauline Gospel, partly by preaching "another Jesus," partly by calling in question the legitimacy of Paul's vocation. They said nothing openly of what was the inevitable and intended issue of all this—the bringing of spiritual Gentile Christendom under the old Jewish yoke. But it is this which goes to the Apostle's soul; he can be nothing but irreconcilably hostile to men who have assumed the guise of apostles of Christ, in order that they may with greater security subvert Christ's characteristic work. Paul dwells on the deceitfulness of their conduct as its most offensive feature; yet he does not wonder at it, for even Satan, he says, fashions himself into an angel of light. It is no great thing, then, if his servants also fashion themselves as servants of righteousness.

We can only tell in a general way what Paul meant when he spoke of Satan, the prince of darkness, transfiguring himself so as to appear a heavenly angel. He may have had some Jewish legend in his mind, some story of a famous temptation, unknown to us, or he may only have intended to represent to the imagination, with the utmost possible vividness, one of the familiar laws in our moral experience, a law which was strikingly illustrated by the conduct of his adversaries at Corinth. Evil, we all know, could never tempt us if we saw it simply as it is; disguise is essential to its power; it appeals to man through ideas and hopes which he cannot but regard as good. So it was in the very first temptation. An act which in its essential character was neither more nor less than one of direct disobedience to God was represented by the tempter, not in that character, but as the means by which man was to obtain possession of a tree good for food (sensual satisfaction), and pleasant to the eyes (æsthetic satisfaction), and desirable to make one wise (intellectual satisfaction). All these satisfactions, which in themselves are undeniably good, were the cloak under which the tempter hid his true features. He was a murderer from the beginning, and entered Eden to ruin man, but he presented himself as one offering to man a vast enlargement of life and joy. This is the nature of all temptations; to disguise himself, to look as like a good angel as he can, is the first necessity, and therefore the first invention, of the devil. And all who do his work, the Apostle says, naturally imitate his devices. The soul of man is born for good, and will not listen at all to any voice which does not profess at least to speak for good: this is why the devil is a liar from the beginning, and the father of lies. Lying in word and deed is the one weapon with which he can assail the simplicity of man.

But how does this apply to the Judaisers in Corinth? To Paul, we must understand, they were men affecting to serve Christ, but really impelled by personal, or at the utmost by partisan, feelings. Their true object was to win an ascendency for themselves, or for their party, in the Church; but they made their way into it as evangelists and apostles. Nominally, they were ministers of Christ; really, they ministered to their own vanity, and to the bigotry and prejudices of their race. They professed to be furthering the cause of righteousness,[96] but in sober truth the only cause which was the better for them was that of their own private importance; the result of their ministry was, not that bad men became good, but that they themselves felt entitled to give themselves airs. Over against all this unreality Paul remembers the righteous judgment of God. "Whose end," he concludes abruptly, "shall be according to their works."

The most serious aspect of such a situation as this is seen when we consider that men may fill it unconsciously: they may devote themselves to a cause which looks like the cause of Christ, or the cause of righteousness; and at bottom it may not be Christ or righteousness at all which is the animating principle in their hearts. It is some hidden regard to themselves, or to a party with which they are identified. Even when they labour, and possibly suffer, it is this, and not loyalty to Christ, which sustains them. It may be in defence of orthodoxy, or in furtherance of liberalism, that a man puts himself forward in the Church, and in either case he will figure to those who agree with him as a servant of righteousness; but equally in either case the secret spring of his action may be pride, the desire to assert a superiority, to consolidate a party which is his larger self, to secure an area in which he may rule. He may spend energy and talent on the work; but if this is the ultimate motive of it, it is the work of the devil, and not of God. Even if the doctrine he defends is the true one—even if the policy he maintains is the right one—the services he may accidentally render are far outweighed by the domestication in the Church of a spirit so alien to the Lord's. It is diabolical, not divine; the Gospel is profaned by contact with it; the Church is prostituted when it serves as an arena for its exercise; when it comes forward in the interest of righteousness, it is Satan fashioning himself into an angel of light.

At this point Paul returns to the idea which has been in his mind since chap. x. 7—the idea of boasting, or rather glorying. He does not like the thing itself, and just as little does he like the mask of a fool, under which he is to play the part: he is conscious that neither suits him. Hence he clears the ground once more, before he commits himself. "Again, I say, let no man think that I *am* foolish; but if that favour cannot be granted, then even as a foolish person receive me, that I also may boast a little." There is a fine satirical reflection in the "also." If he does make a fool of himself by boasting, he is only doing what the others do, whom the Corinthians receive with open arms. But it strikes his conscience suddenly that there is a higher rule for the conduct of a Christian man than the example of his rivals, or the patience of his friends. The tenderness of Paul's spirit comes out in the next words: "What I speak, I speak *not after the Lord*, but as in foolishness, in this confidence of glorying." The Lord never boasted; nothing could be conceived less like Him, less after His mind; and Paul will have it distinctly understood that *His* character is not compromised by any extravagance of which His servant may here make himself guilty. As a rule, the Apostle did speak "after the Lord"; his habitual consciousness was that of one who had "the mind of Christ," and who felt that Christ's character was, in a sense, in his keeping. That ought to be the rule for all Christians; we should never find ourselves in situations in which the Christian character, with all its responsibilities, affecting both ourselves and Him, cannot be maintained. With Christ and His interests removed from the scene, Paul at length feels himself free to measure himself against his rivals. "Since many glory after the flesh, I also will glory." The flesh means everything except the spirit. Where Christ and the Gospel are concerned, it is, according to Paul, an absolute irrelevance, a thing to be simply left out of account; but since they persist in dragging it in, he will meet them on their own ground. What that is, first comes out clearly in ver. 22: but the Apostle delays again to urge his plea for tolerance. "Ye suffer the foolish gladly, being wise yourselves." It answers best to the vehemence of the whole passage to take the first clause here—"Ye suffer the foolish gladly"—as grim earnest, the reference being to the other boasters, Paul's rivals; and only the second clause ironically. Then ver. 20 would give the proof of this: "Ye bear with the foolish gladly ... for ye bear with a man if he enslaves you, if he devours you, if he takes you captive, if he exalts himself over you, if he strikes you on the face." We must suppose that this strong language describes the overbearing and violent behaviour of the Judaists in Corinth. We do not need to take it literally, but neither may we suppose that Paul spoke at random: he is virtually contrasting his own conduct and that of the people in question, and the nature of the contrast must be on the whole correctly indicated. He himself had been accused of weakness; and he frankly admits that, if comparison has to be made with a line of action like this, the accusation is just. "I speak by way of disparagement, as though we had been weak." This rendering of the Revised Version fairly conveys the meaning. It might be expressed in a paraphrase, as follows: "In saying what I have said of the behaviour of my rivals, I have been speaking to my own disparagement, the idea involved[97] being that *I*" (notice the emphatic ἡμεῖς) "have been weak. Weak, no doubt, I was, if violent action like theirs is the true measure of strength: nevertheless, whereinsoever any is bold (I speak in foolishness), I am bold also. On whatever ground they claim to exercise such extraordinary powers, that ground I can maintain as well as they."

Here, finally, the boasting does begin. "Are they Hebrews? so am I. Are they Israelites? so am I. Are they the seed of Abraham? so am I." This is the sum and substance of what is meant by their glorying after the flesh: they prided themselves on their birth, and claimed authority on the strength of it. They may have appealed, not only to the election of Israel as the Old Testament represents it, but to words of Jesus, like "Salvation is of the Jews." The three names for what is in reality one thing convey the impression of the immense importance which was assigned to it. "Hebrews" seems the least significant; it is merely the *national* name, with whatever historical glories attached to it in Hebrew minds. "Israelites" is a *sacred* name; it is identified with the prerogatives of the theocratic people: Paul himself, when his heart swells with patriotic emotion, begins the enumeration of the privileges belonging to his kinsmen after the flesh—"they, who are Israelites." "Seed of Abraham," again, is for the Apostle, and probably for these rivals of his, equivalent to "heirs of the promises"; it describes the Jewish people as more directly and immediately interested—nay, as alone directly and immediately interested—in the salvation of God. No one could read Rom. ix. 4 f. without feeling that pride of race—pride in his people, and in their special relation to God and special place in the history of redemption—was among the strongest passions in the Apostle's heart; and we can understand the indignation and scorn with which he regarded men who tracked him over Asia and Europe, assailed his authority, and sought to undermine his work, on the ground that he was faithless to the lawful prerogatives of Israel. There was not an Israelite in the world prouder of his birth, with a more magnificent sense of his country's glories, than the Apostle of the Gentiles: and it provoked him beyond endurance to see the things in which he gloried debased, as they were debased, by his rivals—made the symbols of a paltry vanity which he despised, made barriers to the universal love of God by which all the families of the earth were to be blessed. Driven to extremity, he could only outlaw such opponents from the Christian community, and transfer the prerogatives of Israel to the Church. "*We*," he taught his Gentile converts to say—"*we are the circumcision, who worship by the Spirit of God, and rejoice in Christ Jesus, and have no confidence in the flesh*" (Phil. iii. 3).

Here he does not linger long over what is merely external. It is a deeper question that he asks in ver. 23, "Are they ministers of Christ?" and he feels like a man beside himself, clean out of his senses (παραφρονῶν)—so unsuitable is the subject for boasting—as he answers, "I more." Many interpret this as if it meant, "I am more than a servant of Christ," and then ask wonderingly, "What more?" but surely the natural meaning is, "I am a servant too, in a higher degree." The proof of this is given in that tale of sufferings which bursts irrepressibly from the Apostle's heart, and sweeps us in its course like a torrent. If he thought of his rivals when he began, and was instituting a serious comparison when he wrote "in labours *more abundantly* [than they]," they must soon have escaped from his mind. It is his own life as a minister of Christ on which he dwells; and after the first words, if a comparison is to be made, he leaves the making of it to others. But comparison, in fact, was out of the question: the sufferings of the Apostle in doing service to Christ were unparalleled and alone. The few lines which he devotes to them are the most vivid light we have on the apostolic age and the apostolic career. They show how fragmentary, or at all events how select, is the narrative in the Book of Acts. Thus of the incidents mentioned in ver. 25 we learn but little from St. Luke. Of the five times nine-and-thirty stripes, he mentions none; of the three beatings with rods, only one; of the three shipwrecks, none (for Acts xxvii. is later), and nothing of the twenty-four hours in the deep. It is not necessary to comment on details, but one cannot resist the impression of triumph with which Paul recounts the "perils" he had faced; so many they were, so various, and so terrible, yet in the Lord's service he has come safely through them all. It is a commentary from his own hand on his own word—"as dying, and, behold, we live!" In the retrospect all these perils show, not only that he is a true servant of Christ, entering into the fellowship of his Master's sufferings to bring blessing to men, but that he is owned by Christ as such: the Lord has delivered him from deaths so great; yes, and will deliver him; and his hope is set on Him for every deliverance he may need (chap. i. 10).

But, after all, these perils are but outward, and the very enumeration of them shows that they are things of the past. In all their kinds and degrees—violence, privation, exposure, fear—they are a historical testimony to the devotion with which Paul has served Christ. He bore in his body the marks which they had left, and to him they were the marks of Jesus; they identified him as Christ's slave. But not to mention incidental matters,[98] there is another testimony to his ministry which is ever with him—a burden as crushing as these bodily sufferings, and far more constant in its pressure: "that which cometh upon me daily, anxiety for all the Churches." Short of this, anything of which man can boast may be, at least in a qualified sense, "after the flesh"; but in this identification of himself with Christ's cause in the world—this bearing of others' burdens on his spirit—there is that fulfilment of Christ's law which alone and finally legitimates a Christian ministry. Nor was it merely in an official sense that Paul was interested in the affairs of the Church. When the Church is once planted in the world, it has a side which is of the world, a side which may be administered without a very heavy expenditure of Christian feeling: this, it is safe to say, is simply out of sight. Paul's anxiety for the Churches is defined in all its scope and intensity in the passionate words of the twenty-ninth verse: "Who is weak, and I am not weak? Who is made to stumble, and I burn not?" His love individualised Christian people, and made him one with them. There was no trembling timorous soul, no scrupulous conscience, in all the communities he had founded, whose timidity and weakness did not put a limit to his strength: he condescended to their intelligence, feeding them with milk, and not with meat; he measured his liberty, not in principle but in practice, by their bondage; his heart thrilled with their fears; in the fulness of his Christ-like strength he lived a hundred feeble lives. And when spiritual harm came to one of them—when the very least was made to stumble, and was caught in the snare of falsehood or sin—the pain in his heart was like burning fire. The sorrow that pierced the soul of Christ pierced his soul also; the indignation that glowed in the Master's breast, as He pronounced woe on the man by whom occasions of stumbling come, glowed again in him. This is the fire that Christ came to cast on the earth, and that He longed to see kindled—this prompt intense sympathy with all that is of God in men's souls, this readiness to be weak with the weak, this pain and indignation when the selfishness or pride of men leads the weak astray, and imperils the work for which Christ died. And this is indeed the Apostle's last line of defence. Nowhere could boasting be less in place than when a man speaks of the lessons he has learned at the Cross: yet these only give him a title to glory as "a minister of Christ." If glorying *here* is inadmissible, it is because glorying in every sense is "folly."

XXVI
STRENGTH AND WEAKNESS

"If I must needs glory, I will glory of the things that concern my weakness. The God and Father of the Lord Jesus, He who is blessed for evermore, knoweth that I lie not. In Damascus the governor under Aretas the king guarded the city of the Damascenes, in order to take me: and through a window was I let down in a basket by the wall, and escaped his hands.

"I must needs glory, though it is not expedient; but I will come to visions and revelations of the Lord. I know a man in Christ, fourteen years ago (whether in the body, I know not; or whether out of the body, I know not; God knoweth), such a one caught up even to the third heaven. And I know such a man (whether in the body, or apart from the body, I know not; God knoweth), how that he was caught up into Paradise, and heard unspeakable words, which it is not lawful for a man to utter. On behalf of such a one will I glory: but on mine own behalf I will not glory, save in *my* weaknesses. For if I should desire to glory, I shall not be foolish; for I shall speak the truth: but I forbear, lest any man should account of me above that which he seeth me *to be*, or heareth from me. And by reason of the exceeding greatness of the revelations—wherefore, that I should not be exalted overmuch, there was given to me a thorn in the flesh, a messenger of Satan to buffet me, that I should not be exalted overmuch. Concerning this thing I besought the Lord thrice, that it might depart from me. And He hath said unto me, My grace is sufficient for thee: for *My* power is made perfect in weakness. Most gladly therefore will I rather glory in my weaknesses, that the strength of Christ may rest upon me. Wherefore I take pleasure in weaknesses, in injuries, in necessities, in persecutions, in distresses, for Christ's sake: for when I am weak, then am I strong."—2 Cor. xi. 30-xii. 10 (R.V.).

The difficulties of exposition in this passage are partly connected with its form, partly with its substance: it will be convenient to dispose of the formal side first. The thirtieth verse of the eleventh chapter—"If I must needs glory, I will glory of the things that concern my weakness"—seems to serve two purposes. On the one hand, it is a natural and effective climax to all that precedes; it defines the principle on which Paul has acted in the glorying of vv. 23-29. It is not of exploits that he is proud, but of perils and sufferings; not of what he has achieved, but of what he has endured, for Christ's sake; in a word, not of strength, but of weakness. On the other hand, this same thirtieth verse indubitably points forward; it defines the principle on which Paul will always act where boasting is in view; and it is expressly resumed in chap. xii., ver. 5 and ver. 9. For this reason, it seems better to treat it as a text than as a peroration; it is the key to the interpretation of what follows, put into our hands by the Apostle himself. In the full consciousness of its dangers and inconveniences, he means to go a little further in this foolish boasting; but he takes security, as far as possible, against its moral perils, by choosing as the ground of boasting things which in the common judgment of men would only bring him shame.

At this point we are startled by a sudden appeal to God, the solemnity and fulness of which strike us, on a first reading, as almost painfully gratuitous. "The God and Father of the Lord Jesus, He who is blessed for ever, knoweth that I lie not." What is the explanation of this extraordinary earnestness? There is a similar passage in Gal. i. 19—"Now touching the things which I write unto you, behold, before God, I lie not"—where Lightfoot says the strength of the Apostle's language is to be explained by the unscrupulous calumnies cast upon him by his enemies. This *may* be the clue to his vehemence here; and in point of fact it falls in with by far the most ingenious explanation that has been given of the two subjects introduced in this paragraph. The explanation I refer to is that of Heinrici. He supposes that Paul's escape from Damascus, and his visions and revelations, had been turned to account against him by his rivals. They had used the escape to accuse him of ignominious cowardice: the indignity of it is obvious enough. His visions and revelations were as capable of misconstruction: it was easy to call them mere illusions, signs of a disordered brain; it was not too much for malice to hint that his call to apostleship rested on nothing better than one of these ecstatic hallucinations. It is because things so dear to him are attacked—his reputation for personal courage, which is the mainstay of all the virtues; his actual vision of Christ, and divinely authorised mission—that he makes the vehement appeal that startles us at first. He calls God to witness that in regard to both these subjects he is going to tell the exact truth: the truth will be his sufficient defence. Ingenious as it is, I do not think this theory can be maintained. There is no hint in the passage that Paul is defending himself; he is glorying, and glorying in the things that concern his weakness. It seems more probable that, when he dictated the strong words of ver. 31, the outline of all he was going to say was in his mind; and as the main part of it—all about the visions and revelations—was absolutely uncontrollable by any witness but his own, he felt moved to attest it thus in advance. The names and attributes of God fall in well with this. As the visions and revelations were specially connected with Christ, and were counted by the Apostle among the things for which he had the deepest reason to praise God, it is but the reflection of this state of mind when he appeals to "the God and *Father of the Lord Jesus,* He who is *blessed for evermore.*" This is not a random adjuration, but an appeal which takes shape involuntarily in a grateful and pious heart, on which the memory of a signal grace and honour still rests. Of course the verses about Damascus stand rather out of relation to it. But it is a violence which nothing can justify to strike them out of the text on this ground, and along with them part or the whole of ver. 1 in chap. xii.[99] For many reasons unknown to us the danger in Damascus, and the escape from it, may have had a peculiar interest for the Apostle; *hæc persequutio,* says Calvin, *erat quasi primum tirocinium Pauli*; it was his "matriculation in the school of persecution." He may have intended, as Meyer thinks, to make it the beginning of a new catalogue of sufferings for Christ's sake, all of which were to be covered by the appeal to God, and have abruptly repented, and gone off on another subject; but whether or not, to expunge the lines is pure wilfulness. The Apostle glories in what he endured at Damascus—in the imminent peril and in the undignified escape alike—as in things belonging to his weakness. Another might choose to hide such things, but they are precisely what he tells. In Christ's service scorn is glory, ignominy is honour; and it is the mark of loyalty when men rejoice that they are counted worthy to suffer shame for the Name.[100]

When we go on to chap. xii., and the second of the two subjects with which boasting is to be associated, we meet in the first verse with serious textual difficulties. Our Authorised Version gives the rendering: *"It is not expedient for me doubtless to glory. I will come to visions and revelations of the Lord."* This follows the Textus Receptus: Καυχᾶσθαι δὴ οὐ συμφέρει μοι· ἐλεύσομαι γὰρ κ.τ.λ., only omitting the γὰρ (*for* I will come). The MSS. are almost chaotic, but the most authoritative editors—Tregelles, Tischendorf in his last edition, and Westcott and Hort—agree in reading Καυχᾶσθαι δεῖ οὐ[101 συμφέρον μὲν ἐλεύσομαι δὲ κ.τ.λ.] This is the text which our Revisers render: *"I must needs glory, though it is not expedient; but I will come to visions and revelations of the Lord."* Practically, the difference is not so great after all. According to the best authorities, Paul repeats that he is being forced to speak as he does; the consciousness of the disadvantages attendant on this course does not leave him, it is rather deepened, as he approaches the highest and most sacred of all subjects—visions and revelations he has received from Christ. Of these two words, revelations is the wider in import: visions were only one of the ways in which revelations could be made. Paul, of course, is not going to boast directly of the visions and revelations themselves. All through the experiences to which he alludes under this name he was to himself as a third person; he was purely passive; and to claim credit, to glory as if he had done or originated anything, would be transparently absurd. But there are "things of his weakness" associated with, if not dependent on, these high experiences; and it is in them, after due explanation, that he purposes to exult.

He begins abruptly. "I know a man in Christ, fourteen years ago (whether in the body, I know not; or whether out of the body, I know not; God knoweth), such a one caught up even to the third heaven." A man in Christ means a Christian man, a man in his character *as* a Christian. To St. Paul's consciousness the wonderful experience he is about to describe was not natural, still less pathological, but unequivocally religious. It did not befall him as a man simply, still less as an epileptic patient; it was an unmistakably Christian experience. He only existed for himself, during it, as "a man in Christ." "I know such a man," he says, "fourteen years ago caught up even to the third heaven." The date of this "rapture" (the same word is used in Acts viii. 39; 1 Thess. iv. 17; Rev. xii. 5: all significant examples) would be about A.D. 44. This forbids us to connect it in any way with Paul's conversion, which must have been twenty years earlier than this letter; and indeed there is no reason for identifying it with anything else we know of the Apostle. At the date in question, as far as can be made out from the Book of Acts, he must have been in Tarsus or in Antioch. The rapture itself is described as perfectly incomprehensible. He may have been carried up bodily to the heavenly places; his spirit may have been carried up, while his body remained unconscious upon earth: he can express no opinion about this; the truth is only known to God. It is idle to exploit a passage like this in the interest of apostolic psychology; Paul is only taking elaborate pains to tell us that of the mode of his rapture he was absolutely ignorant. It is fairer to infer that the event was unique in his experience, and that when it happened he was alone; had such things recurred, or had there been spectators, he could not have been in doubt as to whether he was caught up "in the body" or "out of the body." The mere fact that the date is given individualises the event in his life; and it is going beyond the facts altogether to generalise it, and take it as the type of such an experience as accompanied his conversion, or of the visions in Acts xvi. 9, xxii. 17 f., xviii.

9. It was one, solitary, incomparable experience, including in it a complex of visions and revelations granted by Christ: it was this, at all events, to the Apostle; and if we do not believe what he tells us about it, we can have no knowledge of it at all.

"Caught up even to the third heaven." The Jews usually counted seven heavens; sometimes, perhaps because of the dual form of the Hebrew word for heaven, two; but the distinctions between the various heavens were as fanciful as the numbers were arbitrary. It adds nothing, even to the imagination, to speak of an aerial, a sidereal, and a spiritual heaven, and to suppose that these are meant by Paul; we can only think vaguely of the "man in Christ" rising through one celestial region after another till he came even to the third. The word chosen to define the distance (ἕως) suggests that an impression of vast spaces traversed remained on the Apostle's mind; and that the third heaven, on which his sentence pauses, and which is a resting-place for his memory, was also a station, so to speak, in his rapture. This is the only supposition which does justice to the resumption in ver. 3 of the deliberate and circumstantial language of ver. 2. "And I know such a man—whether in the body or apart from the body (I know not) God knoweth—how that he was caught up into Paradise, and heard unspeakable words that it is not lawful for a man to utter." This is a resumption, not a repetition. Paul is not elaborately telling the same story over again, but he is carrying it on, with the same full circumstance, the same grave asseveration, from the point at which he halted. The rapture had a second stage, under the same incomprehensible conditions, and in it the Christian man passed out and up from the third heaven into Paradise. Many of the Jews believed in a Paradise beneath the earth, the abode of the souls of the good while they awaited their perfecting at the Resurrection (cf. Luke xvi. 23 ff., xxiii. 43); but obviously this cannot be the idea here. We must think rather of what the Apocalypse calls "the Paradise of God" (ii. 7), where the tree of life grows, and where those who overcome have their reward. It is an abode of unimaginable blessedness, "far above all heavens," to use the Apostle's own words elsewhere (Eph. iv. 10). What visions he had, or what revelations, during that pause in the third heaven, Paul does not say; and at this supreme point of his rapture, in Paradise, the words he heard were words unspeakable, which it is not lawful for man to utter. Mortal ears might hear, but mortal lips might not repeat, sounds so mysterious and divine: it was not for *man* (ἀνθρώπῳ is qualitative) to utter them.

But why, we may ask, if this rapture has its meaning and value solely for the Apostle, should he refer to it here at all? Why should he make such solemn statements about an experience, the historical conditions of which, as he is careful to assure us, are incomprehensible, while its spiritual content is a secret? Is not such an experience literally *nothing* to us? No, unless Paul himself is nothing; for this experience was evidently a great thing to him. It was the most sacred privilege and honour he had ever known; it was among his strongest sources of inspiration; it had a powerful tendency to generate spiritual pride; and it had its accompaniment, and its counter-weight, in his sharpest trial. The world knows little of its greatest men; perhaps we very rarely know what are the great things in the lives even of the people who are round about us. Paul had kept silence about this sublime experience for fourteen years, and no man had ever guessed it; it had been a secret between the Lord and His disciple; and they only, who were in the secret, could rightly interpret all that depended upon it. There is a kind of profanity in forcing the heart to show itself too far, in compelling a man to speak about, even though he does not divulge, the things that it is not lawful to utter. The Corinthians had put this profane compulsion on the Apostle; but though he yields to it, it is in a way which keeps clear of the profanity. He tells what he dare tell in the third person, and then goes on: "On behalf of such a one will I glory, but on behalf of myself will I not glory, save in my infirmities." *Removere debemus* τὸ *ego a rebus magnis* (Bengel): there are things too great to allow the intrusion of self. Paul does not choose to identify the poor Apostle whom the Corinthians and their misleading teachers used so badly with the man in Christ who had such inconceivable honour put on him by the Lord; if he does boast on behalf of such a one, and magnify his sublime experiences, at all events he does not transfer his prerogatives to *himself*; he does not say, "*I* am that incomparably honoured man; reverence in me a special favourite of Christ." On the contrary, where *his own* interest has to be forwarded, he will glory in nothing but his weaknesses. The one thing about which he is anxious is that men should not think too highly of him, nor go in their appreciation beyond what their experience of him as a man and a teacher justifies (ver. 6). He might, indeed, boast, reasonably enough; for the truth would suffice, without any foolish exaggeration; but he forbears, for the reason just stated. We are familiar with the danger of thinking too highly of ourselves; it is as real a danger, though probably a less considered one, to be too highly thought of by others. Paul dreaded it; so does every wise man. To be highly thought of, where the character is sincere and unpretentious, may be a protection, and even an inspiration; but to have a reputation, morally, that one does not deserve—to be counted good in respects in which one is really bad—is to have a frightful difficulty added to penitence and amendment. It puts one in a radically false position; it generates and fosters hypocrisy; it explains a vast mass of spiritual ineffectiveness. The man who is insincere enough to be puffed up by it is not far from judgment.

But to return to the text. Paul wishes to be humble; he is content that men should take him as they find him, infirmities and all. He has that about him, too, and not unconnected with these high experiences, the very purpose of which is to keep him humble. If the text is correct,[102] he expresses himself with some embarrassment. "And by reason of the exceeding greatness of the revelations—wherefore, that I should not be exalted overmuch, there was given to me a thorn in the flesh, a messenger of Satan to buffet me, that I should not be exalted overmuch." The repetition of the last word shows where the emphasis lies: Paul has a deep and constant sense of the danger of spiritual pride, and he knows that he would fall into it unless a strong counter-pressure were kept up upon him.

I do not feel called on to add another to the numberless disquisitions on Paul's thorn in the flesh. The resources of imagination having been exhausted, people are returning to the obvious. The thorn in the flesh[103] was something painful, which affected the Apostle's body; it was something in its nature purely physical, not a solicitation to any kind of sin, such as sensuality or pride, else he would not have ceased to pray for its removal; it was something terribly humbling, if not humiliating—an affection which might well have excited the contempt and loathing of those who beheld it (Gal. iv. 14, which probably refers to this subject); it had begun after, if not in consequence of, the rapture just described, and stood in a spiritual, if not a physical, relation to it; it was, if not chronic or periodic, at least recurrent; the Apostle knew that it would never leave him. What known malady, incident to human nature, fulfils all these conditions, it is not possible with perfect certainty to say. A considerable mass of competent opinion supports the idea that it must have been liability to epileptic seizures.[104] Such an infirmity Paul might have suffered under in common with men so great as Julius Cæsar and the first Napoleon, as Mahomet, King Alfred, and Peter the Great. But it does not quite satisfy the conditions. Epileptic attacks, if they occur with any frequency at all, invariably cause mental deterioration. Now, Paul distinctly suggests that the thorn was a very steady companion; and as his mind, in spite of it, grew year after year in the apprehension of the Christian revelation, so that his last thoughts are always his largest and best, the epileptic hypothesis has its difficulties like every other. Is it likely that a man who suffered pretty constantly from nervous convulsions of this kind wrote the Second Epistle to the Corinthians after fourteen years of them, or the Epistles to the Romans, Philippians, Colossians, and Ephesians later still? There is, of course, no religious interest in affirming or denying any physical explanation of the matter whatever; but with our present data I do not think a certain explanation is within our reach.

The Apostle himself is not interested in it as a physical affection. He speaks of it because of its spiritual significance, and because of the wonderful spiritual experiences he has had in connexion with it. It was given him, he says: but by whom? When we think of the purpose—to save him from spiritual pride—we instinctively answer, "God." And that, it can hardly be doubted, would have been the Apostle's own answer. Yet he does not hesitate to call it in the same breath a messenger of Satan. The name is dictated by the inborn, ineradicable shrinking of the soul from pain; that agonising, humiliating, annihilating thing, we feel at the bottom of our hearts, is not really of God, even when it does His work. In His perfect world pain shall be no more. It does not need science, but experience, to put these things together, and to understand at once the evil and the good of suffering. Paul, at first, like all men, found the evil overpowering. The pain, the weakness, the degradation of his malady, were intolerable. He could not understand that only a pressure so pitiless and humbling could preserve him from spiritual pride and a spiritual fall. We are all slow to learn anything like this. We think we can take warning, that a word will be enough, that at most the memory of a single pang will suffice to keep us safe. But pains remain with us, and the pressure is continuous and unrelieved, because the need of constraint and of discipline is ceaseless. The crooked branch will not bend in a new curve if it is only tied to it for half an hour. The sinful bias in our natures—to pride, to sensuality, to falsehood, or whatever else—-will not be cured by one sharp lesson. The commonest experience in human life is that the man whom sickness and pain have humbled for the moment, the very moment their constraint is lifted, resumes his old habit. He does not think so, but it is really the thorn that has been keeping him right; and when its sharpness is blunted, the edge is taken from his conscience too.

Paul besought the Lord, that is Christ, thrice, that this thing might depart from him. The Lord, we may be sure, had full sympathy with that prayer. He Himself had had His agony, and prayed the Father thrice that if it were possible the cup of pain might pass from Him. He prayed, indeed, in express submission to the Father's will; the voice of nature was not allowed in Him to urge an unconditional peremptory request. Perhaps in Paul on this occasion—certainly often in most men—it is nature, the flesh and not the spirit, which prompts the prayer. But God is all the while guarding the spirit's interest as the higher, and this explains the many real answers to prayer which seem to be refusals. A refusal *is* an answer, if it is so given that God and the soul thenceforth understand one another. It was thus that Paul was answered by Christ: "He hath said to me, My grace is sufficient for thee: for [My] strength is made perfect in weakness."

The first point to notice in this answer is the tense of the verb: "He hath said." The A.V. with "He said" misses the point. The sentence is present as well as past; it is Christ's continuous, as well as final, answer to Paul's prayer. The Apostle has been made to understand that the thorn must remain in his flesh, but along with this he has received the assurance of an abiding love and help from the Lord. We remember, even by contrast, the stern answer made to Moses when he prayed that he might be permitted to cross Jordan and see the goodly land—"Let it suffice thee: speak no more unto Me of this matter." Paul also could no more ask for the removal of the thorn: it was the Lord's will that he should submit to it for high spiritual ends, and to pray against it would now have been a kind of impiety. But it is no longer an unrelieved pain and humiliation; the Apostle is supported under it by that grace of Christ which finds in the need and abjectness of men the opportunity of showing in all perfection its own condescending strength. The collocation of "grace" and "strength" in the ninth verse is characteristic of the New Testament, and very significant. There are many to whom "grace" is a holy word with no particular meaning; "the grace of God," or "the grace of the Lord Jesus Christ," is only a vague benignity, which may fairly enough be spoken of as a "smile." But grace, in the New Testament, is force: it is a heavenly strength bestowed on men for timely succour; it finds its opportunity in our extremity; when our weakness makes us incapable of doing anything, it gets full scope *to work*. This is the meaning of the last words—"strength is made perfect in weakness." The truth is quite general; it is an application of it to the case in hand if we translate as in the A.V. (with some MSS.): "*My* strength is made perfect in [thy] weakness." It is enough, the Lord tells Paul, that he has this heavenly strength unceasingly bestowed upon him; the weakness which he has found so hard to bear—that distressing malady which humbled him and took his vigour away—is but the foil to it: it serves to magnify it, and to set it off; with that Paul should be content.

And he is content. That answer to his thrice-repeated prayer works a revolution in his heart; he looks at all that had troubled him—at all that he had deprecated—with new eyes. "Most gladly therefore will I rather glory in my infirmities—that is, glory rather than bemoan them or pray for their removal—that the power of Christ may spread its tabernacle over me." This compensation far outweighed the trial. He has ceased to speak now of the visions and revelations, perhaps he has ceased already to think of them; he is conscious only of the weakness and suffering from which he is never to escape, and of the grace of Christ which hovers over him, and out of weakness and suffering makes him strong. His very infirmities redound to the glory of the Lord, and so he chooses them, rather than his rapture into Paradise, as matter for boasting. "For this cause I am well content, on Christ's behalf,[105] in infirmities, in insults, in necessities, in persecutions and distresses; for when I am weak, then am I strong."

With this noble word Paul concludes his enforced "glorying." He was not happy in it; it was not like him; and it is a triumph of the Spirit of Christ in him that he gives it such a noble turn, and comes out of it so well. There is a tinge of irony in the first passage (chap. xi. 21) in which he speaks of weakness, and fears that in comparison with his high-handed rivals at Corinth he will only have this to boast about; but as he enters into his real experience, and tells us what he had borne for Christ, and what he had learned in pain and prayer about the laws of the spiritual life, all irony passes away; the pure heroic heart opens before us to its depths. The practical lessons of the last paragraphs are as obvious as they are important. That the greatest spiritual experiences are incommunicable; that even the best men are in danger of elation and pride; that the tendency of these sins is immensely strong, and can only be restrained by constant pressure; that pain, though one day to be abolished, is a means of discipline actually used by God; that it may be a plain duty to accept some suffering, or sickness, even a humbling and distressing one, as God's will for our good, and not to pray more for its removal; that God's grace is given to those who so accept His will, as a real reinforcement of their strength, nay, as a substitute, and far more, for the strength which they have not; that weakness, therefore, and helplessness, as foils to the present help of God, may actually be occasions of glorying to the Christian,—all these, and many more, are gathered up in this passionate Apologia of Paul.

XXVII
NOT YOURS, BUT YOU

"I am become foolish: ye compelled me; for I ought to have been commended of you: for in nothing was I behind the very chiefest apostles, though I am nothing. Truly the signs of an apostle were wrought among you in all patience, by signs and wonders and mighty works. For what is there wherein ye were made inferior to the rest of the Churches, except *it be* that I myself was not a burden to you? forgive me this wrong.

"Behold, this is the third time I am ready to come to you; and I will not be a burden to you: for I seek not yours, but you: for the children ought not to lay up for the parents, but the parents for the children. And I will most gladly spend and be spent for your souls. If I love you more abundantly, am I loved the less? But be it so, I did not myself burden you; but, being crafty, I caught you with guile. Did I take advantage of you by any one of them whom I have sent unto you? I exhorted Titus, and I sent the brother with him. Did Titus take any advantage of you? walked we not by the same Spirit? *walked we* not in the same steps?

"Ye think all this time that we are excusing ourselves unto you. In the sight of God speak we in Christ. But all things, beloved, *are* for your edifying. For I fear, lest by any means, when I come, I should find you not such as I would, and should myself be found of you such as ye would not; lest by any means *there should be* strife, jealousy, wraths, factions, backbitings, whisperings, swellings, tumults; lest when I come again, my God should humble me before you, and I should mourn for many of them that have sinned heretofore, and repented not of the uncleanness and fornication and lasciviousness which they committed."—2 Cor. xii. 11-21 (R.V.).

Expositors differ widely in characterising the three or four brief paragraphs into which this passage may be divided: (1) vv. 11-13; (2) vv. 14, 15, and vv. 16-18; (3) vv. 19-21. What is clear is, that we feel in it the groundswell of the storm that has raged through the last two chapters, and that it is not till the beginning of chap. xiii. that the Apostle finally escapes from this, and takes up an authoritative and decisive attitude to the Corinthians. When he does reach Corinth, it will not be to explain and justify his own conduct, either against rivals or those whom rivals have misled, but to take prompt and vigorous action against disorders in the life of the Church.

(1) A review of what he has just written leads to a burst of indignant remonstrance. "I *have* become foolish." The emphasis is on the verb, not on the adjective; it is the painful fact that the eleventh chapter of Second Corinthians is a thing that no wise man would have written if he had been left to himself and his wisdom. Paul, who was a wise man, felt this, and it stung him. He resented the compulsion which was put upon him by the ingratitude and faithlessness of the Corinthians. The situation ought to have been exactly reversed. When he was defamed by strangers, then they, who knew him, instead of hearkening to the calumniators, ought to have stood up in his defence. But they basely left him to defend himself, to plead his own cause, to become a fool by "glorying." This kind of compulsion should never be put upon a good man, especially a man to whom, under God, we ourselves have been deeply indebted. The services he has rendered constitute a claim on our loyalty, and it is a duty of affection to guard his character against disparagement and malice.

Paul, in his deep consciousness of being wronged, presses home the charge against the Corinthians. They had every reason, he tells them, to act as his advocates. When he was among them, he was in nothing inferior to the "superlative" Apostles—this is his last flout at the Judaist interlopers—nothing though he was. The signs that prove a man to be an apostle were wrought among them (the passive expression keeps *his* agency in the background) in all patience, by signs and wonders and mighty deeds. Their suspicions of him, their willingness to listen to insinuations against him, after such an experience, were unpardonable. He can only think of one "sign of the apostle" which was not wrought among them by his means, of one point in which he had made them inferior to the other Churches: he had not burdened them with his support. They were the spoilt children of the apostolic family; and he begs them, with bitter irony, to forgive him this wrong. If they had only been converted by a man who stood upon his rights![106]

"The signs of an apostle" are frequently referred to in Paul's Epistles, and are of various kinds. By far the most important, and the most frequently insisted on, is success in evangelistic work. He who converts men and founds Churches has the supreme and final attestation of apostleship, as Paul conceives it. It is to this he appeals in 1 Cor. ix. 2; 2 Cor. iii. 1-3. In the passage before us Calvin makes "patience" a sign—*primum signum nominat patientiam*. Patience is certainly a characteristic Christian virtue, and it is magnificently exercised in the apostolic life; but it is not peculiarly apostolic. Patience in the passage before us, "every kind of patience," rather brings before our minds the conditions under which Paul did his apostolic work. Discouragements of every description, bad health, suspicion, dislike, contempt, moral apathy and moral licence—the weight of all these pressed upon him heavily, but he bore up under them, and did not suffer them to break his spirit or to arrest his labours. His endurance was a match for them all, and the power of Christ that was in him broke forth in spite of them in apostolic signs. There were conversions, in the first place; but there were also what he calls here "signs [in a narrower sense], and wonders, and mighty deeds." This is an express claim, like that made in Acts xv. 12, Rom. xv. 19, to have wrought what we call miracles. The three words represent miracles under three different aspects: they are "signs" (σημεῖα), as addressed to man's intelligence, and conveying a spiritual meaning; they are "wonders" (τέρατα), as giving a shock to feeling, and moving nature in those depths which sleep through common experience; and they are "mighty works" or "powers" (δυνάμεις), as arguing in him who works them a more than human efficiency. But no doubt the main character they bore in the Apostle's mind was that of χαρίσματα, or gifts of grace, which God ministered to the Church by His Spirit. It is natural for an unbeliever to misunderstand even New Testament miracles, because he wishes to conceive them, as it were, *in vacuo*, or in relation to the laws of nature; in the New Testament itself they are conceived in relation to the Holy Ghost. Even Jesus is said in the Gospels to have cast out devils by the Spirit of God; and when Paul wrought "signs and wonders and powers," it was in carrying out his apostolic work graced by the same Spirit. What things he had done in Corinth we have no means of knowing, but the Corinthians knew; and they knew that these things had no arbitrary or accidental character, but were the tokens of a Christian and an apostle.

(2) In the second paragraph Paul turns abruptly (ἰδοὺ, "behold!") from the past to the future. "This is the third time I am ready to come to you, and I will not burden you." The first clause has the same ambiguity in Greek as in English; it is impossible to tell from the words alone whether he had been already twice, or only once, in Corinth. Other considerations decide, I think,

that he had been twice; but of course these cannot affect the construction of this verse: for the third time he is in a state of readiness—this is all the words will yield. But when he makes the new visit, whether it be his third or only his second, one thing he has decided: he will act on the same principle as before, and decline to be a burden to them. He does not speak of it boastfully now, as in chap. xi. 10, for his adversaries have passed out of view, but in one of the most movingly tender passages in the whole Bible. "I will not lie on you like a benumbing weight, for I seek, not yours, but you." It is not his own interest which brings him to Corinth again, but theirs; it is not avarice which impels him, but love. In a sense, indeed, love makes the greater claim of the two; it is far more to demand the heart than to ask for money. Yet the greater claim is the less selfish, indeed is the purely unselfish one; for it can only be really made by one who gives all that he demands. Paul's own heart was pledged to the Corinthians; and when he said "I seek *you*," he did not mean that he sought to make a party of them, or a faction, in the interest of his own ambition, but that the one thing he cared for was the good of their souls. Nor in saying so does he claim to be doing anything unusual or extraordinary. It is only what becomes him as their father in Christ (1 Cor. iv. 15). "I seek *you*; for the children ought not to lay up for the parents, but the parents for the children." Filial duty, of course, is not denied here; Paul is simply bringing himself as the spiritual father of the Corinthians under the general rule of nature that "love descends rather than ascends." If this seems a hard saying to a child's heart, it is at least true that it descends *before* it ascends. It all begins from God: in a family, it all begins from the parents. The primary duty of love is parental care; and nothing is more unnatural, though at a certain level it is common enough, than the desire of parents to make money out of their children as quickly and as plentifully as possible, without considering the ulterior interests of the children themselves. This kind of selfishness is very transparent, and is very naturally avenged by ingratitude, and the Apostle for his part renounces it. "*I*," he exclaims, with all the emphasis in his power—"*I* have more than a natural father's love for you. I will with all gladness spend, yes, and be spent to the uttermost, for your souls! I will give what I have, yes, and all that I am, that you may be profited." And then he checks that rush of affection, and dams up the overflowing passion of his heart in the abrupt poignant question: "If I love you more abundantly, am I loved less?"[107]

This is not the first passage in the Epistle, nor, near as we are to the end, is it the last, in which Paul shows us the true spirit of the Christian pastor. "Not yours, but you," is the motto of every minister who has learned of Christ; and the noble words of ver. 15, "I will very gladly spend and be spent to the last for your souls," recall more nearly than any other words in Scripture the law by which our Lord Himself lived—not to be ministered unto, but to minister, and to give life a ransom for many. Here, surely, is a sign of apostleship—an unmistakable mark of the man who is specially called to continue Christ's work. That work cannot be done at all except in the spirit of Him who inaugurated it, and though love like Paul's, and love like Christ's, may be mocked and trampled on, it is the only power which has the right to speak in Christ's name. The joy of sacrifice thrills through the Apostle's words, and it is joy in the Holy Ghost; it is a fellowship with Christ in the very life of His life that lifts Paul, for the moment, to the heavenly places. This is the spirit in which wrong is to be met, and suspicion, calumny, and contempt; it is in this, if at all, that we can be more than conquerors. Nature says, "Stand upon your rights; vindicate your position; insist on having all that you conceive to be your due"; but love says, "Spend and be spent, and spare not till all is gone; life itself is not too much to give that love may triumph over wrong."

It is not possible to write long as Paul writes in these two verses (14 and 15). The tension is too great both for him and for his readers. With ἔστω δέ—"But be it so"—he descends from this height. He writes in the first person, but he is plainly repeating what he assumes others will say. "Very well, then, let that pass," is the answer of his enemies to his friends when that passionate protestation is read. "He did not *himself* prove burdensome to us, but being crafty he brought us into his net by guile. He exploited the Church in his own interest by means of his agents." This charge the Apostle meets with a downright denial; he can appeal to the knowledge which the Corinthians themselves possess of the manner in which his agents have conducted themselves. He had no doubt had occasion, far oftener than we know, to communicate with so important and so restless a Church; and he challenges the Corinthians to say that a single one of those whom he had sent had taken advantage of them. He instances—perhaps as the last of his deputies, who had but just returned from Corinth when he wrote this letter; perhaps as the one on whom scandal had chosen to fasten—his "partner" and "fellow-labourer toward them," Titus; and he refers to an unknown brother who had accompanied him. They cannot mean to say (μήτι) that Titus took advantage of them? "Walked we not in the same Spirit?" A modern reader naturally makes "spirit" subjective, and takes it as equivalent to "the same moral temper or principle"; an early Christian reader would more probably think of the Holy Spirit as that which ruled in Paul and Titus alike. In any case the same Spirit led to the same conduct; they walked in the same self-denying path, and scrupulously abstained from burdening the Corinthians for their support.

(3) We feel the meanness of all this, and are glad when the Apostle finally turns his back on it. It is an indignity to be compelled even to allude to such things. And the worst is, that no care a man can take will prevent people from misunderstanding his indignant protest, and from assuming that he is really on his trial before them, and not improbably compromised. Paul's mind is made up to leave the Corinthians no excuse for such misunderstanding and presumption. In ver. 19 he reads their ignoble thought: "Ye have long[108] been thinking"—*i.e.*, all through the last two chapters, and, indeed, more or less all through the Epistle; see chap. iii. 1—"that we are making our defence at your bar. Far from it: at God's bar we speak in Christ." He will not endure, with his visit to Corinth close at hand, that there should be any misapprehension as to their relations. His responsibility as a Christian man is not to them, but to God; He is the Master to whom he stands or falls; it is He alone to whom he has to vindicate his life. The Corinthians had been seating themselves in imagination on the tribunal, and they are summarily set on the floor. But Paul does not wish to be rude or unkind. "You are not my judges, certainly," he seems to say, "but all I have said and done, beloved, all I say and do, is for your building up in Christian life. My heart is with you in it all, and I sincerely intend your good." We cannot sufficiently admire the combination in the Apostle, or rather the swift alternation, of all those intellectual and emotional qualities that balance each other in a strong living character. He can be at once trenchant and tender; inexorable in the maintenance of a principle, and infinitely sympathetic and considerate in his treatment of persons. We see all his qualities illustrated here.

Their edification is the governing thought on which the last verses of the chapter turn, and on which eventually the whole Epistle rests (see chap. xiii. 10). It is because he is interested in their edification that he thinks with misgiving of the journey in prospect. "I fear lest by any means when I come I find you not such as I would, and on my part be found of you not such as ye would." What these two fears imply is unfolded in due order in the remainder of the letter. The Corinthians, such as Paul would not have them, are depicted in vv. 20 and 21; Paul, in a character in which the Corinthians would prefer not to see him, comes forward in chap. xiii., vv. 1-10. It is with the first only of these two fears, the bad condition of the Corinthian Church, that we are here concerned. This first fear has two grounds. The first is the prevalence of sins which may perhaps be summarised as sins of self-will. Strife, jealousy, passions, factions and low factious arts, backbitings, whisperings, swellings, tumults: such is the catalogue. It illustrates what has been well described as "the carnality of religious contention." Almost all the sins here enumerated are directly connected with the existence of parties and party feeling in the Church. They are of a kind which has disgraced the Church all through its history, and the exceeding sinfulness of which is not yet recognised by the great mass of professing Christians. People do not consider that the Church, as a visible society, more or less naturalised in the world, is as capable as any other society of offering a career to ambition, or of furnishing a theatre for the talents and the energies of self-seeking men; and they have a vague idea that the wilfulness, the intriguing and factious arts, the jealousy and conceit of men, are better things when put to the service of the Church than when employed in mere selfishness. But they are not. They are the very same, and they are peculiarly odious when enlisted in His service who was meek and lowly in heart, and who gave Himself for men. Paul's first list of sins is only too life-like, and the fear grounded on it is one which many a modern minister can share. The second list is made up of what might be called, in contrast with sins of self-will, sins of self-indulgence—"uncleanness, fornication, and lasciviousness that they wrought." Both together make up what the Apostle calls the works of the flesh. Both together are the direct opposite of those fruits of the spirit in which the true life of the Church consists. Paul writes as if he were more alarmed about the sins of the latter class. He puts μὴ ("lest") instead of μήπως ("lest by any means": ver. 20), marking thus the climax, and something like the certainty,[109] of his sad apprehension. "I fear," he says, "lest when I come again my God should humble me before you"—or, perhaps "in connexion with you." Nothing could more bow down a true and loving heart like Paul's than to see a Church that he had regarded as the seal of his apostleship—a congregation of men "washed, sanctified, and justified"—wallowing again in the mire of sensual sins. He had been proud of them, had boasted of them, had given thanks to God on their behalf: how it must have crushed him to think that his labour on them had come to this! Yet he writes instinctively "my God." This humiliation does not come to him without his Father; there is a divine dispensation in it, as far as he is concerned, and he submits to it as such. He dare not think of it as a personal insult; he dare not think of the sinners as if they had offended against *him*. He fears he will have to *mourn over* numbers of those who have before sinned, and who will not have repented[110] of these sensualities before he reaches Corinth. In chap. v. 2 of the First Epistle he sums up his condemnation of the moral laxity of the Church in the presence of such evils in the words: *Ye did not mourn*. He himself will not be able to avoid mourning: his heart grows heavy within him as he thinks of what he must see before long. This, again, is the spirit of the true pastor. Selfish anger has nothing healing in it, nor has wounded pride; it is not for any man, however good or devoted, to feel that he is entitled to resent it, as a personal wrong, when men fall into sin. He is not entitled to resent it, no matter how much he may have spent, or how freely he may have spent himself, upon them; but he is bound to bewail it. He is bound to recognise in it, so far as he himself is free from responsibility, a dispensation of God intended to make him humble; and in all humility and love he is bound to plead with the lapsed, not his own cause, but God's. This is the spirit in which Paul confronts the sad duties awaiting him at Corinth, and in this again we see "the signs of the apostle."

The two catalogues of sins with which this chapter closes remind us, by way of contrast, of the two characteristic graces of Christianity: self-will or party spirit, in all its forms, is opposed to brotherly love, and self-indulgence, in all its forms, to personal purity. There is much in this Epistle which would be called by some people theological and transcendent; but no one knew better than Paul that, though Christianity must be capable of an intellectual construction, it is not an intellectual system in essence, but a new moral life. He was deeply concerned, as we have repeatedly seen, that the Corinthians should think right thoughts about Christ and the Gospel; but he was more than concerned, he was filled with grief, fear, and shame, when he thought of the vices of temper and of sensuality that prevailed among them. These went to the root of Christianity, and if they could not be destroyed it must perish. Let us turn our eyes from them to the purity and love that they obscure, and lift up our hearts to these as the best things to which God has called us in the fellowship of His Son.

XXVIII
CONCLUSION

"This is the third time I am coming to you. At the mouth of two witnesses or three shall every word be established. I have said beforehand, and I do say beforehand, as when I was present the second time, so now, being absent, to them that have sinned heretofore, and to all the rest, that, if I come again, I will not spare; seeing that ye seek a proof of Christ that speaketh in me; who to you-ward is not weak, but is powerful in you: for He was crucified through weakness, yet He liveth through the power of God. For we also are weak in Him, but we shall live with Him through the power of God toward you. Try your own selves, whether ye be in the faith; prove your own selves. Or know ye not as to your own selves, that Jesus Christ is in you? unless indeed ye be reprobate. But I hope that ye shall know that we are not reprobate. Now we pray to God that ye do no evil; not that we may appear approved, but that ye may do that which is honourable, though we be as reprobate. For we can do nothing against the truth, but for the truth. For we rejoice, when we are weak, and ye are strong: this we also pray for, even your perfecting. For this cause I write these things while absent, that I may not when present deal sharply, according to the authority which the Lord gave me for building up, and not for casting down.

"Finally, brethren, farewell. Be perfected; be comforted; be of the same mind; live in peace: and the God of love and peace shall be with you. Salute one another with a holy kiss.

"All the saints salute you.

"The grace of the Lord Jesus Christ, and the love of God, and the communion of the Holy Ghost, be with you all."—2 Cor. xiii. (R.V.).

The first part of this chapter is in close connexion with what precedes; it is, so to speak, the explanation of St. Paul's fear (xii. 20) that when he came to Corinth he would be found of the Corinthians "not such as they would." He expresses himself with great severity; and the abruptness of the first three sentences, which are not linked to each other by any conjunctions, contributes to the general sense of rigour. "This is the third time I am coming to you" is a resumption of chap. xii. 14, "This is the third time I am ready to come to you," and labours under the same ambiguity; it is perhaps more natural to suppose that Paul had actually been twice in Corinth (and there are independent reasons for this opinion), but the words here used are quite consistent with the idea that this was the third time he had definitely purposed and tried to visit them, whether his purpose had been carried out or not. When he arrives, he will proceed at once to hold a judicial investigation into the condition of the Church, and will carry it through with legal stringency. "At the mouth of two and (where available) three witnesses shall every question be brought to decision." This principle of the Jewish law (Deut. xix. 15), to which reference is made in other New Testament passages connected with Church discipline (Matt. xviii. 16; 1 Tim. v. 19), is announced as that on which he will act. There will be no informality and no injustice, but neither will there be any more forbearance. All cases requiring disciplinary treatment will be brought to an issue at once, and the decision will be given rigorously as the matter of fact, attested by evidence, requires.[111] He feels justified in proceeding thus after the reiterated warnings he has given them. To these reference is made in the solemn words of ver. 2. English readers can see, by comparing the Revised Version with the Authorised, the difficulties of translation which still divide scholars. The words which the Authorised Version renders "*as if I were* present" (ὡς παρών) are rendered by the Revisers "*as when I was present.*" All scholars connect this ambiguous clause with τὸ δεύτερον: "the second time." Hence there are two main ways in which the whole passage can be rendered. The one is that which stands in the Revised Version, and which is defended by scholars like Meyer, Lightfoot,[112] and Schmiedel: it is in effect this—"I have already forewarned, and do now forewarn, as I did on the occasion of my second visit, so also now in my absence, those who have sinned heretofore, and all the rest, that if I come again I will not spare." This is certainly rather cumbrous; but assuming that chap. ii. 1 gives strong ground for believing in a second visit already paid to Corinth—a visit in which Paul had been grieved and humbled by disorders in the Church, but had not been in a position to do more than warn against their continuance—it seems the only available interpretation. Those who evade the force of chap. ii. 1 render here in the line of the Authorised Version: "I have forewarned [viz., in the first letter, *e.g.* iv. 21], and do now forewarn, as though I were present the second time, although I am now absent, those who have sinned," etc. So Heinrici. This, on grammatical grounds, seems quite legitimate; but the contrast between presence and absence, which is real and effective in the other rendering, is here quite inept. We can understand a man saying, "I tell you in my absence, just as I did when I was with you that second time": but who would ever say, "I tell you as if I were present with you a second time, although in point of fact I am absent"? The absence here comes in with a grotesque effect, and there seems hardly room to doubt that the rendering in our Revised Version is correct. Paul had, when he visited Corinth a second time, warned those who had sinned before that visit; he now warns them again, and all others with them who anticipated his coming with an evil conscience, that the hour of decision is at hand. It is not easy to say what he means by the threat not to spare. Many point to judgments like that on Ananias and Sapphira, or on Elymas the sorcerer; others to the delivering of the incestuous person to Satan, "for the destruction of the flesh"; the supposition being that Paul came to Corinth armed with a supernatural power of inflicting physical sufferings on the disobedient. This uncanny idea has really no support in the New Testament, in spite of the passages quoted; and probably what his words aim at is an exercise of spiritual authority which might go so far as totally to exclude an offender from the Christian community.

The third verse is to be taken closely with the second: "I will not spare, since ye seek a proof of Christ that speaketh in me, who to you-ward is not weak, but is powerful in you." The friction between the Corinthians and the Apostle involved a higher interest than his. In putting Paul to the proof, they were really putting to the proof the Christ who spoke in him. In challenging Paul to come and exert his authority, in defying him to come with a rod, in presuming on what they called his weakness, they were really challenging Christ. The description of Christ in the last clause—"who towards you is not weak, but is powerful in you, or among you"—must be interpreted by the context. It can hardly mean that in their conversion, and in their experience as Christian people, they had evidence that Christ was not weak, but strong: such a reference, though supported by Calvin, is surely beside the mark. The meaning must rather be that for the purpose in hand—the restoration of order and discipline in the Corinthian Church—the Christ who spoke in Paul was not weak, but mighty. Certainly any one who looked at Christ in Himself might see proofs, in abundance, of weakness; going directly to the crowning one, "He was *crucified*," the Apostle says, "*in virtue of weakness.*" Sin was so much stronger than He, in the days of His flesh, that it did what it liked with Him. Sin mocked Him, buffeted Him, scourged Him, spit upon Him, nailed Him to the tree—so utter was His weakness, so complete the triumph of sin over Him. But that is not the whole story:

"He liveth in virtue of the power of God." He has been raised from the dead by the glory of the Father; sin cannot touch Him any more: He has all power in heaven and on earth, and all things are under His feet. This double relation of Christ to sin is exemplified in His Apostle. "For we also are weak in Him; but we shall live with Him, in virtue of God's power, toward you." The sin of the Corinthians had had its victory over Paul on the occasion of his second visit; God had humbled him then, even as Christ was humbled on the cross; he had seen the evil, but it had been too strong for him; in spite of his warnings, it had rolled over his head. That "weakness," as the Corinthians called it, remained; to them he was still as weak as ever—hence the present ἀσθενοῦμεν: but to the Apostle it was no discreditable thing; it was a weakness "in Christ," or perhaps, as some authorities read, "with Christ." In being overpowered by sin for the moment, he entered into the fellowship of his Lord's sufferings; he drank out of the cup his Master drank upon the cross. But the cross does not represent Christ's whole attitude to sin, nor does that incapacity to deal with the turbulence, disloyalty, and immorality of the Corinthians represent the whole attitude of the Apostle to these disorders. Paul is not only crucified with Christ, he has been made to sit with Him in the heavenly places; and when he comes to Corinth this time, it will not be in the weakness of Christ, but in the victorious strength of His new life. He will come clothed with power from on high to execute the Lord's sentence on the disobedient.

This passage has great practical interest. There are many whose whole conception of the Christian attitude toward evil is summed up in the words: "He was crucified through weakness." They seem to think that the whole function of love in presence of evil, its whole experience, its whole method and all its resources, are comprehended in bearing what evil chooses, or is able, to inflict. There are even bad people, like the Corinthians, who imagine that this exhausts the Christian ideal, and that they are wronged if they are not allowed by Christians to do what they like to them with impunity. And if it is not so easy to act on this principle in our dealings with one another— though there are people mean enough to try it—there are plenty of hypocrites who presume on it in their dealings with God. "He was crucified through weakness," they say in their hearts; the cross exhausts His relation to sin; that infinite patience can never pass over to severity. But the assumption is false: the cross does *not* exhaust Christ's relation to sin; He passed from the cross to the throne, and when He comes again it is as Judge. It is the sin of sins to presume upon the cross; it is a mistake that cannot be remedied to persist in that presumption to the end. When Christ comes again, *He* will not spare. The two things go together in Him: the infinite patience of the cross, the inexorable righteousness of the throne. The same two things go together in men: the depth with which they feel evil, the completeness with which they suffer it to work its will against them, and the power with which they vindicate the good. It is the worst blindness, as well as the basest guilt, which, because it has seen the one, refuses to believe in the other.

The Corinthians, by their rebellious spirit, were putting Paul to the proof; in ver. 5 he reminds them sharply that it is their own standing as Christians which is in question, and not his. "Try *yourselves*," he says, with abrupt emphasis, "*not me*; try *yourselves*, if ye are in the faith; put *yourselves* to the proof; or know ye not as to *your own selves*, that Jesus Christ is in you?—unless, indeed, ye be reprobate." The meaning here is hardly open to doubt:[113] the Apostle urges his readers individually to examine their Christian standing. "Let each," he virtually says, "put himself to the proof, and see whether he is in the faith." There is, indeed, a difficulty in the clause, "Or know ye not as to your own selves, that Jesus Christ is in you?—unless, indeed, ye be reprobate." This may be read either as a test, put into their hands to direct them in their self-scrutiny; or as an appeal to them after—or even before—the scrutiny has been made. The manner in which the alternative is introduced—"unless, indeed, ye are reprobates"—a manner plainly suggesting that the alternative in question is *not* to be assumed, is in favour of taking it in the sense of an appeal. After all, they are a Christian Church with Christ among them, and they cannot but know it. Paul, again, on his side cannot think that they are reprobate, and he hopes they will recognise that *he* is not, but on the contrary a genuine Apostle, attested by God, and to be acknowledged and obeyed by the Church. Very often that temper which judges others, and calls legitimate spiritual authority in question, is due, as in part it was among the Corinthians, to inward misgivings. It is when people ought to be putting themselves to the proof, and are with cause afraid to begin, that they are most ready to challenge others. It was a kind of self-defence—the self-defence of a bad conscience—when the Corinthians required Paul to demonstrate his apostolic claims before he meddled with their affairs. It was a plea, the sole purpose of which was to enable them to live on as they were, immoral and impenitent. It is properly retorted when he says, "Try *yourselves* if ye are in the faith; it is in every sense of the word an impertinence to drag in anybody else."

In both cases Paul hopes the result of the trial will be satisfactory. He would not like to think the Corinthians ἀδόκιμοι ("reprobate"), and no more would he like them to regard him in that light. Still, the two things are not on exactly the same footing in his mind; *their* character is much dearer to him than his own reputation, provided they are what they ought to be, he does not care what is thought of himself. This is the general sense of vv. 7 to 9, and except in ver. 8 the details are clear enough. He prays to God that the Corinthians may do no evil. His object in this is not that he himself may appear approved; indeed, if his prayer is granted, he will have no opportunity of exercising the disciplinary authority of which he has said so much. It will be open to any one then to say that he is ἀδόκιμος, reprobate, a person to be rejected because he has not demonstrated his claim to apostolic authority by apostolic action. But as long as they act well, which is the real object of his prayer, he does not care, though he *has* to pass as ἀδόκιμος. He can bear evil report as well as good report, and rejoice to fulfil his vocation under the one condition as well as the other. This is only one aspect of that sacrifice of self to the interest of the flock which is indispensable in the good shepherd. As compared with any single member of his congregation, a minister may be more in the eye of the world, more still in the eye of the Church; and it is natural for him to think that some self-assertion, some recognition and reputation, are due to his position. It is a mistake: no man who understands the position at all will dream of asserting his own importance against that of the community. The Church, the congregation even, no matter how much it may be indebted to him, no matter if it owes to him, as the Corinthian Church to Paul, its very existence in Christ, is always greater than he; it will outlive him; and, however tender he may naturally be of his own position and reputation, if the Church prosper in Christian character, he must be as willing to let these dear possessions go, and to count them worthless, as to part with money or any material thing.

The real difficulty here lies in the eighth verse, where the Apostle explains, apparently, why he acts on the principle just stated. "I pray this prayer for you," he seems to say, "and I am content to pass as a reprobate, while you do that which is honourable; for I can do nothing against the truth, but for the truth." What is the connexion of ideas alluded to by this "for"? Some of the commentators give up the question in despair; others only remind one of the French pastor who said to some one who preached on Romans: "Saint Paul est déjà fort difficile et ... vous veniez après." As far as one can make out, he seems to say: "I act on this principle because it is the one which furthers the truth, and therefore is obligatory upon me; I am not able to act on one which would injure or prejudice the truth." The truth, in this interpretation, would be synonymous, as it often is in the New Testament, with the Gospel. Paul is incapable of acting in a way that would check the Gospel, and its influence over men; he has no choice but to act in its interest; and therefore he is content to let the Corinthians think what they please of him, provided his prayer is answered, and they do no evil, but rather that which is good before God. For this is what the Gospel requires. "Content," indeed, is not a strong enough word. "We *rejoice*," he says in ver. 9, "when we are weak, and you are strong: this we also pray for, even your perfecting." "Perfecting" is perhaps as good a word as can be got for κατάρτισις: it denotes the putting right of all that is defective or amiss.

It is in favour of this interpretation of the eighth verse that the reason seems at first out of proportion to the conclusion. With an idealist like Paul it is always so. He appeals to the loftiest motives to influence the lowliest actions,—to faith in the Incarnation, as a motive to generosity—to faith in the Resurrection Life, as a motive to patient continuance in well-doing—to faith in the heavenly citizenship of believers, as a motive to separation from the licentious. In the same way he appeals here to a universal moral rule to explain his conduct in a particular case. His principle everywhere is, not to act in prejudice of (κατά) the Gospel, but in furtherance of it (ὑπέρ); he has strength available for this last purpose, but none at all for the former. It is the rule on which every minister of Christ should always act; and if the line of conduct which it pointed out sometimes led men to disregard their own reputation, provided the Gospel was having free course, the very strangeness of such a result might turn to the furtherance of the truth. It is by-ends that explain nine-tenths of spiritual inefficiency; singleness of mind like this would save us our perplexities and our failures alike.

It is because he has an interest like this in the Corinthians that Paul writes as he has done while absent from Corinth. He does not wish, when he comes among them, to proceed with severity. The power the Lord gave him would entitle him to do so; yet he remembers that this power was given him, as he has remarked already (x. 8), for building up, and not for casting down. Even casting down with a view to building up on a better basis was a less natural, if sometimes a necessary, exercise of it; and he hopes that the severity of his words will lead, even before his coming, to such voluntary action on the part of the Church as will spare him severity in deed.

This is practically the end of the letter, and the mind involuntarily goes back to the beginning. We see now the three great divisions of it plainly before our eyes. In *the first seven chapters* Paul writes under the general impression of the good news Titus has brought from Corinth. It has made him glad, and he writes gladly. The one case that he had been concerned about has been disposed of in a way that he can consider satisfactory; the Church, in the majority of its members, has acted well in the matter. *The eighth and ninth chapters* are a digression: they are concerned solely with the collection for the poor at Jerusalem, and Paul inserts them where they stand perhaps because the transition was easy from his joy over the change at Corinth to his joy over the liberality of the Macedonians. In *chaps, x. 1-xiii.* 10 he evidently writes in a very different strain. The Church, as a whole, has returned to its allegiance, especially on the moral question at issue; but there are Jewish interlopers in it, subverting the Gospel, and reconverting

Paul's converts to their own illiberal faith; and there are also, as it would appear, numbers of sensual people who have not yet renounced the vilest sins. It is these two sets of persons who are in view in the last four chapters; and it is the utter inconsistency of Judaic nationalism on the one hand, and Corinthian licence on the other, with the spiritual Gospel of the Son of God, that explains the seventy of his tone. "The truth" is at stake—the truth for which he has suffered all that he recounts in chap. xi.—and no vehemence is too passionate for the occasion. Yet love controls it all, and he speaks severely that he may not have to act severely; he writes these things that, if possible, he may be spared the pain of saying them.

And then the letter, like almost every letter, hastens in disconnected sentences to its close. "Finally, brethren, farewell." He cannot but address them affectionately at parting; when the heart recovers from the heat of indignation, its unchanging love speaks again as before. Some would render χαίρετε "rejoice," instead of "farewell"; to Paul's readers, no doubt, it had a friendly sound, but "rejoice" is far too strong. In all the imperatives that follow there is a reminiscence of their faults as well as a desire for their good: "be perfected, be comforted, be of the same mind, live in peace." There was much among them to rectify, much that was inevitably disheartening to overcome, much dissension to compose, much friction to allay; but as he prays them to face these duties he can assure them that the God of love and peace will be with them. God can be characterised by love and peace; they are His essential attributes, and He is an inexhaustible source of them, so that all who make peace and love their aim can count confidently to be helped by Him. It is, as it were, the first step of obedience to these precepts—the first condition of obtaining the presence of God which has just been promised—when the Apostle writes, "Greet one another with a holy kiss." The kiss was the symbol of Christian brotherhood; in exchanging it Christians recognised each other as members of one family. To do this even in form, to do it with solemnity in a public assembly of the whole Church, was to commit themselves to the obligations of peace and love which had been so set at naught in their religious contentions. It is a generous encouragement to them to recognise each other as children of God when he adds that all the Christians about him recognise them in that character. "All the saints salute you." They do so because they are Christians and because you are; acknowledge each other, as you are all acknowledged from without.

The letter is closed, like all that the Apostle wrote, with a brief prayer. "The grace of the Lord Jesus [Christ], and the love of God, and the communion of the Holy Spirit, be with you all." Of all such prayers it is the fullest in expression, and this has gained for it pre-eminently the name of the apostolic benediction. It would be too much to say that the doctrine of the Trinity, as it has been defined in the creeds, is explicitly to be found here; there is no statement at all in this place of the relations of Christ, God, and the Holy Spirit. Still, it is on passages like this that the Trinitarian doctrine of God is based; or rather it is in passages like this that we see it beginning to take shape: it is based on the historical fact of the revelation of God in Christ, and on the experience of the new divine life which the Church possesses through the Spirit. It is extraordinary to find men with the New Testament in their hands giving explanations, speculative or popular, of this doctrine, which stand in no relation either to the historical Christ or to the experience of the Church. But these things hang together; and whatever the worth may be of a Trinitarian doctrine which is not essentially dependent on the Person of Christ and on the life of His Church, it is certainly not Christian. The historical original of the doctrine, and the impulse of experience under which Paul wrote, are suggested even by the order of the words. A speculative theologian may try to deduce the Triune nature of God from the borrowed assumption that God is love, or knowledge, or spirit; but the Apostle has only come to know God as love through the grace of the Lord Jesus Christ. It is this which reveals God's love and assures us of it; it is this by which God commends His own love to us. "No man cometh unto *the Father* but by *Me*," Jesus said; and this truth, pre-announced by the Lord, is certified here by the very order in which the Apostle instinctively puts the sacred names. "The communion of the Holy Spirit" stands last; it is in this that "the grace of the Lord Jesus and the love of God" become the realised possessions of Christian men. The precise force of "the communion" is open to doubt. If we take the genitive in the same sense as it bears in the previous clauses, the word will mean "the fellowship or unity of feeling which is produced by the Spirit." This is a good sense, but not the only one: what Paul wishes may rather be the joint participation of them all *in* the Spirit, and in the gifts which it confers. But practically the two meanings coincide, and our minds rest on the comprehensiveness of the blessing invoked on a Church so mixed, and in many of its members so unworthy. Surely "the grace of the Lord Jesus Christ, and the love of God, and the communion of the Holy Ghost" were with the man who rises so easily, so unconstrainedly, after all the tempest and passion of this letter, to such a height of love and peace. Heaven is open over his head; he is conscious, as he writes, of the immensities of that love whose breadth and length and depth and height pass knowledge. In the Son who revealed it—in God who is its eternal source—in the Spirit through whom it lives in men—he is conscious of that love and of its workings; and he prays that in all its aspects, and in all its virtues, it may be with them all.

FOOTNOTES:

[1] *Einleitung*, 2nd ed., p. 255 f.

[2] The same view is strongly held by Schmiedel. He infers from chap. vi. 9 that Paul's sufferings had been interpreted at Corinth as a divine chastisement; in opposition to this the Apostle shows that they are divinely intended to profit the Corinthians. Hence the opening of the letter is not a simple outpouring of his heart, but is delicately calculated to set aside a reproach without naming it. The same purpose rules in the assumption that the Corinthians will intercede and give thanks on his behalf; it takes for granted their reconciliation to him.

[3] The text is incurably perplexed. The variations can be seen in any critical edition. The MS. authority does not justify any confident decision, and the happiest suggestion yet made seems to be that of Professor Warfield, who would omit altogether the words καὶ σωτηρίας (*and salvation*). The MSS. vary most in regard to these words, inserting, omitting, and transposing them. Hence they are very probably an old gloss, and their omission simplifies both the grammar and the sense.

[4] Notice the perfect ἐσχήκαμεν. We *had* this experience, and in its fruit—a newer and deeper faith in God—we *have* it still. It is a permanent possession in this happy form. The same idea is expressed in the pft. ἠλπίκαμεν, ver. 10.

[5] The doubtful words here are καὶ ῥύεται in ver. 10 of the Received Text, from DC, E, F, G, K, etc. ("*and doth deliver*," in the Authorised Version). They are not found in A, D, Syr., Chrys., while the most authoritative MSS., ℵ, B, C, P, have καὶ ῥύσεται ("and *will* deliver," of the Revised Version). Most editors take the last reading, as best attested; but on internal grounds two of the most recent and acute interpreters, Schmiedel and Heinrici, prefer the Received Text. The present tense ("*doth* deliver") presupposes that the danger

to which Paul had been exposed in some form or in some sense continued. If this were the case, of course it could not have been, as Hofmann supposes, the shipwreck in which the Apostle spent a night and a day in the deep. Otherwise this would be a plausible and tempting supposition.

[6] To render διὰ πολλῶν *prolixe*, copiously, is at least precarious; and to take πρόσωπα as "faces" ("that from many faces upturned in prayer to God"), though lexically admissible, seems on all other grounds out of place.

[7] For χάριν, (benefit) אC, B, L, P, have χαράν (joy.) Though Westcott and Hort put this in the text, and χάριν in the margin, most scholars are agreed that χάριν is the Apostle's word, and χαράν a slip or a correction.

[8] Mention may be made here of another interpretation of ver. 17, modifications of which recur from Chrysostom to Hofmann. In substance it is this: "The things that I purpose, do I purpose according to the flesh (*i.e.*, with the stubborn consistency of a proud man, who disposes as well as proposes), that with *me* (ἐμοί emphatic: *me*, as if *I* were God, always to do what I would like to do) the Yes should be yes, and the No, no—*i.e.*, every promise inviolably kept?" This is grammatically quite good, but contextually impossible.

[9] According to Schmiedel, in the words δι' ἡμῶν ... δι' ἐμοῦ καὶ Σιλουανοῦ καὶ Τιμοθέου we ought to discover an emphatic reference, by way of contrast, to Judaising opponents of Paul in Corinth. These are said to have brought *another* Jesus (xi. 4), who was *notì* God's ἴδιος υἱός in Paul's sense (Rom. viii. 32), and in whom there *was* Yea and Nay—namely, the confirmation of the promises to the Jews or those who became Jews to receive them, and the refusal of the promises to the Gentiles as such. It needs a keen scent to discover this, and as the Corinthians read without a commentator it would probably be thrown away upon them.

[10] Observe the play on the words in βεβαιῶν εἰς Χ ρ ι σ τ ό ν and Χ ρ ί σ α ς.

[11] When we consider the New Testament use of this idea (cf. Rom. iv. 11; Rev. vii. 2 ff.; Eph. i. 13 f., and this passage), and remember that Paul and John can have had nothing to do with the Greek mysteries, it will be apparent that to adduce the ecclesiastical use of σφραγίς as a proof that

the conceptions current in these mysteries had a powerful influence from the earliest times on the Christian conception of baptism is beside the mark. One of the earliest examples outside the New Testament is in the Shepherd of Hermas, *Simil.*, viii. 6: οἱ πιστεύσαντες καὶ εἰληφότες τὴν σφραγῖδα καὶ τεθλακότες αὐτὴν καὶ μὴ τηρήσαντες ὑγιῆ. This figure of *breaking the seal*, by falling into sin and losing what baptism confers, is common. Sometimes it is varied: "Keep the flesh pure, καὶ τὴν σφραγῖδα ἄσπιλον," in 2 Clem. viii. 6. This may be made to carry superstition, but there is nothing superstitious or unscriptural in it to begin with.

[12] The R.V. "forbare to come" has the same vagueness as οὐκέτι ἦλθον, which may mean (1) "I came not as yet"—so A.V.; or (2) "I came not again"; or (3) "I came no more."

[13] To suppose the reference to be to an epistle carried by Titus and now lost, is to suppose what is incapable of proof or disproof. To take ἔγραψα as "epistolary" aorist, and translate "I write," is grammatically, but only grammatically, possible. The supposed reference to chaps, x. i-xiii. 10 as a separate epistle is noticed in the Introduction.

[14] On the identity of the person referred to, see Introduction.

[15] This meaning of ἐπιβαρεῖν, taken as intransitive, is rather vague, but I believe substantially correct. If the word is to be taken as virtually transitive, the object must be the partisans of the offender. It would "bear hardly" on them, to assume that *they* had been grieved by what Paul considered an offence. They had not been grieved. That is why he excludes them from πάντας ὑμᾶς by ἀπὸ μέρους.

[16] This suits with either idea as to the identity of the man. (1) If he were the incestuous person of 1 Cor. v., the minority would consist of those who abused the Christian idea of liberty, and were "puffed up" (1 Cor. v. 2) over this sin as an illustration of it. (2) If he were one who had personally insulted Paul, the minority would probably consist of the Judaistic opponents of the Apostle.

[17] This is the force of the καὶ before ἔγραψα in ver. 9.

[18] In spite of the Vulgate, which has *in persona Christi*; of Luther, who gives *an Christi Statt*; and of the English versions, Authorised and Revised, which both give "in the person of Christ" (though the R.V. puts *presence* in the

margin), there seems no room to doubt that "in the presence of Christ" is the true meaning. The same words in chap. iv, 6 are admittedly different in import; and in the only passages where ἐν προσώπῳ occurs with a genitive, it means "in presence of." These are Prov. viii. 30, where ἐν προσώπῳ αὐτοῦ is = וָיִנָּפֵל; and Sir. xxxii. 6, where "Thou shalt not appear *before the Lord* empty" is ἐν π. Κυρίου.

[19] The perfect ἔσχηκα seems at first sight out of place, but it is more expressive than the aorist. It suggests the *continuous* expectation of relief which was always anew disappointed.

[20] See Grimm's Lexicon *s.v.*, or Lightfoot on Col. ii. 15.

[21] In τὴν ὀσμὴν τῆς γνώσεως, γνώσεως is gen. of apposition: the ὀσμὴ and the γνῶσις are one.

[22] "The many" (οἱ πολλοί) seems to be the true reading. "The rest" (οἱ λοιποί) would be stronger still in its condemnation. But probably Paul is not thinking of the Church in general, but of the teachers as a body who crossed and thwarted him in his chosen field. The transition which is immediately made to the case of his opponents (τινὲς, iii. 1), and to the comparison of the old and new covenants, suggests that his Judaistic adversaries in Corinth (see chap. xi.) are in view.

[23] The true reading of the last words in ver. 3 is doubtful. The Received Text has ἐν πλαξὶ καρδίας σαρκίναις. This is as old as Irenæus and Origen, and is found in many versions. Almost all MSS. give the reading which is translated in the Revised Version: ἐν πλαξὶ καρδίαις σαρκίναις(א, A, B, C, D, etc.); and this is adopted by most of the purely critical editors. Some, however, and many exegetes, suspect a primitive error, affecting all MSS. and versions. Schmiedel would omit καρδίαις or καρδίας, as a marginal note, suggested by Prov. vii. 3, Jer. xvii. 1; Westcott and Hort, on the other hand, think that πλαξὶ may be a primitive interpolation. No certainty is possible; but considering Old Testament usage, one would expect Paul to write ἐν πλαξὶ καρδίας almost unconsciously.

[24] The true reading in Matt. xxvi. 28 omits "new," but the reference is unmistakable.

[25] Grammatically, it is probable that γράμματος and πνεύματος in ver. 6 depend, not on διαθήκης, but on διακόνους; but the sense is all one.

[26] The contrast of "letter" and "spirit" has, as is well known, been taken in various ways. That which is given above undoubtedly represents St. Paul's mind, and may be called the historical interpretation. An interpretation so common in early times that it might fairly be called the patristic, would explain the words as meaning that the *literal* sense of the Scriptures, especially of the Old Testament, is fatally misleading, and that we must find what that literal sense represents to the laws of allegory, if we would make it a word of life (cf. in Rev. xi. 8, "the great city, which *spiritually* is called Sodom and Egypt, where also our Lord was crucified"). There is another interpretation still, which may be called the literary or practical one. According to this, the Apostle means that the spiritual life, whether of intelligence or conscience, is strangled by literalism; we must regard not words as such, but the spirit and purpose of their author, if we are to have life and progress. This is perfectly true, but perfectly irrelevant, and is a good example of the free-and-easy way in which the Bible is quoted by those who do not study it.

[27] Chrysostom explains ἐν τούτῳ τῷ μέρει by κατὰ τὸν τῆς συγκρίσεως λόγον, and this is substantially right. But I think the words merely anticipate εἵνεκεν τῆς ὑπερβαλλούσης δόξης.

[28] In the LXX. ἐλπίζω is often used as the rendering of הָבַט *confidere*.

[29] Attempts have been made to render πρὸς τὸ μὴ ἀτενίσαι otherwise: *e.g.*, πρὸς has been taken as in Matt. xix. 8, which would give the meaning, "considering that the children of Israel did not look on," etc. Moses would thus veil himself in view of the fact that they did not see: the veil would be the symbol of the judicial blindness which was henceforth to fall on them.

[30] I cannot suppose that ἐπὶ τῇ ἀναγνώσει τῆς π. διαθήκης means anything different from ἡνίκα ἂν ἀναγινώσκηται Μωϋσῆς. It conveys no sense, that I can see, to sau that there are *two veils*, one upon the reading, and another upon the e(art. Uet many take it so.

[31] The present, where we might expect the future, conveys the certainty and decisiveness of the result.

[32] The subject of the verb ἐπιστρέψῃ ("turn") is not in point of grammar very clear. It may be Israel, or the heart on which a veil lies, or any one, taken indefinitely. Practically, the application is limited to those who live under the old covenant, and yet have its nature hidden from them. Hence it is fair to render, as I have done, "when *they* turn to the Lord."

[33] The peculiarity of the passage has given occasion to conjectures, of which by far the most ingenious is Baljon's: Οὐ δὲ ὁ Κύριος, τὸ Πνεῦμά ἐστιν, οὗ δὲ τὸ Πνεῦμα Κυρίου, ἐλευθερία: "Where the Lord is, the Spirit is; and where the Spirit of the Lord is, there is liberty."

[34] *Hom.* vii. on 2 Cor., p. 486, E.: Οὐ μόνον ὁρῶμεν εἰς τὴν δόξαν τοῦ Θεοῦ, ἀλλὰ καὶ ἐκεῖθεν δεχόμεθά τινα αἴγλην.

[35] So Meyer, from whom the particulars in this sentence are taken.

[36] The idea of the mirror is not to be omitted, as of no consequence. It is essential to the figure: "we see not yet face to face."

[37] Expositors seem to be agreed that in this passage there is a reference, more or less definite and particular, to the Judaising opponents of St. Paul at Corinth. This may be admitted, but is not to be forced. It is forced, *e.g.*, by Schmiedel, who habitually reads St. Paul as if (1) he had been expressly accused of everything which he says he does not do, and (2) as if he deliberately retorted on his opponents every charge he denied. Press this as he does, and whole passages of the Epistles become a series of covert insinuations—a kind of calumnious conundrums—instead of frank and *bona fide* statements of Christian principle. The result condemns the process.

[38] "Il voulut se servir de la supériorité de ce génie, comme les rois de leur puissance; il crut tout soumettre, et tout abaisser par la force."

[39] Grammarians differ much as to the relation of τῶν ἀπίστων ("which believe not") to ἐν οἷς ("in whom"). I have no doubt they are the same. The natural way for the Apostle to express himself would have been: "it is veiled in them that are perishing, whose minds the god of this world blinded." But he wished to include the moral aspect of the

case, the side of the personal responsibility of the perishing, as of equal significance with the agency of Satan; and this is what he does by adding τῶν ἀπίστων. Hence, though the expression is capable of being grammatically tortured into something different (the perishing becoming only *a part* of the unbelieving—so Meyer), it is, by its sheer grammatical awkwardness, exempted from liability to such rigorous treatment, and brought under the rules, not of grammar, but of common sense.

[40] Σὺν Ἰησοῦ is the true reading: sameness of kind is meant, not of time.

[41] Διὰ τῶν πλειόνων is construed in the R.V. with πλεονάσασα (so Meyer): De Wette takes it as above; in the A.V. the διὰ is made to govern τὴν εὐχαριστίαν. There is no grammatical decision certain here.

[42] The Hebrew Psalm cxvi. 10 is at this precise point practically unintelligible, but that does not justify any one in saying that the fine thought of the Apostle is utterly foreign to the original text. The open confession of God, as a duty of faith, pervades the psalm from this point to the end (the verses beginning Ἐπίστευσα διὸ ἐλάλησα make a psalm by themselves in the LXX.).

[43] The true rendering here is that in the margin of the R.V.

[44] This translation is Schmiedel's. For the use of διὰ cf. Rev. xxi. 24: Καὶ περιπατήσουσιν τὰ ἔθνη διὰ τοῦ φωτὸς αὐτης. It cannot mean "by" faith, in the sense of "according to" faith, or as faith directs. Nor can it be proved that εἶδος ever means "sight."

[45] The φανερωθῆναι of the last judgment, ver. 10, has as good as taken place—for God.

[46] According to Winer ἐξέστη in Mark iii. 21 has the present sense = *insanity*; and so it might be with ἐξέστημεν here. The verb occurs fifteen times in the New Testament, and except in these two passages has always the sense of being amazed or astonished beyond measure.

[47] The "we" in the first clause of ver. 16 is emphatic.

[48] As Heinrici does.

[49] See the excellent section on Paul and the Historical Christ in Sabatier's *The Apostle Paul* (English Translation, pp. 76-85).

[50] Observe the aorist παρῆλθεν.
[51] Chap. ii. 14, 17, and chap. iii. 14, are more limited.
[52] Perhaps the use of ἐν Χριστῷ here may be determined by the wish to express tacitly his opposition to those who claimed to be in a special sense τοῦ Χριστοῦ. Paul's formula really asserts a much more intimate relation to Christ than theirs.
[53] This seems to be the force of ὡς: it is a violent supposition that it means "since," or "for," and that ὅτι is a marginal interpretation of it which has crept into the text.
[54] This makes λογιζόμενος a true present, not an imperfect participle. It quite dislocates the sentence if it is co-ordinated with καταλλάσσων, and not with θέμενος.
[55] Observe that it is ὡς Θεοῦ διάκονοι, not διακόνους.
[56] Some, because of the want of the article, make it equivalent to "veracity."
[57] Beet, however, takes it in the technical sense: justification by faith is the preacher's sword and shield.
[58] *Rara et præsentissima appellatio* (Bengel).
[59] An ingenious defence of the place of these verses has been made by Godet in his Introduction to St. Paul's Epistles. At chap. vi. 10 the Apostle suddenly stops, amazed, as it were, at himself and at what the Spirit has just dictated to him. His heart swells, and he longs to embrace the thankless Church to which he writes. What *can* be the cause of its ingratitude? It is this. He has inexorably exacted from them a sacrifice claimed by their Christian profession—abstinence from banquets, etc., in idol temples (1 Cor. x.). But he has had no choice; the promises God makes to His sons and daughters are made on condition of such separation. Hence the entreaty in vii. 2 f., "Make room for me in your hearts: I have not deserved ill of any one by what I have done."— *Introduction*, p. 381.
[60] So freely that Ewald thinks the words from κἀγὼ εἰσδέξομαι onward are a quotation from some unknown source: as, *e.g.*, Eph. v. 14.
[61] But see on chap. ii. 5-11.
[62] This is, I think, the only possible meaning of πολλή μοι παῤῥησία πρὸς ὑμᾶς.
[63] So Schmiedel.

[64] It is difficult to fix either the text or the punctuation in ver. 8, and agreement among critics is quite hopeless. Practically they are at one in omitting the γάρ of the Received Text after βλέπω: and Schmiedel agrees with Lachmann and Westcott and Hort that the original reading was probably βλέπων. The R.V. has the same punctuation as the A.V., which probably means that the Revisers could not get a sufficient majority to change it, not that it is quite satisfactory as it stands. It certainly seems better to connect εἰ καὶ μετεμελόμην with what follows (νῦν χαίρω) than with what precedes; but the sense is not affected.

[65] But see on chap. ii. 5-11.

[66] This is the true text. Instead of ἐπὶ τῇ παρακλήσει in ver. 13 all critical editions read ἐπὶ δὲ τῇ π., and make these words begin a new paragraph.

[67] Ἁπλότης is literally simplicity or singleness of heart, the disposition which, when it gives, does so without *arrière-pensée*: in point of fact this is identical with the liberal or generous disposition. Cf. chap. ix. 11, 13; Rom. xii. 8; James i. 5.

[68] Previous to his recent visit? So Schmiedel. Or simply = formerly?

[69] This, according to Hermann (quoted by Meyer), is often the force of ἀλλά, which is certainly a surprising word here.

[70] Translating it, of course, *"was* poor," or "lived poor": which is not impossible in itself.

[71] The προ in προενήρξασθε seems to mean "before the Macedonians."

[72] The order of "do" and "will" is peculiar and has not been clearly explained.

[73] Αὐθαίρετος ἐξῆλθεν: the aorists all through this passage are virtually epistolary—ἐξῆλθεν = he is going; συνεπέμψαμεν = I am sending with him.

[74] *Our* (ἡμῶν), not *your* (ὑμῶν), is the true reading. The precise sense is doubtful. It may be as the R.V. gives it, though this completely upsets the balance of the clauses πρὸς τὴν τοῦ Κυρίου δόξαν and καὶ προθυμίαν ἡμῶν. The meaning should rather be: "which is ministered by us, that the Lord may be glorified, and that we may be made of good heart";

only Paul's spirits seem a small thing side by side with the Lord's glory. There is something to say for the conjecture that the καὶ before προθυμίαν should be κατά, even though this could only be connected with χειροτονηθείς: "elected as we earnestly desired."

[75] The T.R. has ἐνδείξασθε here, and so Westcott and Hort read in text, with ℵ, C, D**, etc. Most editors read with B, D*, E, F, G, etc., ἐνδεικνύμενοι. The imperative certainly seems to be a change made to facilitate the construction. Reading the participle, we must supply ἐνδείξεσθε, and put a comma after ἐνδεικνύμενοι: "in showing it to them, [you will show it] before the Churches." This is the same kind of ellipsis as in ver. 23.

[76] This is the force of τὸ γράφειν.

[77] The R.V. renders πλεονεξία "extortion"—the πλεονέκται being those who *get* the money; but it seems to me more natural to render "avarice," in which case both εὐλογία and πλεονεξία apply to the Corinthians.

[78] Ἐπ' εὐλογίαις: "so that blessings are associated therewith" (Winer): the full hand in sowing makes a full hand in reaping.

[79] Λειτουργία: for the general sense of "service," especially charitable service, quite apart from priestly associations, see Phil. ii. 25, 30: and Grimm's Lexicon.

[80] On Hausrath's view that this was a letter between our Ep. I. and Ep. II. see the Introduction.

[81] This is the only place in the New Testament where ταπεινὸς ("lowly") is used in a bad (contemptuous) sense: in Christian lips it is a term of praise (Matt. xi. 29); the speakers here had not learned its Christian meaning.

[82] The dative in δυνατὰ τῷ Θεῷ is the same as in Jonah iii. 3, Acts vii. 20. A vague rendering like "divinely powerful" is probably nearest the meaning.

[83] This is the reading adopted by Westcott and Hort with most MSS. except B.

[84] The difficult τε in ἐάν τε γὰρ is most easily explained by the ellipse of a corresponding καί: of several reasons he might adduce, Paul adduces only one (Schmiedel).

[85] The ninth verse, Ἵνα μὴ δόξω κ.τ.λ. is most naturally taken with what precedes, and most simply explained by supplying something like, "but I say no more about it, *i.e.* about my authority, that I may not seem," etc. To say more would look like trying to frighten them. Others make it protasis to ver. 11, ver. 10 being then a parenthesis.

[86] The following sentence from a letter of H. E. M. (a sister of James Mozley's) is an interesting illustration of this truth: "I consider Mr. Rickards as the type and model of a country parish and domestic priest. *All* his powers and energies are expended on and exerted for teaching, preaching, and talking. *Bodily presence is his vocation*: unlike some, writers and others, he must be seen to be felt; and unlike others again, writers and others, the more he is seen, the more he is felt."

[87] See note.

[88] "Woods, trees, meadows, and hills are my witnesses that I drew on a fair match betwixt Christ and Anwoth."—S. Rutherford.

[89] The words καὶ τῆς ἁγνότητος are bracketed by Westcott and Hort. They are very strongly attested (by ℵ, B, F, gr., G, etc.); but as they are found in some authorities *before,* instead of *after,* τῆς ἁπλότητος, it is not improbable that they may be a gloss on these last words, suggested by ἁγνὴν in ver. 2, and incorporated in the text. They rather blur than emphasise the thought.

[90] It is worth appending two ingenious notes on this. Bengel, who holds that the suppositions are untrue, says: "Ponit conditionem, ex parte rei, impossibilem; ideo dicit in imperfecto *toleraretis*: sed pro conatu pseudo-apostolorum, non modo possibilem, sed plane præsentem; ideo dicit in præsenti, *prædicat.*" Schmiedel, who holds that the suppositions are true, explains the impft. by saying that Paul resolved, while dictating, to add the apodosis *in the historical tense* to the timeless protasis, because the fact which it described actually lay before him. They *were tolerating* the other teachers: that is why Paul says ἀνείχεσθε. He happily compares Plato, *Apol.*, 33 A.: Εἰ δέ τίς μου λέγοντος ... ἐπιθυμεῖ ἀκούειν ... οὐδενὶ πώποτε ἐφθόνησα. Still, he prefers the present.

[91] It is gratuitous to drag in a reference to the first Apostles, and then to suppose the Corinthians drawing the inference—"if he is not inferior to them, still less is he inferior to our new teachers." Such an inference depends on a traditional conception of apostleship which the Corinthians were not likely to share, and it is equally unnecessary and improbable.

[92] Probably either ἐν παντὶ or ἐν πᾶσιν, the latter of which is omitted in some authorities, is a gloss.

[93] This (observe the aorist λαβών) implies that he brought some money with him from Macedonia to Corinth.

[94] That is, the two ἵνα are co-ordinate.

[95] That is, the ἵνα are not co-ordinate, but the second is subordinate to τῶν θελόντων ἀφορμήν.

[96] There has been some discussion as to the precise force of δικαιοσύνη ("righteousness") in this place. It seems to me most natural to take it, without suspicion, in a perfectly simple sense: a minister of righteousness is the truly good character which these bad men affect. To suppose a covert sneer at their "legalism," or that they had pointed to such matters as are discussed in 1 Cor. v., viii., and x., as indicating the need of a gospel which would pay more attention to righteousness than Paul's, is surely too clever.

[97] This is the force of the ὡς: it leaves it open whether the idea has reality answering to it or not.

[98] This, which is the second alternative given in the margin of the Revised Version, seems to me the true meaning of χωρὶς τῶν παρεκτός.

[99] This is done by a number of critics, including Holsten and Schmiedel.

[100] Godet gives the incident a peculiar turn, more ingenious than convincing. "No doubt the list I have given is one of mere infirmities. I might well boast of things apparently more glorious—as when the whole of that great city, Damascus, was raised against me, and I could only escape secretly."—*Introduction au Nouv. Test.*, p. 393.

[101] In their margin Westcott and Hort read δὲ οὐ.

[102] The editors vary greatly in punctuation, especially as they do or do not insert διὸ before the first ἵνα μὴ ὑπεραίρωμαι. Westcott and Hort suspect some primitive error.

[103] For the meaning "thorn," not "stake" or "cross," see Ezek. xxviii. 24; Hosea ii. 8 (6); Num. xxxiii. 55.

[104] I should lay no stress here on what some so much insist upon—the use of ἐξεπτύσατε in Gal. iv. 14, and the fact that *morbus despui suctus* is a name for epilepsy: ἐκπτύειν does not mean *despuere*, and after ἐξουθενεῖν it is necessarily metaphorical.

[105] Construe ὑπὲρ Χριστοῦ with εὐδοκῶ.

[106] Αὐτὸς ἐγώ in ver. 13 has a peculiar emphasis, not easily explained. It cannot mean "*I* did not, though my assistants did," for this is denied in ver. 18. Neither can it mean "*I* did not, though the Judaists did," for whatever is opposed to αὐτὸς ἐγώ must nevertheless be conceived here as belonging to the same category, which the Judaists did not. Possibly it only separates the *person* expressly from his *works*, just recited, and has the same sort of value as in Rom. ix. 3, where it emphasises the person as opposed to the heart and conscience.

[107] This is the reading of our Revisers, and of Westcott and Hort's text. In their margin they read: "I will very gladly spend, etc., if loving you [ἀγαπῶν instead of ἀγαπῶ] more abundantly I am loved the less." This reading and punctuation are adopted by a number of scholars, but explained in two ways:—(1) As in the Authorised Version, "*though* the more abundantly," etc. But εἰ ("if"), which is the true reading (not εἰ καί), cannot be translated "though." (2) By others it is rendered, "I will very gladly spend, etc., if the more abundantly I love you the less I am loved": that is, "if things have come to such a pass between us that the natural relations are utterly inverted, I will make any sacrifice to restore them to a better footing." This is insipid and flat to the last degree: textual and psychological considerations combine to support the Revisers text.

[108] Πάλαι is the true reading, not πάλιν. Westcott and Hort retain the interrogation.

[109] This is also suggested by the reading ταπεινώσει, which Tischendorf adopts in ver. 21, with B, D, E, F, etc. ℵ, A, K, followed by Westcott and Hort, have ταπεινώσῃ.

[110] It is more natural to construe ἐπὶ τῇ ἀκαθαρσια κ.τ.λ. with μετανοησάντων than with πενθήσω.

[111] Although it is supported by commentators like Chrysostom and Calvin, it is difficult to treat otherwise than as a whim the idea that Paul's two or three visits to Corinth make *him* equal to the two or three witnesses required by the law. So also Godet, who counts the three thus: (1) a warning by word of mouth during his second visit; (2) this letter; (3) his actual arrival for the third time.

[112] See *Biblical Essays*, p. 274.

[113] Another interpretation is worth mentioning. "Try *yourselves*, I say; put *yourselves* to the proof; *do not leave it for me to do* when I come. Why, do you not recognise as to your own selves that Jesus Christ is among you, so that you have spiritual competence to proceed in correcting the disorders of the Church?—unless, indeed, ye are reprobates: which is an impossible supposition. But ἑαυτοὺς certainly suggests that in the implied contrast Paul is *object*, not *subject*."